The Diocese of
Allentown
A History

by
John Hanley

The Diocese of Allentown

Published by
Éditions du Signe
BP 94 - 67038 Strasbourg - Cedex 2 - France
Tel (++33) 388 789 191
Fax (+33) 388 789 199
info@editionsdusigne.fr

Publishing Director
Christian Riehl

Publishing Assistant
Marc de Jong

Design and Layout
Juliette Roussel

Photography
John Glover

Photoengraving
Éditions du Signe - 107932

Éditions du Signe 2010
ISBN: 978-2-7468-2517-8

Table of Contents

Foreword

OFFICE OF THE BISHOP
Mailing Address
POST OFFICE BOX F
ALLENTOWN, PENNSYLVANIA
18105-1538

4029 WEST TILGHMAN STREET
ALLENTOWN, PENNSYLVANIA 18104
(610) 437-0755
Fax (610) 433-7822

Dear Faithful,

In January 1961, Pope John XXIII created the Diocese of Allentown from the five northern counties of the Archdiocese of Philadelphia. In 2011, we celebrate our 50th anniversary.

This book features pictures and stories about the heroic people who first sowed the seeds of faith in this part of Pennsylvania dating back centuries before our Diocese was created. There are also stories of the heroes who nurtured that faith over the years until it was strong enough to flourish as the local church it is today.

Here too, are pictures and histories of the parishes that are and have been the backbone of this Diocese.

I hope this pictorial history of our beloved local church will become a valued keepsake. It provides us with a wonderful reference and memento of our past, but also propels us into our 21st century embrace of "holiness and mission" in the Diocese of Allentown.

Sincerely in Christ,

+ John O. Barres

Most Reverend John O. Barres
Bishop of Allentown

The History
OF THE DIOCESE OF ALLENTOWN

CHAPTER 1:

The First Jesuit Mission at Goshenhoppen: The Chapel of Saint Paul (1741)

Goshenhoppen was the former name of the Perkiomen Valley in Pennsylvania. Prior to 1740, the Jesuit missionaries in Maryland had learned the numbers and places of residence of the scattered Catholics in Pennsylvania. Because many of these were Germans, application was made through the Provincial in England to the Provincials of the Order in Germany to send some German priests to minister to their countrymen in the colony of Pennsylvania. Before 1741, Father Ferdinand Farmer and other priests of Saint Joseph's Church of Philadelphia made missionary visits to the Goshenhoppen area. Goshenhoppen is now known as Bally where Most Blessed Sacrament Church traces its roots to these humble beginnings.

Father Joseph Greaton, the founder of the Church in Philadelphia, saw the need of a German priest and applied for one. The earliest letter making reference to Father Schneider was dated July 16, 1740 and from Father Retz, the General of the Society of Jesus, to Father Boult, the provincial at Liege. Father Retz's letter two months later revealed that the Provincial had granted Father Schneider leave for the Pennsylvania Mission. On April 8, 1741, Father Retz wrote to Father Boult and informed him that Father Scheneider and Father Wappler had arrived at their Pennsylvania Missions.

On September 19, 1740, Father Schneider was ordered by the General of the Society to go to Pennsylvania. A few days later he departed from Germany; going by way of Cologne, and Aachen to Liege, then to London, to leave from there to Maryland. Father Schneider did not waste much time in Maryland. He and Father Wilhelm Wappler almost immediately began their activities in Pennsylvania. Father Wappler immediately went to Conewago. Not long after arriving in Philadelphia, Father Schneider left to take up residence in Goshenhoppen.

When Father Schneider came to Goshenhoppen in 1741, he resided with the John Kuhn family. From the church registers, we can see that John Kuhn's house was used six times for religious functions in 1742. Father Schneider first said Mass in the homes of the people until he acquired a residence in a two-story frame house and made it his rectory and parish school. The earliest record of Jesuit missionary work in the vicinity was the first baptismal record dated August 23, 1741 at Falkner's Swamp. The first mention of Goshenhoppen was the baptism of George Melchoir on February 13, 1743. By February 1743, Father Theodore Schneider had his own residence. This house served as temporary church, school and rectory. It was a small two-story building, with one room on each floor. Father Schneider may have rented the Goshenhoppen property from Ulrich Beidler prior to 1747. Ownership of the property begins with the purchase of 121 acres from Ulrich Beidler by Father Henry Neale on March 1, 1747. The remaining 378 acres was purchased from Ulrich Beidler by Father Joseph Greaton on August 3, 1752.

The letters of Father Schneider have not been located and all that remains of his writings are quotations from the letters that were published in a Jesuit periodical referred to as "Der Neue Welt-Bott." Among those pages are excerpts from a letter from either 1749 or 1750 where Father Theodore Schneider states:

Title page of Father Schneider's Goshenhoppen Sacramental Register (1741)

Sketch of Saint Paul's Chapel- includes the original
1753 chapel and the 1796 renovation

"Last Summer they have finished as large & elegant a Church as any in the province, for public worship about 35 miles from Town; & by all accounts their numbers increase greatly."

Another letter referring to Saint Paul's Chapel was written by Conrad Weiser to Governor Morris on July 23, 1755, where he states that: "the Catholics in Cussahoppen... they have a very magnificent chapel." This letter also confirms that the chapel was in existence in 1755. The layout of the original 1754 chapel as suggested by documents appears to be the sanctuary, a choir loft and the nave. Father Schneider's chapel actually extended to the present side altars ; and the roofline of the chapel was no higher than the old sanctuary and the sacristy walls.

"I go around with the thought to build on my farm, a new church; and for me a new dwelling. Although I will have to get the necessary money, which I do not have at present, I hope to obtain the same through the great generosity of European benefactors. In short, I hope to get it together from the rich alms I have received from you, Reverend Rector, and some benefactors, especially after I have paid the creditor from whom I bought this farm."

One of the great achievements of Father Schneider's pastorate was the founding of the first Catholic parish school in Pennsylvania. Father Schneider himself was the teacher and school was located at his residence. By 1763, the school was large enough to justify hiring a schoolmaster named Henry Fretter and building a separate schoolhouse.

Father Schneider's plan to build a new church suggests that there was an old church. The "new church" is the Saint Paul's Chapel that resides behind the sanctuary of Most Blessed Sacrament and was built in 1754. The suggested old church, traditionally dated to 1743, may not have been anything more than the "priest house" mentioned in the register in 1744. Other likely candidates for Father Schneider's old church are the Beidler farmhouse, a tenant house or the Mennonite Meetinghouse that was on the Beidler farmland. A letter from Will Smith to Thomas Penn on May 1, 1755, mentions the building of Saint Paul's Chapel in the summer of 1754 and states:

Father Theodore Schneider
(1702-1764) is buried in the
floor of St. Paul's Chapel

"What is said about Roman Catholics is too strong; but it seems to mean only that the common privilege of a universal Toleration is too much Encouragement to them, considering our Vicinity to a popish Enemy."

In addition to Goshenhoppen, Father Schneider also ministered to the German Catholics of Philadelphia until February 6, 1758. In 1764, he became ill and sent word to Philadelphia for one of the missionary Fathers to assist him at Saint Paul's. In the weeks before his death, he was assisted by Father Ferdinand Farmer. Father Schneider died on July 10, 1764 and was buried in the floor of Saint Paul's Chapel. Father Farmer looked after the parish until Father de Ritter was appointed as pastor one year later.

Father John Baptist de Ritter, S.J. was appointed pastor of Saint Paul's in 1765 and served until 1787. He arrived in America on May 31, 1765 and his first baptism in Goshenhoppen was on July 14, 1765. Father de Ritter led the parish during the Revolutionary War. He made

Father John Baptist de
Ritter (1717-1878) is buried in
the floor of St. Paul's Chapel

Original bell from St. Paul's Chapel- now in the Monsignor Charles Allwein Museum

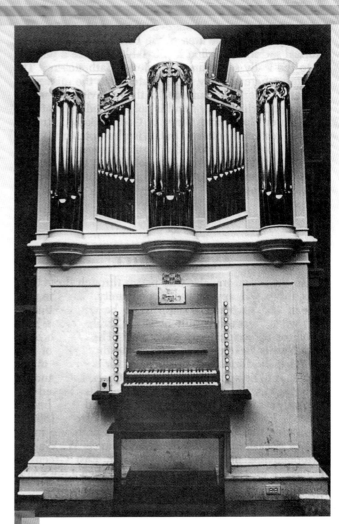

Krauss Organ- built in 1799

many missionary trips during his pastorate throughout Pennsylvania to Reading, Easton, Northampton and Haycock Run. With Father de Ritter's arrival, there is evidence of the use of the first graveyard. In 1765, a death was recorded in the registers which states that Mary Martin was buried in the church graveyard. Father de Ritter died on February 3, 1787 at the age of 70 years. His body was also buried in the floor in front of the old altar beside the remains of Father Schneider.

Father Peter Helbron served as pastor of Goshenhoppen from November 1787 until 1791. Father Hebron found the parish buildings run down and began repairs. He built a steeple and added the chapel bell in 1789. The bell, originally cast in Paris in 1706, had been purchased by Father Schneider in Philadelphia years earlier. In order to install the chapel bell, the roof over the sanctuary of Saint Paul's was modified in 1789. Father Nicholas Delvaux served as pastor from 1791 until 1793. Father Paul Erntzen served as pastor from 1793 until 1818. It is during the early part of his pastorate that Bishop John Carroll of Baltimore visited Goshenhoppen in 1793. Father Erntzen records this visit and Confirmation among the marriages as follows:

"April 19, 1793, being confessed and having made his First Communion this same day Anthony Reichard, son of William Reichard and his wife Elizabeth Redert, was confirmed by the Right Reverend John Carroll, bishop of Baltimore."

Father Erntzen did much to improve and repair the church. He commissioned John Strauss to build an organ for the church in 1797. The new organ was consecrated on March 10, 1799. Two secular priests attended to Saint Paul's from 1818 until October 1819. Father Schoenfelder from Reading served from 1818 to 1819 and Father Brennewitz served only until October 1819. On October 8, 1819, Father Paul Kohlmann, S.J. was appointed as pastor and served until 1822.

Father Boniface Corvin, S.J. was appointed as pastor in 1822. In conjunction with Father E. McCarthy, another Missionary Jesuit, he made

Father Boniface Corvin (1777-1837) is buried in the floor of St. Paul's Chapel

Most Blessed Sacrament Church interior about 1866

Father Bally and school children at St. Aloysius Academy in 1866

Rev. Nicholas Steinbacher as deacon, the Rev. Henry Herzog, as subdeacon. Above three thousand persons are supposed to have been present on the occasion. The old church erected about the year 1765 has been converted into a spacious sanctuary (40 feet square) and sacristy, and an addition made of 80 feet by 50. The edifice is one of the most elegant in the Diocese, highly creditable to the liberality of the congregation, and still more so to the zeal of the pious Pastor. The baptismal Register preserved in the adjoining pastoral residence begins in the year 1741, when the Rev. Theodore Schneider, S.J. settled there, and from it visited several places, to perform the Missionary duties. Philadelphia appears to have had one resident pastor at that time, as a Baptism is reported, performed by the above Missionary in the Chapel at Philadelphia. Another Baptism is registered for the following year; and not until 1744 is the number of three Baptisms in one year credited to our city, where now, perhaps, a thousand take place."

many long trips to Berks, Lebanon, Lehigh, Montgomery and Schuylkill Counties from 1827 until 1829. During the tenure of Father Corvin, a small community grew up around the area of Saint Paul's Chapel which became known as Churchville. Father Corvin set out to build a new church and, although unfinished, the church was dedicated on October 11, 1835. An article on the dedication of the new "Church of the Most Holy Sacrament" appeared in *The Catholic Herald* on October 15, 1835 and read:

"The elegant and spacious church lately erected by the exertions of the Rev. Bonifacius Corvin, S.J. in the settlement called Goshenhoppen, Berks County, was dedicated to divine worship on Sunday the 11th October, by the Rt. Rev. Joachim Fernandez Madrid y Canal, Bishop of Tenegra in partibus. After the solemn benediction of the church, the Rev. Nicholas Steinbacher, preached in German, and after the Gospel, the Rev. Peter Richard Kenrick preached in English. Mass was celebrated in Pontifical vesture by the Rt. Rev. prelate, the Rev. Corvin acting as assisting priest, the

Father Corvin did not live to see the church completed and died suddenly while in Philadelphia on October 11, 1837. The old chapel of Saint Paul was included in the new dimensions of the church and the new edifice was named the Church of the Most Blessed Sacrament. The new Most Blessed Sacrament was built out of the nave of Saint Paul's and expanded outward.

Father Augustin Bally, S.J. was appointed as pastor on October 31, 1837. Upon arrival, his first work was to finish the church construction started by Father Corvin. The 80-foot extension was completed in 1838. Father Bally built a new

Father Augustin Bally

Most Blessed Sacrament Church in 1870

Most Blessed Sacrament Church interior with side altars about 1870

schoolhouse which was a one-story red brick double building that he named Saint Aloysius Academy in 1850. The attendance grew to around 65 to 70 children. A few years later, an addition was built onto the school building. Father Bally became ill on November 1, 1881 and Father John Meurer, S.J. was appointed to assist him. Father Bally's death occurred on January 20, 1882. He is buried in the new cemetery which he established on the hill across from the church in 1876.

Father Meurer served as pastor from 1882 until 1889. In 1883, Nicholas Andre and Father Meurer went to the postal

Three Sisters of St Francis at Most Blessed Sacrament Church in Bally- Sisters Crispina, Enesius and Petrania

authorities in Philadelphia and requested that a post office be established in Churchville with the name "Bally." The request was granted and a new post office was opened with the name "Bally" on August 7, 1883. The name of Bally gradually replaced Churchville, but it was not until 1912 that the Borough of Bally was incorporated. The Sisters of Saint Francis from Glen Riddle arrived on August 1, 1889 and were the first religious community to teach at Bally. The school was opened by the Sisters on September 1, 1889. The Jesuit Order turned Most Blessed Sacrament Church over to the Archdiocese of Philadelphia in 1889. The property included the church, house, school and a small portion of land.

Father Aloysius Mistle served as pastor from 1889 to 1898. During his pastorate, a new school was built on the site of the original school and mission house in 1893. Father Anthony Nathe became pastor on October 1, 1898 and served until 1902. Priests from Saint Paul's Church in Reading served the parish until Father Charles Saunders was appointed pastor in 1903. Father Saunders was succeeded as pastor by Father Peter Fuengerlings, who served from 1912 until 1921. Father Aloysius Scherf served as pastor from August 1921 until 1951. During his pastorate, the convent for the Sisters of Saint Francis was built in 1922.

On May 22, 1952, Father Charles L. Allwein was appointed pastor and his first concern was to build a new school. A plot of ground at the corner of Seventh and Pine Streets in Bally was obtained and ground was broken for the school on March 1, 1953. The new Most Blessed Sacrament School was opened for classes on September 10, 1953 and dedicated on April 9, 1954. Monsignor Allwein opened a parish museum in 1957.

Saint Francis Academy Regional School in Bally

Most Blessed Sacrament Church with 1850 schoolhouse and new cemetery about 1900

Restoration and renovation of Most Blessed Sacrament Church took place between 1984 and 1991. Renovations of the historic Saint Paul's Chapel began on July 8, 1991 and were completed in November 1991. Most Blessed Sacrament Church, the oldest parish in the Allentown Diocese and the fourth oldest in the original Thirteen Colonies, celebrated its 250th anniversary from September 22, 1991 through October 11, 1992. In 1993, the Sisters of Saint Francis left Most Blessed Sacrament School after 109 years of service. The school became a regional school and the name was then changed to Saint Francis Academy Regional School in honor of the Sisters of Saint Francis in September 1993. In May 1997, the church's historic Krauss organ was rededicated and the parish museum was named for Monsignor Charles Allwein.

Monsignor Charles Allwein

Most Blessed Sacrament is the oldest parish in the Diocese of Allentown. The school is recognized as the oldest Catholic-public school in the Thirteen Original Colonies. Most Blessed Sacrament Church has preserved many antiquities in its Monsignor Charles Allwein Museum. The parish's baptismal records are the oldest continuous baptismal records in the Thirteen Original Colonies and are kept in the archives at Saint Charles Seminary in Philadelphia. The artworks of Most Blessed Sacrament Church begin with a unique 1756 oil painting of the Last Supper that was a present to Father Schneider in 1764 from Prince-Elect Carl Theodore of Germany. Most Blessed Sacrament Church is also fortunate to have had an important religious artist of Germany and America,

Berthold von Imhoff, who painted a number of ceiling and wall murals including: The Virgin Mary and a traditional rendition of Da Vinci's Last Supper. The Stations of the Cross were donated to the church in 1886. The original wood altar, built when Saint Paul's Chapel was constructed, can still be seen in the Chapel. Five early Jesuit priests are also buried in the floor of the Chapel including Father Theodore Schneider (1764), Father John Baptist de Ritter (1787), Father Peter Helbron (1791), Father Paul Erntzen (1818) and Father Boniface Corvin (1837).

The painting of the Last Supper given to Father Schneider

CHAPTER 2:
The Goshenhoppen Missionary Trail (1741-1808)

Before and during the American Revolutionary War, Catholics in the thirteen colonies were under the ecclesiastical jurisdiction of the bishop of the Apostolic Vicariate of the London District in England. On June 6, 1784, Father John Carroll was confirmed by Pope Pius VI as Superior of the Missions in the United States of North America. This act established a hierarchy in the United States and removed them from the authority of the Vicar Apostolic of the London District. Pope Pius VI then established the Apostolic Prefecture of the United States on November 26, 1784.

Bishop John Carroll of Baltimore

On March 12, 1788, the Roman Catholic clergy of the United States requested permission from Rome to elect their first bishop. Pope Pius VI granted permission for this on July 12, 1788. Father Carroll was elected as bishop by the clergy in April 1789. Pope Pius VI approved the election of Bishop John Carroll and established the Diocese of Baltimore on November 6, 1789.

Goshenhoppen was truly a base for missionary operations in Pennsylvania in the years before and after the American Revolution. Some of the earliest stops on the missionary trail from Goshenhoppen made by Fathers Schneider, de Ritter and Helbron were between 1741 and 1793 and included: Falkner's Swamp (1741), Pottsville (1742), Haycock (1742), Allemangel (1742), Bethlehem (1742), Oley (1742), Reading (1744), Cedar Creek (1744), Macungie (1750s), Sharp Mountain (1766), Easton (1768), Milton (1774), Pottsgrove (1775), Allentown

(1776), Douglassville (1780), Mount Pleasant (1793), Obolds (1793), Moselem Springs (1800s), Lackall, Hereford, Long Swamp, Maiden Creek, Ruscombmanor, Windsor, Nockamixon, Rockhill, Tinicum, Denikum, Linn Township, Weissenburg and Frankford. The priests from Goshenhoppen went to Hamburg, Port Clinton, Schuylkill Haven, Ashland and as far as Sunbury; they also branched off at Pottsville and passing through the Schuylkill Valley, visited all the little towns such as Port Carbon, Middleport, Brockton (then called Patterson), Tuscarora and Tamaqua toward Buck Mountain and Mauch Chunk. From Goshenhoppen they also went to Kutztown. Another trail from Goshenhoppen went to Vera Cruz, Emaus, Catasauqua, Slatington, Berlinsville, Walnutport and Parryville.

The earliest record of Jesuit missionary work in the vicinity of Goshenhoppen is found in the sacramental registers of Father Schneider in Goshenhoppen. This first record was the baptism of Albertina Kohl by Father Schneider that took place in the home of John M. Utzman at Falkner's Swamp on August 23, 1741.

Falkner's Swamp, the site of Father Schneider's first entry in his register, was one of the centers of German activity on what then could be considered the western frontier of Pennsylvania. It is located on what was then known as the Great Road, now known as the Swamp Pike in New Hanover Township, Montgomery County. It was here that the pioneer Jesuit first administered the sacraments. For a few years he used the house of John Utzman as a gathering place, but after establishing his own residence, he no longer included Falkner's Swamp on his mission circuit since it was only a few miles from Goshenhoppen.

In Father Schneider's time, the Manatawny or Ridge Road ran from the Trappe through Pottsgrove to Douglassville in Berks County. Today, this highway is

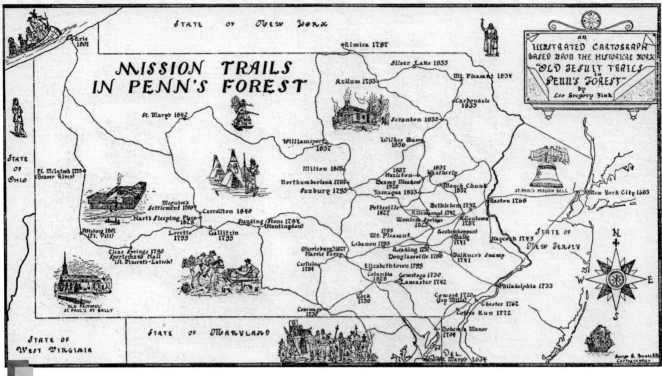

Early Jesuit Missionary Trails in Pennsylvania

known as Route 422. In colonial days, this road veered off at Douglassville and continued on to Oley. Father Schneider traveled this road frequently in the early days of his mission circuit. Douglassville had been the site of a Swedish settlement and the area was known as Morlatten. By the middle of the eighteenth century, a number of Irish immigrants had located there and were the object of the early ministry of Father Schneider. In the eighteenth century, Pottstown was known as Pottsgrove and Father Farmer visited Pottsgrove in March 1775 and November 1776.

By 1740, a number of English and Irish Catholics had settled in Upper Bucks County in Haycock and Nockamixon Townships. By 1742, Father Schneider was in contact with these Catholic families and had developed a schedule of visitation. Father Schneider performed a baptism in Haycock Run on May 27, 1742. Services were first held in the homes of the various Catholics until Nicholas Carty built a new house just prior to the American Revolution to be used as a place of worship. Saint John the Baptist Church in Haycock was built in 1798. Closely associated with the Catholics of upper Bucks County were those of the Easton and "Bethlehem" area. Father Schneider recorded a baptism at Wendelin Heifer's house in «Bethlehem County" in March 1742. In the early days of Fathers Schneider and de Ritter, Catholics of the Easton area journeyed to Haycock. About 1768, Nicholas Hucki settled near Easton and his house was used frequently as a mission station by Father de Ritter.

In the Northwest corner of Berks County, Father Schneider first visited Allemangel in 1742, and it was to be a place of regular visitation until the close of the eighteenth century. Services were first held in the home of Jacob Pawlitz. After the war with France, more Catholic families settled here, including Christian Henrich, whose home was on Sharp Mountain and consistently used as a Mass House until his death in 1798.

Father Schneider's 1st baptismal entry at Falkner's Swamp in 1741

Lying south of Allenmangel are Kutztown in Maxatawny Township and Moselem Springs in Richmond Township in Berks County, both frequently referred to in the registers. In this area, Moselem Forge was established in 1760 and among its early workers were some Catholics. The number of Catholics increased to the point that a congregation was organized early in the nineteenth century. Saint Henry's Church in Moselem Springs was built in 1823, but the parish closed in 1865.

Father Ferdinand Farmer

As early as 1744, Father Schneider visited Redding (Reading) Furnace in Chester County and refers to it as "Branson's Iron Works." He found a number of Catholics, mostly Irish, whom he visited periodically. A place of worship existed at least by the year 1756. Recorded in Will Book "2" at the Reading courthouse is the will of Peter Bingaman dated May 13, 1756, in which he bequeaths to a son ... "a house in Reading which lies opposite the Roman Catholic Church ..." Sammy Weiser was active in the development of the city and wrote that the property on which the first Catholic Church was built was selected by Father Schneider. The first mention of Reading in the records of Goshenhoppen occurs in the first entry by Father de Ritter in July 1765, when he administers a Baptism in the city but no specific site is mentioned. The first mention of a chapel "at Reading" occurs on May 11, 1766. The first mention of a cemetery in the city is found in a death entry for Anna Maria Chaumont on November 11, 1765, when it states that she was buried "in the catholic graveyard at Reading." Based on the records of Father de Ritter, there was a chapel and cemetery at Reading at the beginning of his pastorate. In all probability, the site of this early Catholic center was on the east side of Duke Street, now Seventh Street. The old chapel was razed in 1790 and a small brick church dedicated to Saint Peter was erected. In the *Readinger Zeitung* issue dated August 10, 1791, appeared the following notice:

"*Those who wish to see the solemn ceremony of laying the cornerstone of a ROMAN CATHOLIC CHAPEL, to be built at READING, are invited to attend at READING, on the Seventeenth day of August instant.*"

No site is mentioned for the event, but no doubt this new chapel was built on the Duke Street property. It was not until March 1, 1809, that the Roman Catholic congregation at Reading received a deed for the Duke Street property from John Coates. This deed represents the first record of title to this property, which had most likely been used by the Catholics of Reading since 1751.

It was not until the time of Father Helbron that the Goshenhoppen priests ventured beyond the Schuylkill on a regular basis prior to 1793. It was he who started regular visitations to the house of Philip Schmidt in Obolds or Mt. Pleasant near Bernville. These visitations by priests from Goshenhoppen were continued until the death of

St. Peter's Church in Reading

Father Erntzen in 1818, when the Catholics served at the Schmidt homestead were required to go to Reading.

Oley, or the Oley Hills, so often referred to in the registers, were also one of the earliest mission centers of Father Schneider. His first mention of this area occurs in 1742 when he called the area "New Forge near Jotter's Mill." He later refers to the area as the Oley Hills or Oley Forge. Macungie was the scene of Catholic activity from the beginning of Father Schneider's ministry. This place, as with most others encountered in the early registers, encompassed a much larger area of modern Lehigh County than the present town of Macungie. In the early years of his work, Father Schneider resided for periods of time with John Kuhn. After this, it seems that the Catholics of the area went to Oley or Cedar Creek for the administration of the Sacraments. At the end of Father Schneider's tenure and during the time of Father Ritter, Macungie again became a regular mission station. The home of Philip Schmidt was used as a Mass house until his death in 1775.

The city of Allentown was laid out in 1762 and was named after its founder William Allen, but came to be known as the town of Northampton until 1838. At the western edges of Allentown is Cedar Creek in South Whitehall Township. The first mention of Cedar Creek occurred in April 1744 when Father Schneider baptized a son of John Koch in the home of Henry and Margaret Kuhn. Father de Ritter made Cedar Creek a frequent mission stop and used the home of Margaret Kuhn as a Mass house until her death in 1773. In 1757, Father Schneider records that there were 159 Catholics in Northampton County. In 1766, Father de Ritter records the death of a son of Peter Bishop "tailor at Allentown." On September 25, 1767, the Catholics of Northampton petitioned the Governor of Pennsylvania for permission to collect money for a Catholic Church in the area. The permission was asked because the Catholics desired to obtain some financial aid from non-Catholics for the construction of a church. Plans never materialized with the start of the American Revolution. As early as 1774, the home of Francis Cooper was used as a Mass house for several years. During the Revolution, Cooper moved to Philadelphia and very little is known of any Catholic activity in Allentown for the remainder of the eighteenth century.

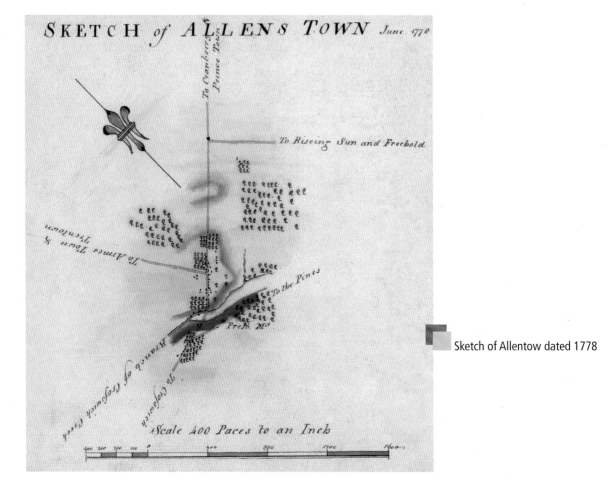

Sketch of Allentow dated 1778

CHAPTER 3:
Early Parishes and Missions
under the Diocese of Philadelphia (1808-1875)

The Diocese of Philadelphia was established by Pope Pius VII on April 8, 1808 from territories of the Archdiocese of Baltimore. Originally the diocese included all of Pennsylvania, Delaware and seven counties of New Jersey. The Most Reverend Michael Francis Egan, O.F.M. was named the first Bishop of Philadelphia and served as bishop until his death on July 22, 1814. The Diocese of Philadelphia was without a bishop for 5 years from 1814 to 1819, while a successor was sought by the Holy See.

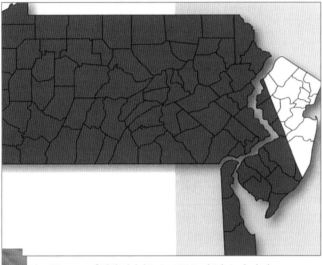

The Diocese of Philadelphia in 1808 which included Pennsylvania, Delaware and western New Jersey

The Most Reverend Henry Conwell was named the second Bishop of Philadelphia on November 26, 1819. He was consecrated bishop in London on August 24, 1820 and arrived in Philadelphia on December 2, 1820. Bishop Conwell served as bishop until his death on April 22, 1842. During his tenure as bishop, 8 parishes and missions were established including: Saint Henry Parish in Moselem Springs (1823), Saint Patrick Parish in Pottsville (1827), Saint Bernard Parish in Easton (1829), Saint John the Baptist Parish in Haycock (1833), Saint Jerome Parish in Tamaqua (1833), Saint Patrick Parish in Nesquehoning (1839), Saint John the Baptist Parish in Pottsville (1841), and Saint Mary Parish in Beaver Meadows (1841).

The Most Reverend Francis Patrick Kenrick was named the third Bishop of Philadelphia on April 22, 1842. He served as bishop until he was installed as the sixth Archbishop of Baltimore on October 9, 1851. During his tenure as bishop, 9 parishes and missions were established including: Saint Vincent de Paul Parish in

Bishop Michael Francis Egan, O.S.F.:
1st Bishop of Philadelphia

Bishop Henry Conwell:
2nd Bishop of Philadelphia

St. Jerome's Church in Tamaqua:
2nd church built in 1855

St. Mary's Church in Beaver Meadows- 1st church built in 1847

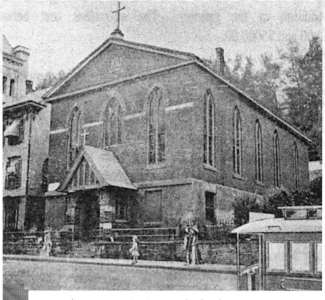

Immaculate Conception in Mauch Chunk

Minersville (1842), Saint Aloysius Mission in Pottsville (1846), Saint Bartholomew Parish in Brockton (1846), Saint Stephen Parish in Port Carbon (1847), Saint Raphael Parish in Tuscarora (1848), Immaculate Conception Parish in Mauch Chunk (1848), Saint Joseph Parish in Summit Hill (1850), Saint Joseph Mission in Laurytown (1850), and Saint Ambrose Parish in Schuylkill Haven (1851).

Bishop Francis Patrick Kenrick- 3rd Bishop of Philadelphia

The Most Reverend John Nepomucene Neumann, C.SS.R. was named the fourth Bishop of Philadelphia in 1852. He was installed as bishop in March 1852 and served as bishop until his death on January 5, 1860. He was later canonized as Saint John Neumann by Pope Paul VI on June 19, 1977. Of all the early bishops and archbishops of Philadelphia, Bishop Neumann made the most missionary travels throughout the See of Philadelphia. During his tenure as bishop, 11 parishes and missions were established including: Saint Joseph Parish in Easton (1852), Saint Boniface Parish in Saint Clair (1853), Saint Mary Parish in Hamburg (1854), Immaculate Conception Parish in Tremont (1854), Our Lady of Mount Carmel Parish in Minersville (1855), Saint Mauritius Parish in Ashland (1856), Saint Joseph Parish in Ashland (1856), Immaculate Conception of the Blessed Virgin Mary Parish in Allentown (1857), Annunciation of the Blessed Virgin Mary Parish in Catasauqua (1857), Saint Kyran/Kieran Parish in Heckscherville (1857), and Saint Lawrence the Martyr Parish in Catasauqua (1858).

The Most Reverend James Frederick Wood was named the fifth Bishop of Philadelphia on January 5, 1860. He served as bishop until the Archdiocese of Philadelphia was established and he was named its first Archbishop on February 12, 1875. During his tenure as bishop, 18 parishes and missions were established including: Saint Paul Parish in Reading (1860), Holy Infancy Parish in Bethlehem (1861), Saint Canicus Parish in Mahanoy City

Bishop (later Saint) John Neumann- 4th Bishop of Philadelphia

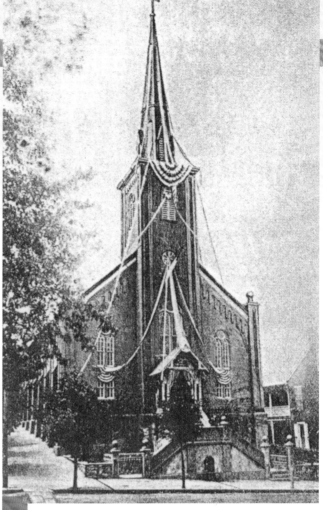

Notes concerning Saint Joseph's Church in Easton made by Bishop John Neumann

(1862), Saint Fidelis Parish in Mahanoy City (1863), Saint Mary Parish in Saint Clair (1863), Saints Peter and Paul Mission in Tower City (1865), Holy Family Parish in New Philadelphia (1866), Sacred Heart of Jesus Parish in Allentown (1869), Saint Patrick Parish in Beaver Brook (1869), Holy Family Parish in Shenandoah (1870), Annunciation of the Blessed Virgin Mary Parish in Shenandoah (1870), Saint Joseph Parish in Girardville (1870), Holy Ghost Parish in Bethlehem (1871), Saint Joseph Parish in Mauch Chunk (1871), Saint Casimir Parish in Shenandoah (1872), Holy Rosary Parish in Mahanoy Plane, Saint Nicholas Mission in Berlinsville (1872), and the German Fireline Mission in Bowmansville (1872).

Sacred Heart Church in Allentown- 1st church built in 1870

Immaculate Conception Church in Mauch Chunk (now Jim Thorpe)- 1st church built in 1852

Annunciation Church and rectory in Shenandoah- built in 1872

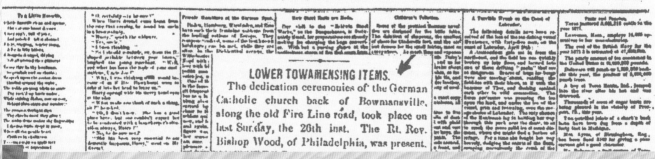

Dedication of the Old German Fireline Church from the Carbon Democrat newspaper on June 6, 1872

CHAPTER 4:
Parish and Mission expansion under the Archdiocese of Philadelphia (1875-1961)

The Archdiocese of Philadelphia was established on February 12, 1875 when the Diocese of Philadelphia was elevated to an Archdiocese by Pope Pius IX. Bishop James Frederick Wood was named the first Archbishop of Philadelphia and served as archbishop until his death on June 20, 1883. During his tenure as archbishop, two parishes were established including: Saint Mary Magdalen Parish in Lost Creek (1879) and Assumption of the Blessed Virgin Mary Parish in Slatington (1883).

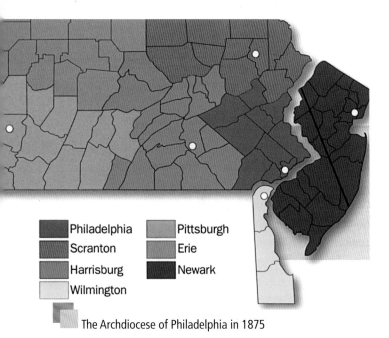

■ Philadelphia	▨ Pittsburgh
▨ Scranton	▨ Erie
▨ Harrisburg	■ Newark
▢ Wilmington	

The Archdiocese of Philadelphia in 1875

Reading (1895), Saint Francis of Assisi Parish in Minersville (1895), Sacred Heart of Jesus Parish in Newtown (1896), Saints Peter and Paul Parish in Tower City (1896), Our Lady of Mount Carmel Parish in Roseto (1897), Saint Stanislaus Parish in Shenandoah (1898), Saint Stephen Parish in Shenandoah (1899), Immaculate Conception Parish in Keylares (1899), Saint Andrew Parish in Catasauqua (1902), Our Lady of Pompeii of the Most Holy Rosary Parish in Bethlehem (1902), Holy Rosary Parish in Reading (1904), Immaculate Conception Parish in Saint Clair (1905),

The Most Reverend Patrick John Ryan was named the second Archbishop of Philadelphia on June 8, 1884. He was installed as archbishop on August 20, 1884 and served as archbishop until his death on February 11, 1911. During his tenure as archbishop, 43 parishes and missions were established including: Saints Peter and Paul Parish in Lehighton (1885), Saint Mary Star of the Sea Parish in Branchdale (1886), Saint Mary Parish in Reading (1888), Saint Joseph Parish in Mahanoy City (1888), Saint Joseph in Reading (1891), Saints Cyril and Methodius Parish in Bethlehem (1891), Saint George Parish in Shenandoah (1891), Saint Michael the Archangel Parish in Lansford (1891), Saint Mary's Parish in Mahanoy City (1892), Saint Mary of the Assumption Parish in Coaldale (1892), Saint Casimir Parish in Mahanoy City (1893), Saint Mary of the Assumption Parish in McAdoo (1893), Saint Kunegunda Parish in McAdoo (1893), Saint Joseph Parish in Sheppton (1894), Sacred Heart Parish in New Philadelphia (1895), Saints Cyril and Methodius Parish in

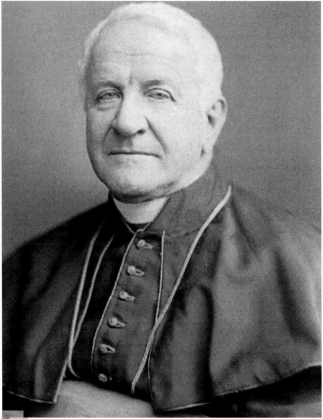

Archbishop James Frederick Wood- 5th Bishop and 1st Archbishop of Philadelphia

Archbishop Patrick John Ryan- 2nd Archbishop of Philadelphia

Little Servants of the Immaculate Conception at St. Mary's Church in Reading in 1926

Sacred Heart Church in Palmerton- built 1908

Gathering of Slovak-American clergy at the cornerstone dedication of St. Michael's Church in Lansford on May 30, 1908

Archbishop Edmond Prendergast

The Little Mission Church of the Nativity served as the first parish church for Saints Simon and Jude in Bethlehem

Sacred Heart Hospital was established by Monsignor Peter Masson in 1911

Saint Stanislaus Kostka Parish in Minersville (1905), Saint John the Baptist Parish in Allentown (1906), Saint Stanislaus Parish in Bethlehem (1906), Saint Vincent de Paul Parish in Girardville (1907), Sacred Heart Parish in Mahanoy City (1907), Saint Louis Parish in Maizeville (1907), Saint Anthony of Padua Parish in Cumbola (1907), Saint Ann Parish in Lansford (1907), Saints Peter and Paul Parish in Lansford (1907), Saint Michael Mission in Easton (1907), Saint Michael Parish in Tresckow (1908), Holy Family Parish in Nazareth (1908), Sacred Heart Parish in Palmerton (1908), Saint Anthony of Padua Parish in Easton (1909), Saint Joseph Parish in Frackville (1909), and Saints Peter and Paul Parish in Tamaqua (1911).

The Most Reverend Edmond Francis Prendergast was named the third Archbishop of Philadelphia on May 27, 1911. He was installed as archbishop on July 26, 1991 and served as archbishop until his death on February 27, 1918. During his tenure as archbishop, 19 parishes and missions were established including: Saints Peter and Paul Parish in Allentown (1912), Saint Casimir Parish in Saint

Cardinal Dennis Joseph Dougherty- 4th Archbishop of Philadelphia

Interior of Sacred Heart Church in Bethlehem

Clair (1912), Saint Joseph Parish in Bethlehem (1913), Our Lady of Mount Carmel Parish in Little Italy (1913), Saint Barbara Mission in Minersville (1913), Saint Anthony Parish in Reading (1913), Saint Anthony of Padua Parish in Reading (1914), Our Lady of Mount Carmel Parish in Shenandoah (1914), Immaculate Conception Parish in Nesquehoning (1914), Saint John the Baptist Parish in Coaldale (1914), Saint Stephen of Hungary Parish in Allentown (1915), Our Lady of Good Counsel Mission in Gordon (1915), Our Lady of Good Counsel Parish in Bangor (1915), Immaculate Conception of the Blessed Virgin Mary Parish in Birdsboro (1916), Saint Michael Parish in Easton (1916), Saint Bartholomew Parish in Tresckow (1917), Annunciation of the Blessed Virgin Mary Parish in Frackville (1917), Saints Simon and Jude Parish in Bethlehem (1917), and Sacred Heart Parish in West Reading (1917).

Three priests, called by one writer "Diocesan Missioners of Christ," played a large role in the formation of many of these parishes. They are Monsignors George Bornemann, William Heinen and Peter Masson.

The Most Reverend Dennis Joseph Dougherty was named the fourth Archbishop of Philadelphia on May 1, 1918. He was installed as archbishop on July 10, 1918 and was created a Cardinal by Pope Benedict XV on March 7, 1921. Cardinal Dougherty served as archbishop until his death on May 31, 1951. During his tenure as

Sisters from St Michael's Parish in Lansford

Cardinal John Francis O'Hara- 5th Archbishop of Philadelphia

in Reading (1920), Sacred Heart Parish in Bath (1920), Mary Queen of Peace Parish in Pottsville (1920), Saints Cyril and Methodius Parish in Coaldale (1920), Saint Columbkill Parish in Boyertown (1921), Saint John Mission in Oneida (1922), Our Lady of Good Counsel Parish in Gordon (1922), Assumption of the Blessed Virgin Mary Parish in Northampton (1922), Saint Francis de Sales Parish in Mount Carbon (1922), Saint Mary Parish in Ringtown (1923), Saint Ann Parish in Frackville (1924), Saint Barbara Parish in Minersville (1924), Saint Vincent de Paul Mission in Portland (1925), Saint Theresa of the Child Jesus Parish in Hellertown (1925), Saint Catharine of Siena Parish in Reading (1925), Our Lady Help of Christians Parish in Allentown (1927), Saint Peter Parish in Coplay (1927), Saint John the Baptist Parish in Whitehall (1927), Saint Joseph Parish in Limeport (1927), Assumption of the Blessed Virgin Mary Mission in Colesville (1927), Holy Trinity Parish in Egypt (1928), Saint Francis of Assisi Parish in Allentown (1928), Saint Paul Parish in Allentown (1928), Saint Anne Parish in Bethlehem (1929), Holy Guardian Angels Parish in Reading (1929), Saint Elizabeth of Hungary Parish in Pen Argyl (1929), Saint Rocco Parish in Martins Creek (1929), Saint Ann Parish in Emmaus (1931), Sacred Heart Parish in Bethlehem (1936), Saint Roch Parish in West Bangor (1937), Saint Elizabeth Parish in Fullerton (1941), Saint Mary Mission in Easton (1943), Saint Joseph the Worker Parish in Fogelsville (1948), Immaculate Heart of Mary Mission in Middleport (1948), Saint John Baptist de La Salle Parish in Shillington (1948), Saint Theresa of Avila Mission in Pottsville (1950), and Saint Richard of Chichester Parish in Barnesville (1950).

archbishop, 43 parishes and missions were established including: Saints Peter and Paul Parish in Saint Clair (1918), Saint Mary Parish in Kutztown (1919), Saint Catharine of Siena Parish in Allentown (1919), Saint Aidan Parish in Ellengowan (1919), Saint Ursula Parish in Fountain Hill (1919), Saint Jane Frances de Chantal Parish in Wilson Borough (1920), Saint Margaret Parish

Church of Notre Dame in Bethlehem in April 1954

The Most Reverend John Francis O'Hara was named the fifth Archbishop of Philadelphia on November 23, 1951. Pope John XXIII made him a Cardinal on December 15, 1958. Cardinal O'Hara served as archbishop until his death on August 28, 1960. During his tenure as archbishop, 3 parishes and missions were established including: Assumption of the Blessed Virgin Mary Mission in Colesville (1952), Notre Dame Parish in Bethlehem (1954), and Saint Benedict Parish in Mohnton (1955).

Cardinal John O'Hara, Archbishop of Philadelphia, died on August 28, 1960. The day after his death, Auxiliary Bishop Joseph McShea summoned the diocesan consultors to meet with him to elect an administrator for the Archdiocese of Philadelphia until Pope John XXIII appointed a successor. Bishop McShea was elected as administrator. Prior to this, he had already been in contact with the Apostolic Delegation about the division of the Archdiocese. On September 10, 1960, Bishop McShea wrote to the Apostolic Delegation about the condition of the Archdiocese and with a few recommendations.

"I make bold to speak on the problem of the dismemberment of the Archdiocese... I was requested on several occasions, as a bishop, to urge the late cardinal to go ahead with the division of the Archdiocese. Cardinal O'Hara always responded that he had refrained from doing this because he wished to erect secondary schools in the territory to be severed from the mother diocese. In fact, he did build these schools in the years preceding his death. I refrain from giving other details concerning the matter, but I am convinced in conscience that the dismemberment would work great good for soul and religion. The priests and people of the upstate region feel they are abandoned and really not part of the great urban Archdiocese. The late cardinal was convinced that this step should be taken at some later date, and when discussing the erection of a new seminary... with characteristic generosity, he said that it should be built in one of the outlying counties so that the new diocese would have its own seminary."

"The See City of the new diocese, which would be comprised of Berks, Lehigh, Carbon, Northampton and Schuylkill Counties, might be

Archbishop John Krol

either Bethlehem, with a population of 75,000 of which approximately 50 percent are Catholic; or Allentown with a population of about 111,000 of whom 25 percent are Catholic. The cathedral of the new diocese could be the beautiful Church of SS. Simon and Jude in Bethlehem; or in Allentown the Church of St. Catharine of Siena."

The Archdiocese of Philadelphia was taken by surprise by the announcements from Rome on February 15, 1961. Archbishop Egidio Vagnozzi, the Apostolic Delegate to the United States, announced to the public that not only had Auxiliary Bishop John Krol of Cleveland been named the new Archbishop of Philadelphia on February 11, 1961, but that the Holy See had also established the new Diocese of Allentown with Bishop Joseph McShea as its founding bishop. Archbishop Krol had been in Rome when the news of his appointment was released. Shortly after his return to Cleveland, Archbishop Krol met with Bishop McShea to discuss the state of the Archdiocese of Philadelphia and to make preliminary arrangements for their separate installations.

CHAPTER 5:
The Diocese of Allentown (1961)

The first idea for the establishment of a diocese in East Central Pennsylvania can be traced back to 1852, when Bishop John Neumann of Philadelphia proposed the erection of a diocese in Pottsville to the 8th Provincial Council of Baltimore. The Council presented the proposal for submission to the Holy See. Bishop Neumann was also willing to become the first Bishop of Pottstville but sadly, the proposal was not approved. Over 100 years later, that new diocese would finally be created from the northern part of the Archdiocese of Philadelphia. The Diocese of Allentown, Pennsylvania was created by Pope John XXIII in an apostolic letter dated January 28, 1961. Pope John XXIII wrote that:

Diocesan papal bull

"The metropolitan Church of Philadelphia for Catholics of the Latin Rite is so extensive in territory and includes so many faithful that it is deemed opportune and of great advantage to the Christian community to erect from it another diocese, as one bud sprouting from another. Therefore....we separate the territory of Berks, Carbon, Lehigh, Northampton, and Schuylkill Counties, from which we establish a new diocese to be known as the Diocese of Allentown. The Cathedral City of this Diocese will be the city of Allentown."

Another apostolic letter dated February 11, 1961, Pope John XXIII appointed Bishop Joseph McShea as one "especially suited to the labors" to the office of first Bishop of Allentown. On February 15, 1961 Archbishop Egidio Vagnozzi, Apostolic Delegate to the United States, in an official statement to the public and news media announced that,

"His Holiness, Pope John XXIII has divided the archdiocese of Philadelphia... to form the new diocese of

Allentown... At the same time the Holy Father has named...the Most Reverend Joseph McShea... to be Bishop of the new See of Allentown."

On April 11, 1961, Bishop Joseph McShea was formally installed as the first Bishop of Allentown by Archbishop Egidio Vagnozzi in the Cathedral Church of Saint Catharine of Siena in the city of Allentown. In his sermon on the day of that solemn ceremony, Bishop McShea spoke about the new Diocese of Allentown.

Bishop Joseph McShea

"This Diocese begins its life with countless resources...but most of all it has almost a quarter of a million Catholic souls. This is a day of birth. The Diocese of Allentown springs forth as another flowering of the Catholic Church, the mighty tree born of the smallest of

seeds... This is a day of dedication. I, your shepherd, and you, my co-workers and flock, offer ourselves without reservation to the spreading of God's Kingdom on earth."

The Diocese of Allentown was entitled to send its clerical students to Saint Charles Borromeo Seminary in Wynnewood. The diocese was also allowed to publish its news in the Catholic Standard and Times. All of the pertinent records relating to the Diocese of Allentown were transferred from the Archdiocese of Philadelphia and included: all the records of the Allentown priests, the spiritual and financial reports of the parishes and institutions of the new diocese, and all of the necessary deeds and titles. For the convenience of Bishop McShea, the controller's office in Philadelphia continued to

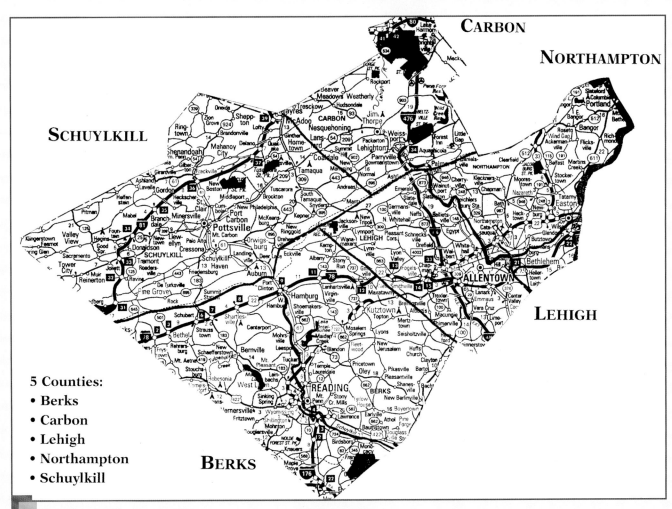

5 Counties:
• Berks
• Carbon
• Lehigh
• Northampton
• Schuylkill

The Diocese of Allentown in 1961

The Diocese of Allentown

administer the financial affairs of Allentown until June 30, 1961. The bishops of Philadelphia and Allentown soon reached an equitable agreement for the division of funds and the financial settlement was finalized in June 1962.

Bishop McShea later stated that there had originally been three possibilities for the location of the diocese: Allentown, Bethlehem and Reading. He had felt that Allentown was better suited because of its central location and the parish of Saint Catharine of Siena was better suited to be the cathedral; it had all the resources and would not have been a burden on the new diocese. So it was at Bishop McShea's suggestion that Allentown and Saint Catharine of Siena were chosen as the See city and the cathedral for the Diocese.

In 1961, the Diocese of Allentown covered 2,773 square miles and the counties of Berks, Carbon, Lehigh, Northampton and Schuylkill. These five counties served a total of 243,260 Catholics out of a total population of 897,325 people. The new diocese included a total of 150 parishes, 98 Catholic elementary schools with 30,000 students, 14 diocesan high schools with 7,000 students, 275 diocesan priests, 60 religious priests, numerous religious orders of men and women, a Vincentian house of theological studies, a Jesuit novitiate at Wernersville, 3

orphanages, 2 schools for special needs children, a training school for girls, 3 hospitals and 4 homes for the convalescent and the aged. Allentown was the seventh suffragan See of the Archdiocese of Philadelphia. The other six dioceses previously created included Pittsburgh (1843), Erie (1853), Scranton (1868), Harrisburg (1868), Altoona-Johnstown (1901), and Greensburg (1951).

The Coat of Arms of the Diocese of Allentown was created in 1961. The golden ring on the silver bar symbolizes Saint Catharine of Siena, the titular saint of the Cathedral of the Diocese of Allentown. The ring designates her mystical marriage to Christ, a ring given to her by our Lord in an apparition. The red background of the diocesan shield signifies the sufferings of Catharine at the hands of her parents, and recalls her devotion to the Church leading to the persuasion of Pope Gregory XI to return from Avignon to Rome. The two silver fleurs-de-lis are taken from the coat of arms of His Holiness, Pope John XXIII, to honor the Pontiff who established the Diocese of Allentown. The silver roundel bearing the red cross was derived from the coat of arms of the Archdiocese of Philadelphia to commemorate the See which gave the Counties of Berks, Carbon, Lehigh, Northampton, and Schuylkill to form the entire territory of the Diocese of Allentown.

The Coat of Arms of the Diocese of Allentown

CHAPTER 6:

The Cathedral of Saint Catharine of Siena in Allentown (1961)

Saint Catharine of Siena Parish was founded by Archbishop Dennis Cardinal Dougherty of Philadelphia on October 8, 1919. He appointed Father John C. Phelan as the first pastor of the new church in the west end of Allentown. Property was soon acquired from Mrs. Leonard Sefring. The Sefring home was converted into a rectory and chapel. Father Phelan celebrated two Masses at the rectory on November 16, 1919. By the spring of 1920, parishioners began converting a stable and carriage house into a chapel.

The chapel was completed by September 1920 and served the parishioners of Saint Catharine of Siena until 1927. Funds were raised for the construction of a combination church, school, and convent in June 1926. They were completed in time for the celebration of Mass on December 25, 1927. The building still stands as the Cathedral Elementary School McShea Building at 210 North Eighteenth Street. Saint Catharine of Siena School was opened on September 4, 1928 with an enrollment of sixty-one pupils and a faculty of four Sisters of Saint Joseph. At its opening, the school included only the first five grades. A grade was added each year and all eight grades were functioning by September 1931. In 1937, the Sisters moved into a new convent, permitting the school to expand to the third floor.

Father John Phelan- 1st pastor of St. Catharine of Siena Parish in Allentown

North Eighteenth Street in May 1957. The School Annex was built at the corner of Eighteenth and Emmet Streets in 1958. The School Annex housed six classrooms for the seventh and eighth grades, with the upper floor serving as a gymnasium.

The year 1961 brought the news of the creation of the Diocese of Allentown, carved from the Archdiocese of Philadelphia and consisting of five counties in eastern Pennsylvania that included: Berks County, Carbon County, Lehigh County, Northampton County and Schuylkill County. The Diocese of Allentown was created by Pope John XXIII on January 28, 1961. On that same day, Pope John XXIII bestowed a great honor on Saint Catharine of Siena Parish by naming it the Cathedral Church of the new Diocese of Allentown.

In the years between 1937 and 1954, the parish experienced rapid growth, coupled with all-around improvements to the parish complex. In 1944, extensive repairs were made to the building which served as the church and school. A cafeteria was also formed about that time. In November 1949, the parish debts were retired and the parishioners looked forward to building a new and larger church. On June 9, 1952, Monsignor Leo Fink turned over the first spade of earth at the blessing and groundbreaking for the new church at Eighteenth and Turner Streets. The cornerstone for the church was laid by the Most Reverend Joseph M. McShea on April 26, 1953. The new and completed church was dedicated on April 25, 1954. The parish complex continued to grow during this period. The convent was expanded with the purchase of property at 213

The old rectory

The original chapel that was converted from a stable and carriage house in 1920

In 1964, the School Annex building was renovated. What had been a spacious gymnasium, now housed nine classrooms on two floors. This brought the number of classrooms in the Annex to fifteen. That same year, the kindergarten was closed to provide more space for primary education classes. The school reached peak enrollment of 1,400 and 30 classrooms from September 1965 until June 1968. In 1968, a school was built at neighboring Saint Thomas More Parish. The Cathedral School also enrolled 732 children in twenty-two classrooms from grades 1 through 8. The first Parish Council was established in June 1969, when over 1,000 parishioners elected 12 members to work alongside 6 clergy that included Monsignor Francis J. Donnelly. Bishop McShea concelebrated a Mass of Thanksgiving on October 5, 1969, marking the 50th anniversary of the founding of the Cathedral Parish. Among the 900 persons attending the Mass were 40 members of the parish's original families and many priests and Sisters who had served the parish or who had entered religious life from the parish.

The Most Reverend Joseph McShea, D.D. was installed as the first Bishop of Allentown at the Cathedral Church of Saint Catharine of Siena in Allentown on April 11, 1961. In May 1961, the Bishop presided over the first ordination rites to be held in the Allentown Cathedral. By September 1961, the Cathedral Choir had been established. The parish was now moving into the years of the Second Vatican Council and many changes were evident.

When the parish church of Saint Catharine of Siena was designated as the Cathedral Church of the Diocese in 1961, a small problem existed. Although the church had a seating capacity of 830 persons, the sanctuary was not adequate for the various pontifical ceremonies which must

The interior of the old St. Catharine of Siena Church in 1944

Monsignor Leo Fink turns over the first spadeful of earth at the ground breaking of the church on June 8, 1952

Auxiliary Bishop Joseph McShea lays the cornerstone for the church on April 26, 1953

be celebrated in the Cathedral Church. The difficulties became even more pronounced following the promulgation of the various liturgical directives of the Second Vatican Council (1962) and the First Synod of Allentown (1968). In order to solve the problem, a major program of renovation was undertaken. In 1972, Bishop McShea began the renovation of the Cathedral. Renovation of the sanctuary was modeled after Santa Maria in Piazza Campitelli in Rome. Changes were also needed in the interior of the church in order for it to look more like a cathedral. Under the guidance of Bishop McShea, four large floor candlesticks containing a carving of the bishop's shield were placed around the altar. Five medallions were placed on the side walls near the top. The medallions on the left side contained the images of the historic events in the diocese's brief history and on the

Interior of the Cathedral of St. Catharine of Siena about 1970

right contain images of the oldest church in each county in the diocese. The baptismal font was moved from the back of the church (which became the back sacristy) to the front left side of the nave. The sanctuary was considerably enlarged without any appreciable loss of seats. Further, the church has been greatly enriched by the addition of new sanctuary furnishings of high artistic quality.

In 1980, Bishop McShea commissioned Dana Van Horn to paint murals for the north and south sanctuary walls of the Cathedral depicting events in the life of Saint Catharine of Siena. The canvass paintings were done on Jack Beal's farm in Oneonta, New York. On April 29, 1981, Bishop McShea celebrated a Pontifical Mass of Dedication in the Cathedral Church of Saint Catharine of Siena. During the solemn liturgy, the Cathedral was consecrated by Bishop McShea in celebration of the 20th anniversary of the founding of the Diocese of Allentown. Bishop McShea also signed the Decree of Dedication at that time. Dana Van Horn's beautiful murals were installed and dedicated by Bishop McShea on November 14, 1982. The north wall painting depicts Saint Catharine leading Pope Gregory XI from Avignon to Rome and Blessed Raymond of Capua, Saint Catharine's spiritual director, riding an ox. The south wall painting shows Saint

Catharine addressing Pope Urban VI with Blessed Raymond behind the Pope, serving as advisor and translator. In 1983, Most Reverend Thomas J. Welsh was installed as the second Bishop of Allentown.

The early 1980s was also a time for new additions to the school. A new library was constructed in 1983 and named in honor of the school's late Vice Principal, Betty Johnson. The Bishop Thompson Scholarship Fund was established and raised $50,000 to assist families with tuition costs in 1986-1987. In 1998, Most Reverend Edward P. Cullen was installed as the third Bishop of the Allentown Diocese. In October 1998, a state-of-the-art computer lab was opened in the Annex Building. The Cathedral Pre-School was opened in the fall of 1997. The kindergarten was increased to a full day program and the Extended Care Program was begun.

In June 1999, Monsignor Alfred Ott began a renovation plan for the parish and announced the purchase of six properties. Eventually, the Walson Center was built next to the McShea Building (old school building). The convent and Tribunal Office were torn down and two parking lots were constructed next to the Annex Building, located across from the Cathedral Church. The Parish Hall, below the church, was also renovated and is now known as the Parish Activity Center.

Bishop Cullen led the way for more renovations and additions to the interior of the Cathedral in 2005. A cathedra, the seat of the diocesan bishop, was positioned on the left hand side of the sanctuary. A huge white marble cross replaced the statue of the Virgin Mother holding the infant Messiah. This was located in the middle of the sanctuary right behind the tabernacle. Surrounding the crucifix there was a large golden mosaic installed. A statue of Mary with the Child Jesus and a statue of Saint Catharine of Siena were placed on the left and right front walls, respectively. A new Crawford ceiling with medallions of the image of Bishop Cullen's shield replaced the old ceiling. A new pulpit was finally situated in the right side of the sanctuary in 2009. Most Reverend John Oliver Barres was installed as the fourth Bishop of Allentown in the Cathedral Church of Saint Catharine of Siena on July 30, 2009.

Cathedral School (now St. John Vianney Regional) in Allentown

The Cathedral

CHAPTER 7:
Bishop Joseph M. McShea
1ˢᵗ Bishop of Allentown 1961~1983

Pope John XXIII, in an apostolic letter dated February 11, 1961, appointed Bishop Joseph Mark McShea to be the first Bishop of the Diocese of Allentown. His appointment as bishop was officially announced in a statement by Archbishop Egidio Vagnozzi, Apostolic Delegate to the United States on February 15, 1961. On April 11, 1961, Bishop Joseph M. McShea was formally installed as the first Bishop of Allentown at the Cathedral Church of Saint Catharine of Siena in Allentown by Archbishop Egidio Vagnozzi. Bishop McShea had previously laid the cornerstone for the future Cathedral of the Diocese of Allentown on April 26, 1953.

Bishop Joseph McShea 1ˢᵗ Bishop of Allentown

The Coat of Arms for Bishop McShea was created in 1961. The left half of the shield contains the coat of arms of the Diocese of Allentown; on the right half the personal arms of Bishop McShea are impaled. On the left half the golden ring on the silver bar symbolizes the mystical marriage to Christ of Saint Catharine of Siena, the titular saint of the Cathedral of the Diocese of Allentown. Her sufferings and devotion to the Church are recalled by the red background. The two silver fleurs-de-lis from the coat of arms of Pope John XXIII honor the Pontiff who established the Diocese. The silver roundel bearing the red cross is taken from the coat of arms of the Archdiocese of Philadelphia and commemorates the

See from which the Diocese of Allentown was split. The Bishop's arms on the right following the arms of the McShea Family of Ireland, is divided into blue and gold partitions by an indented diagonal line. The lily honors Saint Joseph the baptismal patron of Bishop McShea. The reverse cross on which Saint Peter died and the motto "Sub Umbra Petri" (in the shadow of Peter) commemorate Bishop McShea's service to the See of Peter in the Roman Curia and in the Apostolic Delegation in Washington, D.C.

Joseph Mark McShea was born in Lattimer, Pennsylvania on February 22, 1907. He was the son of Roger Aloysius McShea and Jeanette Beach McShea and one of seven children. The McShea family, Irish immigrants from County Donegal, had originally settled

Bishop McShea installed as bishop at the Cathedral of St Catharine of Siena in Allentown on April 11, 1961

in Allentown in 1870. After living there a short time, his grandparents moved to Luzerne County. Bishop McShea spent his early boyhood in his native coal region town, near Hazleton, until the McShea family moved to Philadelphia in 1918. He attended West Philadelphia Catholic High School and entered Saint Charles Borromeo Seminary in 1923. In 1926, he was selected to complete his seminary course at the Pontifical Roman Seminary and the Lateran University in Rome. Joseph McShea was ordained a priest in the chapel of the Roman Seminary by Francesco Cardinal Marchetti-Selvaggiani, the Cardinal Vicar of Rome, on December 6, 1931. He received doctorates in philosophy (Ph.D.) and theology (S.T.D.) and completed his studies in Rome in July 1932.

The Coat of Arms of Bishop Joseph McShea

Bishop McShea taught at Saint Charles Borromeo Seminary from 1932 until March 1935. He returned to Rome to serve as secretary to the Sacred Congregation for the Oriental Churches from 1935 to 1938. In September 1938, he was recalled to the United States to serve as secretary to the Papal Delegate in Washington, D.C. and served under Amleto Cardinal Cicognani until February 1952. Cardinal Cicognani relied heavily on then-Monsignor McShea. During World War II, there was no official diplomatic relationship between the U.S. and the Vatican. Because of his knowledge of Italy and his proficiency in the Italian language, Monsignor McShea was a key conduit between the U.S. government and the Vatican during the Allied effort to retake Italy from the Axis powers. On February 8, 1952, he was named Titular Bishop of Mina and Auxiliary Bishop of Philadelphia. He was consecrated a bishop by Amleto Cardinal Cicognani at the Cathedral of Saints Peter and Paul in Philadelphia on March 19, 1952. In addition to his duties as Auxiliary Bishop, he was also a diocesan consultor and pastor of Saint Francis de Sales in Philadelphia from 1952 to 1961. Bishop McShea was elected as administrator of the Archdiocese of Philadelphia on August 28, 1960, following the death of John Cardinal O'Hara. He served as Auxiliary Bishop and administrator of Philadelphia until April 11, 1961, when he was formally installed as the first Bishop of Allentown on April 11, 1961.

On March 20, 1961, a Tudor-style home located on Chew Street in the city's west end was purchased as the bishop's residence. The home also served as a meeting hall for the assembly of the school board, charity board and diocesan consultors. On April 11, 1961, Bishop McShea named Monsignor Leo Fink to serve as vicar general and Monsignor David Thompson to serve as chancellor. Twelve diocesan consultors were also named to aid in the administration of the diocese. In late 1961, Pope John XXIII appointed Bishop McShea as a member of the Pontifical Commission of Religious for the preparatory sessions of the Second Vatican Council and consultor for the Sacred Congregation for the Oriental Churches. He left for Rome to attend the meetings on January 10, 1962 and was received in a private audience by Pope John XXIII on January 24, 1962. The opening of the Second Vatican

Bishop McShea installed as 1st bishop

Monsignor Leo Fink

On January 28, 1964, Bishop McShea established a Diocesan Liturgical Commission to implement the Constitution on the Sacred Liturgy from the Second Vatican Council. On March 3, 1965, he made a request for the Holy See to designate "Mary, Mother of the Church" as the Patroness of the Diocese of Allentown. Pope Paul VI officially granted the request on April 21, 1965. In early 1966, Bishop McShea called for a initial diocesan modernization plan. On October 11, 1966, he announced extensive changes in the administrative and pastoral structures of the diocese according to the decrees of Vatican II and the norms implementing those decrees. Changes in the administrative and pastoral structures included: the appointment of an additional vicar general, the formation of new deaneries and the election of deans, the establishment of a Council of Priests and the formation of a Pastoral Council. Monsignor David Thompson was appointed to act as the chancellor and the

Bishop McShea and Monsignor David Thompson with Pope Paul VI during a visit to Rome in 1969

Council took place on October 11, 1962. On October 22, 1962, Bishop McShea was elected to the Commission for Religious and was one of only 18 Americans elected to the ten commissions which facilitated the Council's work before returning to Allentown on December 7, 1962.

On February 7, 1962, the diocese purchased land to construct Holy Family Manor and the home for the aged was opened on January 13, 1963. Bishop McShea dedicated the Villa Maria Retreat Center in Wernersville on August 26, 1962. On September 6, 1962, he announced a multi-million dollar education expansion program for the Diocese. The program included plans for a new college, three new high schools, and additions to three existing high schools. An intensive fund drive was undertaken. These funds provided for the creation of four new school buildings including: Holy Name High School in Reading (1964), Bethlehem Catholic High School in Bethlehem (1964), Marian Catholic High School in Tamaqua (1964) and Allentown College of Saint Francis de Sales in Center Valley (1965). The three new parishes also established were Our Lady of Perpetual Help Parish in Bethlehem (1963), Saint Ignatius Loyola Parish in Sinking Spring (1965) and Saint Thomas More Parish in Allentown (1966).

Bishop David Thompson, one of three priests of the Diocese of Allentown who became bishops. He was the first Chancellor of the Diocese of Allentown. He was Vicar General of the Diocese and rector of the Cathedral when he was appointed Bishop of Charleston, SC in 1989. He retired in 1999.

Bishop McShea breaks ground for Allentown College of Saint Francis de Sales on May 17, 1964

Bishop McShea signs the statutes of the 1st Synod of Allentown 1968

second vicar general. Bishop McShea also announced the formation of two new deaneries and the expansion of the duties and powers of the deans. Lehigh County, which previously did not have the status of a deanery because it contained the See city, was made a deanery. The second new deanery was formed from the division of the Schuylkill County Deanery into two distinct districts: East Schuylkill County Deanery and West Schuylkill County Deanery.

In January 1967, planning for the First Synod of Allentown began with the specific goal of the synod being the practical implementation on a diocesan and parish level of the spirit and specific teaching of the Second Vatican Council. On April 3, 1967, Bishop McShea formally announced his intention to convoke a diocesan synod. At that time he appointed a Promoter of the Synod and a Central Commission of eight priests to serve as a managing and coordinating group to guarantee the efficient and proper functioning of the entire synodal

BISHOP'S OFFICE
1729 TURNER STREET
ALLENTOWN, PENNSYLVANIA

To the
Clergy, Religious and Laity
of the
Diocese of Allentown

Dearly Beloved in Christ,

May 1, 1968, was a historic day for the Diocese of Allentown. With the participation of our priests, religious and widely representative groups of the laity the First Synod of Allentown was held in the Cathedral of Saint Catharine of Siena. That ceremonial and canonical observance was the climax of long months of intense consultation and study. I am confident that the doctrinal statements and the statutes enacted represent the best collective thinking of the total Church in the Diocese of Allentown. All were invited to contribute their suggestions; these were carefully weighed and evaluated. For the rest, I am confident that the First Synod of Allentown will through the years prove a valid aid and support to our ministry of salvation.

It is my prayerful plea that the legislation enacted be accepted and observed with the traditional loyalty and love of the Church which have ever been so characteristic of the clergy, laity and religious of our diocese.

+ Joseph M°Shea
Bishop of Allentown

procedure. Thirteen Special Commissions were also designated to formulate doctrine, statutes and recommendations in particular areas of concern. Each Special Commission consisted of a chairman, secretary and at least eight members. Forty-five lay people served in an official capacity on the commissions. These thirteen Special Commissions included: Commission on Worship and Prayer, Commission on Pastoral Government, Commission on the Clergy, Commission on Religious, Commission on the Laity, Commission on Christian Education, Commission on Christian Social Action, Commission on Catholic Schools, Commission on Church Unity, Commission on Marriage and the Family, Commission on Temporal Goods, Commission on Ceremonies and Commission on Press, Radio and Television. A

Letter from Bishop McShea regarding the 1st Synod of Allentown 1968

Holy Family Villa in Bethlehem

Bishop McShea with Allentown's 1ˢᵗ group of permanent deacons after their ordination at the Cathedral on October 16, 1982

unique characteristic of the synodal process was a successful effort to achieve the widest possible involvement of the priests, religious, and laity of the Diocese. A most enthusiastic response on the part of the laity resulted in over 10,000 suggestions during a three-month period. The revised first drafts of the Special Commissions were published as the "Yellow Book" in November 1967. The Central Commission drew up a synthesis of the doctrine and statutes found in the "Yellow Book" and this synthesis was published as the "Blue Book" on December 6, 1967. The final review and synthesis of the "Blue Book" resulted in the publication of the "Red Book" in April 1968. The solemn celebration and promulgation of the First Synod

Bishop McShea with Mother Teresa during her visit to the Diocese of Allentown in 1976

of Allentown was held on May 1, 1968. The Central Committee studied the "Red Book" and made minor revisions from May-December, 1968. The publication and distribution of the "First Synod of Allentown" official document took place on January 1, 1969. The Allentown Diocese was among the first few dioceses in the country to attempt such an intensive modernization after the Second Vatican Council.

On April 19, 1970, Catholics of the Allentown Diocese were introduced to the Catholic Mass in English. Saturday evening Mass was first celebrated throughout the diocese on June 27, 1970. The Diocese of Allentown was the center for two national movements: National Shut-in Day and Operation Rice Bowl. National Shut-in Day was founded in Reading by Monsignor Felix Losito in October 1970. Operation Rice Bowl was founded in the Allentown area in 1975. Holy Family Villa was opened in Bethlehem for retired priests of the diocese on June 16, 1974. In September 1979, Bishop McShea welcomed 35 men into the first Permanent Deacon Program in the diocese and all 35 were later ordained as deacons in the spring of 1982. On April 29, 1981, the Cathedral of Saint Catharine of Siena in Allentown was consecrated by Bishop McShea on the occasion of the 20th anniversary of the Diocese of Allentown.

Bishop McShea observed the 50th anniversary of his ordination to the priesthood at a Golden Jubilee Mass at the Cathedral of Saint Catharine of Siena on December 6, 1981. On February 22, 1982, he submitted a letter of resignation to Pope John Paul II on his 75th birthday according to the established procedures of the Church. On February 8, 1983, the Holy Father accepted his resignation and named the Most Reverend Thomas Welsh as the 2nd Bishop of Allentown. Bishop Joseph McShea died in Allentown at the age of 84 years on November 28, 1991. A two-hour funeral Mass for Bishop Joseph Mark McShea, the 1st Bishop of Allentown was held at the Cathedral of Saint Catharine of Siena on December 4, 1991.

Cardinal Anthony Bevilacqua sprinkles holy water on the casket of Bishop McShea at his burial on the grounds of the Cathedral of St. Catharine of Siena in 1991

CHAPTER 8:
Bishop Thomas J. Welsh
2nd Bishop of Allentown 1983-1998

Thomas Jerome Welsh was born December 20, 1921 in Weatherly, Carbon County, Pennsylvania, to Edward and Mary Doheny Welsh. Bishop Welsh attended Saint Nicholas Grade School and Schwab High School, both in Weatherly. In 1937, he entered Saint Charles Borromeo Seminary, Philadelphia, to begin studies for the priesthood. The late Dennis Cardinal Dougherty ordained him a priest on May 30, 1946 in the Cathedral of SS. Peter and Paul, Philadelphia. After his ordination, Bishop Welsh was sent to do graduate studies in canon law at the Catholic University of America, Washington, D.C. from 1946 to 1949, where he earned a doctorate in canon law. He was then appointed a professor at the former Southeast Catholic High School in Philadelphia where he served for two years. He later served as an assistant pastor at a parish in Philadelphia.

Bishop Thomas Welsh - 2nd Bishop of Allentown

In 1958, Bishop Welsh was appointed a member of the Archdiocesan Metropolitan Marriage Tribunal. In 1963 he was appointed Vice Chancellor of the Archdiocese. Pope Paul VI named him a Monsignor in September of 1965 and in 1966 John Cardinal Krol, Archbishop of Philadelphia appointed Bishop Welsh rector of Saint Charles Borromeo Seminary. Pope Paul VI named him Titular Bishop of Scattery Island and Auxiliary Bishop of Philadelphia on February 18, 1970. He was consecrated a bishop on April 2, 1970 by Cardinal John Krol in the Cathedral of Saints Peter and Paul in Philadelphia. On June 6, 1974, Bishop Welsh was appointed founding bishop of the newly formed Diocese of Arlington by Pope Paul VI and was formally installed on August 13, 1974.

On February 8, 1983, Pope John Paul II accepted the resignation of Bishop Joseph McShea, founding Bishop of the Diocese of Allentown and appointed Bishop Thomas Welsh to succeed him. He was installed as the Second Bishop of Allentown on March 21, 1983 at the Cathedral of Saint Catharine of Siena in Allentown by Cardinal John Krol of Philadelphia and Archbishop Pio Laghi, Apostolic Delegate to the United States.

Immediately after his installation Bishop Welsh gave indications that he wanted to be a pastor among his people. He held six regional celebrations throughout the diocese to which he invited not only the faithful of the area, but also religious and civic leaders.

Bishop Welsh in 1974

On August 14, 1983, Bishop Welsh initiated the "Stand Up for Life" campaign to promote pro-life educational efforts throughout the diocese in parishes, schools and organizations. He held two one-day workshops on Natural Family Planning and on the papal encyclical Humanae Vitae for the priests of the diocese. Bishop Welsh also personally led a group of couples preparing for marriage through three sessions of the diocesan marriage preparation dialogues. In November 1983, Bishop Welsh was selected by Pope John Paul II to be a member of the six-man Presidential Commission of the Pontifical Council for the Family.

In June 1984, Bishop Welsh established the first Youth Ministry Office in the diocese and raised $13 million in an endowment campaign for diocesan schools and other educational efforts. He was a member of the Board of Trustees and Executive Committee of the National Shrine of the Immaculate Conception in Washington, D.C. In 1989, Bishop Welsh founded the Diocesan newspaper, The AD Times.

Bishop Welsh was a champion for many causes, one of which was the preservation of Catholic schools. On September 29, 1984, he announced the "Forward With Christ" education endowment campaign for diocesan schools and other educational quests. Thanks to the overwhelming generosity of the people of the Diocese of Allentown, the six-month campaign exceeded its goal of $8 million and raised nearly $13 million. In May 1985, the Diocesan Development Office was established by Bishop Welsh as a consequence of the "Forward With Christ" campaign.

Evangelization throughout the diocese was the cornerstone of Bishop Welsh's spiritual agenda. He was the impetus behind the establishment of PEACE (Perpetual Eucharistic Adoration Centers for Evangelization) throughout the diocese. He also coordinated a pair of FIRE (Faith, Intercession, Repentance and Evangelism) rallies at Lehigh University in Bethlehem during 1986, 1989 and 1996. Bishop Welsh highlighted the RCIA as the foremost area of evangelization efforts.

Bishop Welsh celebrated the 50th anniversary of his ordination while attending the annual pilgrimage to the Basilica of the National Shrine of the Immaculate Conception in Washington, D.C. on May 2, 1996. In December 1997, Pope John Paul II accepted Bishop Welsh's resignation as Bishop of Allentown. After the installation of Bishop Edward Cullen as his successor in February 1998, Bishop Welsh remained

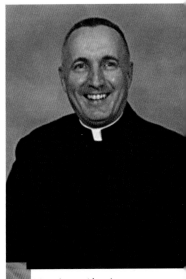

Bishop Welsh with Mother Teresa during her visit to the Diocese of Allentown in 1995

Bishop Welsh's installation on March 21, 1983 with Cardinal Krol, Archbishop Pio Laghi and Bishop McShea

Monsignor Aloysius Callaghan served with the Congregation for Religious and Secular Institutes from 1986-1991 and then with the Congregation for Bishops from 1991-1995.

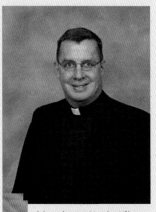

Monsignor Nevin Klinger served with the Congregation for Divine Worship and Discipline of the Sacraments from 1991-1996.

active and administering the Sacrament of Confirmation at churches throughout the Diocese.

Bishop Welsh, then Bishop of the Diocese of Arlington, spearheaded a project to help people around the world with limited time or no access to religious study to be able to obtain the knowledge of God that they needed in 1983. The result was the Catholic Distance University (CDU), an educational facility and the first catechetical institute in the United States that offered the Catechetical Diploma with approval from the Vatican Congregation for Clergy. Bishop Welsh continued to oversee the CDU after his installation as the Bishop of Allentown in 1983. In celebration of the 15th anniversary of the CDU, Bishop Welsh led the faithful from the Dioceses of Allentown, Arlington and Baltimore, and the Archdiocese of Philadelphia on a 10-day pilgrimage to Rome in March 1999.

Bishop Thomas Welsh died in Allentown on February 19, 2009. Memorial Masses were celebrated for Bishop

Funeral Mass for Bishop Thomas Welsh at the Cathedral on February 28, 2009

Welsh at the Cathedral of Saint Catherine of Siena in Allentown on February 26th-27th, 2009. A vigil service was also held at the Cathedral on February 27, 2009. A Mass of Christian Burial was held at the Cathedral on February 28, 2009 and was followed by his burial in Saint Nicholas Cemetery in Weatherly.

The Pilgrimage to Rome with Bishop Welsh in honor of the 15th anniversary of the Catholic Distance University in 1999

Bishop Welsh talks with Pope John Paul II during World Youth Day in Denver in August 1993

Bishop Welsh and Mother Teresa outside St. Joseph Church in Mahanoy City during her historic visit to Schuylkill County in June of 1995

CHAPTER 9:
Bishop Edward P. Cullen
3rd Bishop of Allentown 1998-2009

Edward Peter Cullen was born March 15, 1933 in Philadelphia, Pennsylvania, to Edward Peter and Julia Catherine Leahy Cullen. He was raised in Yeadon, and was the second of five children. Cullen attended Saint Louis School in Yeadon and West Philadelphia Catholic High School for Boys. Following his graduation from West Catholic in 1951, he studied engineering at the Drexel Institute of Technology. In 1953, he entered St. Charles Borromeo Seminary in Overbrook, from where he obtained Bachelor of Arts degree in 1958.

Bishop Edward Cullen- 3rd Bishop of Allentown

Bishop Cullen's installation ceremony on February 9, 1998

On May 19, 1962, Bishop Cullen was ordained to the priesthood by Archbishop John Krol in the Cathedral of Saints Peter and Paul in Philadelphia. His first assignment was as assistant pastor at Saint Maria Goretti Church in Hatfield from 1962-1965. He then served as assistant pastor of Saint Bartholomew Church in Philadelphia from 1965-1968 and as chaplain at Saint Hubert Catholic High School for Girls from 1967-1968. In 1968, he was named assistant director of Catholic Social Services in Philadelphia and served as resident chaplain at the Sisters of Mercy Convent in Merion from 1970-1979.

Bishop Cullen was sent by Archbishop Krol to study social work at the University of Pennsylvania, later earning his Master of Social Work degree in 1970. This was followed by a Master of Religious Education from La Salle University in 1971 and a Master of Divinity from Saint Charles Borromeo Seminary in 1974. From 1979-1993, he served as a chaplain at Saint Edmond's Home for Children in Bryn Mawr. Bishop Cullen was named an Honorary Prelate of His Holiness in April 1982, and served as director of Catholic Social Services from 1983-1988. In August 1988, he was named Vicar General of the Archdiocese of Philadelphia. Bishop Cullen was appointed Auxiliary Bishop of Philadelphia and Titular Bishop of Paria in Proconsolare by Pope John Paul II on February 8, 1994. He received his episcopal consecration on April 14, 1994 from Cardinal Bevilacqua. He selected "Christ, Church, Compassion" as his episcopal motto.

Pope John Paul II accepted the resignation of Bishop Welsh and named Bishop Edward Cullen as the third Bishop of Allentown on December 16, 1997. He was formally installed by Cardinal Anthony Bevilacqua of Philadelphia at the Cathedral of Saint Catharine of Siena in Allentown on February 9, 1998.

In January 1999, Bishop Cullen reorganized diocesan administration and created the Secretariat Model. He formed five secretariat offices that included: the Secretariat for Clergy, the Secretariat for Catholic Life and Evangelization, the Secretariat for Temporal Affairs, the Secretariat for Catholic Education and the Secretariat for Catholic Human Services. Bishop Cullen was responsible for the creation of the Priest Personnel Board and Commission for

The Coat of Arms
of Bishop Edward Cullen

Women. Under his direction, the Offices of Adult Formation, Banking and Investments, and Prison Ministry were also created. Bishop Cullen relocated all the diocesan offices into more modern facilities.

Bishop Cullen introduced the spiritual program RENEW 2000 to the diocese. RENEW 2000 strove to replenish spirituality and strengthen evangelization by forming closer ties within the parish community through small prayer communities that intensified and promoted spirituality and faith sharing. In 2003, Bishop Cullen launched the capital campaign, "Strengthening Our Future in Faith," to which the people of the Diocese pledged more than $54 million.

Bishop Cullen changed the name of Catholic Social Agency to Catholic Charities, Diocese of Allentown. Under Bishop Cullen's guidance Catholic Charities, Diocese of Allentown procured for the first time professional accreditation after a five-year process. He also established a two-tiered governance system for Catholic Charities: a Board of Members and a Board of Trustees.

The Institute for Lay Ministry (ILM), a three-year formation program for the laity , which certified them as

From left to right: Monsignor Andrew Baker, an Allentown priest then assigned to the Vatican's Congregation for Bishops; Pope John Paul II; Bishop Cullen and Monsignor Alfred Schlert, the Diocese's Vicar General during the Bishop's ad limina visit to Rome in 2004.

Bishop Cullen and Father Michael Camilli gather with members of the new diocesan Commission for Women on June 23, 2004

Bishop Cullen speaks at the Strengthening Our Future in Faith campaign dinner on May 27, 2003

Bishop Cullen signs the decree promulgating 27 statutes of the 2nd Synod of Allentown on December 10, 2006 at the Cathedral

qualified to provide leadership in various ministries in the diocese, was established under Bishop Cullen's guidance.

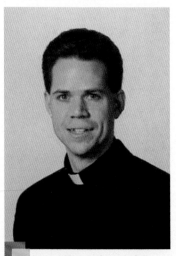

Monsignor Andrew Baker served with the Congregation for Bishops from 2001-2009.

Under Bishop Cullen, Project Rachel was also implemented in the diocese. This post-abortion reconciliation and healing program linked anyone suffering abortion's aftermath with Project Rachel-trained priests and counselors. In the area of interfaith relations, Bishop Cullen hosted a number of meetings with ecumenical leaders of the area and accompanied Jewish survivors of the Holocaust who spoke at Allentown Central Catholic High School, Bethlehem Catholic High School and Notre Dame High School.

Bishop Cullen has led the Cause for the Canonization of Shenandoah native, Father Walter J. Ciszek, S.J. Under his direction, required documentation was completed and forwarded to the Vatican's Congregation for the Causes of Saints, an essential step required in pursuing Father Ciszek's canonization. Bishop Cullen also formally affiliated the religious order Apostles of Jesus (AJ) into

diocesan pastoral ministry. He invited the Sisters of Peace Pentecost into the diocese to minister at the Peace Retreat House in Weatherly. Bishop Cullen's tenure has seen the construction of Seton Manor in Orwigsburg and the establishment of Holy Family Assisted Living at Saint Francis Center in Orwigsburg. Bishop Cullen was intricately involved in the renovation of the Cathedral in 2005.

Bishop Cullen endorsed and participated in the formulation of the Charter for the Protection of Children and Young People. He ensured that the Diocese of Allentown was in full compliance with the charter in all of the audits conducted by the United States Conference of Catholic Bishops.

Bishop Cullen was elected by his brother bishops as chairman of the standing USCCB committee on Women in the Church and served two terms as a trustee of the Catholic University of America.

The academic community honored Bishop Cullen. He was awarded honorary degrees and invited to speak at commencement ceremonies by La Salle University, Muhlenberg College, De Sales University, Alvernia University and Albright College.

Bishop Cullen convoked the Second Synod of Allentown in 2005. The process began with hundreds of people attending listening sessions in each of the six deaneries of the diocese to offer input on the Synod topics. The Solemn Synod Closing Mass was held on December 10, 2006 at the Cathedral of Saint Catharine of Siena in Allentown and Bishop Cullen signed the Statutes of the Synod. The Synod produced 26 statutes, one of which called for the establishment of a Diocesan Pastoral

Bishop Cullen celebrates Mass at the Cathedral marking his 10th anniversary as Bishop of Allentown on February 10, 2008

Council. "The 23 member council was established and charged with the implementation of the 26 Synod statutes, three of which concerned the consolidation and restructuring of parishes. Deanery Region Committees made recommendations on restructuring where necessary, using criteria developed by the Diocesan Pastoral Council and applied uniformly across the Diocese. The Diocesan Pastoral Council and the Council of Priests reviewed the recommendations before the Bishop acted on them.

A letter from Bishop Cullen was read during the Masses at each parish in the six Deaneries of the Diocese of Allentown the weekend of June 1, 2008. In the letter, the plans for parish restructuring were announced and Bishop Cullen wrote:

> *"These decisions have not been made easily or without deliberation. The Listening Sessions, the Second Synod of Allentown, Deanery Region Committees, the Diocesan Pastoral Council, and the Council of Priests represent the advice of thousands of people in this matter. Nonetheless, this decision may cause disappointment or even pain for not a few parishioners. Such feelings truly are understandable. As you have supported the Church with your prayers throughout this process, know that I, along with all who advised me in this process, also support you with our prayers."*

In May 2008 Bishop wrote a pastoral letter entitled, "Experiencing the Love of Our Triune God" and this was followed by a second pastoral letter in February 2009 entitled, "The Cross and Suffering." The content for both of these pastoral letters was drawn heavily from the bishop's personal prayer journal.

In March 2008, Bishop Cullen submitted his resignation to the Holy See, as required under church law on his 75th birthday. Pope Benedict XVI accepted his resignation one year later and named Monsignor John Oliver Barres, Chancellor of the Diocese of Wilmington, as the fourth Bishop of the Diocese of Allentown on May 27, 2009. Bishop-elect Barres was installed as the fourth Bishop of Allentown on July 30, 2009.

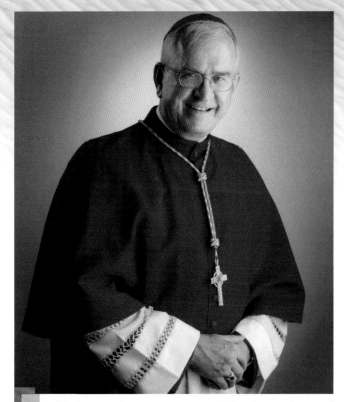

Archbishop Joseph Kurtz was a pastor in the Diocese, director of the Social Action Bureau and President of the Board of Directors of Catholic Charities here. He was appointed Bishop of Knoxville, TN in 1999 and then Archbishop of Louisville in 2007.

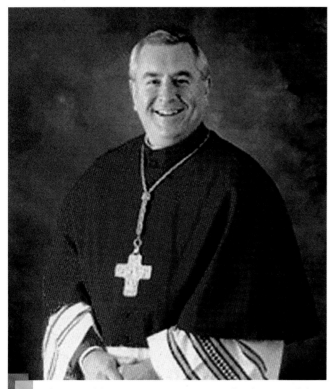

Bishop Ronald Gainer. He was a pastor, Judicial Vicar and the Secretary for Catholic Life and Evangelization in the Diocese. He was appointed Bishop of Lexington, KY in 2002

CHAPTER 10
Bishop John O. Barres
4th Bishop of Allentown 2009

Bishop Barres was born on September 20, 1960 and is a native of Larchmont, New York. His parents, Oliver (a native of Bethlehem, PA) and Marjorie Barres, are convert Protestant ministers who met each other at the Yale Divinity School and entered the Catholic Church in 1955. The story of their conversion is told in Oliver Barres' book, One Shepherd, One Flock, which was published by Sheed and Ward in 1955 and again in 2000 by Catholic Answers. Bishop Barres is the fifth of six children and has seven nephews and four nieces.

Bishop Barres is a graduate of Phillips Academy, Princeton University, and the New York University Graduate School of Business Administration. His theological education includes an STB and an STL in Systematic Theology from the Catholic University of America (where he received seminary formation at Theological College), and a JCL in Canon Law and an STD in Spiritual theology from the Pontifical University of the Holy Cross in Rome. His 1999 doctoral dissertation is entitled Jean-Jacques Olier's

Priestly Spirituality: Mental Prayer and Virtue as the Foundation for the Direction of Souls.

Bishop Barres was baptized by Bishop Fulton J. Sheen in 1960 while his father was working for the Bishop at the Propagation of the Faith in New York City. He was ordained to the priesthood for the Diocese of Wilmington October 21, 1989 by Bishop Robert Mulvee now Bishop Emeritus of the Diocese of Providence. He served as an associate pastor at Holy Family Church in Newark, DE and St. Elizabeth's parish in Wilmington, DE After further study in Rome with residence at the Pontifical North American College, he served as Vice-Chancellor and then Chancellor for Bishop Michael Saltarelli and then Bishop W. Francis Malooly.

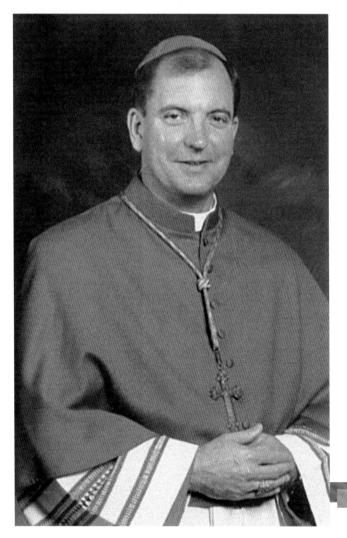

Bishop John Barres played three years of JV basketball at Princeton University during the Coach Pete Carril era.

Bishop John Barres- 4th Bishop of Allentown

Bishop Barres' ordination 1989

Bishop Cullen and Bishop-elect Barres at a press conference May 27, 2009

Pope John Paul II named him a "Chaplain to His Holiness" in July 2000 with the title of "Monsignor." Pope Benedict XVI named him a "Prelate of Honor" in November 2005. In addition to serving on various diocesan boards and committees in Wilmington, Bishop Barres has served on the Administrative Board of the Maryland Catholic Conference, the Board of St. Francis Hospital and the Board of the Cathedral Foundation in Baltimore.

Bishop Barres with Pope John Paul II in Rome 1996

Bishop Edward Cullen submitted his resignation to the Holy See, as required under church law, at the age of 75 in March 2008. Pope Benedict XVI accepted his resignation one year later and named Monsignor John Oliver Barres, Chancellor of the Diocese of Wilmington, as the fourth Bishop of the Diocese of Allentown on May 27, 2009. Bishop-elect Barres was ordained a Bishop and installed as the fourth Bishop of Allentown by His Eminence, Justin Cardinal Rigali, Archbishop of Philadelphia at a special Mass at the Cathedral of Saint Catharine of Siena in Allentown on July 30, 2009. The ceremony was historic because it marked the first time that a priest was ordained a bishop for the Diocese of Allentown since its founding in 1961.

All three previous bishops were already bishops when they were installed as Bishop of Allentown. During the ceremony, Bishop Barres spoke of the signs of the times and hinted at a new evangelization by stating that:

"There are so many signs of hope on the horizon of the 21st century. Together, we in the Diocese of Allentown will read the signs of the times so that we can discern the will of the Holy Spirit with the guidance of Peter... Now is the time for that springtime. Now is the time for evangelization- using every means of modern technology at our disposal to spread the Gospel. And at the heart of evangelization is catechesis."

In the Coat of Arms of Bishop Barres, the red and silver bars are a canting device recalling the Bishop's family surname "Barres". The Bishop's immigrant ancestor was Jacob Barres, who came from Prussia and first settled in Lehigh County in 1852. The blue eagle with the halo is the symbol of Saint John the Evangelist, honoring the Bishop's baptismal name patron. The cross keys symbolically express the Bishop's dedication and fidelity to the See of Peter and to the Most Holy Father, as did the arms of Bishop Barres' predecessor, Bishop Cullen. The dolphin is taken from the arms of Saint John Fisher, and the rose represents Saint Thomas More, particularly his chain of office as Lord Chancellor of England. Pope John Paul II, by motu proprio in 2000, declared Saint Thomas More the Patron of Statesmen, Politicians, and Lawyers. Both of these saints, one a prelate and one a layman, were martyrs for the Faith and remained loyal to the Church and the Holy See. Their symbols are depicted in red to indicate their martyrdom. The axe represents Abraham Lincoln of whom Bishop Barres is a great admirer. The arms are completed with current episcopal indicia authorized by Pope Paul VI in 1969, which are a gold processional cross placed in back of the shield extending above and below it and a round wide-brimmed green "gallero" hat containing a tassel on each side of the hat's crown. Suspended from the gallero are six additional tassels in three rows on each side of the green shield.

The Coat of Arms of Bishop John Barres

Bishop Barres' motto is "Holiness and Mission." It is derived from a phrase in the final section of Pope John Paul II's 1990 encyclical, Redemptoris Missio. Entitled "The True Missionary is the Saint," His Holiness, Pope John Paul II wrote:

"The call to mission derives, of its nature, from the call to holiness. A missionary is really such only if he commits himself to the way of holiness: 'Holiness must be called a fundamental presupposition and an irreplaceable condition for everyone in fulfilling the mission of salvation in the Church.' The universal call to holiness is closely linked to the universal call to mission. Every member of the faithful is called to holiness and to mission. This was the earnest desire of the Council, which hoped to be able 'to enlighten all people with the brightness of Christ, which gleams over the face of the Church, by preaching the Gospel to every creature.' The

Cardinal Rigali blesses Bishop Barres at his 2009 installation

Bishop Barres' installation ceremony 2009

Church's missionary spirituality is a journey towards holiness."

On August 4, 2010 Bishop Barres issued a Pastoral Letter to the priests of the Diocese of Allentown on the 150th Anniversary of the Death of St. John Marie Vianney, the Cure of Ars. In that letter, he stated: "So many of you over the course of many years have served our parishes and our people with humility, charity, pastoral intelligence, grace and finesse. You are the pastoral artists, both young and old, to whom Pope John Paul II refers... The solid peace that radiates from a priest's face, a face that contemplates the face of Christ in silence, in Word and in Sacrament, moves hearts and reflects a heart ablaze with love. The peace on a dedicated priest's face naturally evangelizes."

Bishop Barres celebrates the annual Ciszek Mass at St. Casimir Church in Shenandoah in October 2009

On May 22, 2010, upon receiving an honorary degree from DeSales University, Bishop Barres said these words to the DeSales University Class of 2010:

"Saint Paul writes in his first letter to the Corinthians: "Eye has not seen, ear has not heard…what God has prepared for those who love him." And a great Churchman, Cardinal Merry del Val, put it this way in his spiritual journal: "Receive everything from God and your life will be the first stanza of an eternal hymn, the dawn of a happiness without sunset."

This eternal "happiness without sunset" is where your focus should be. It is precisely this focus that will shed light on every practical detail, every item on your to-do list of every day.

The goal for you and your future spouse is the spirit of holiness and mission that will lead both of you to Eternal Life. Pope Benedict XVI, like Pope John Paul II before him, has repeatedly said that he wants to canonize married couples. Why shouldn't some of those future couples be members of the DeSales University Class of 2010?"

Bishop Barres has initiated a vibrant diocesan-wide St. Thomas More Society for lawyers, "Encountering the Merciful Savior" designed to bring Catholics back to the Sacrament of Penance, and an aspirancy program for young men considering a call to the priesthood. Understanding that periods of renewal in the Church are periods of intense catechesis, the Bishop places a strong emphasis on catechesis at every level, a catechesis that reaches the mind, heart and imagination.

Father Walter Ciszek, who died in 1984, was a native of Shenandoah who became a Jesuit missionary to Russia. He was arrested as a Vatican spy in 1941 and was held captive for 22 years. His cause for canonization is now under review at the Vatican.

The Parishes
OF THE DIOCESE OF ALLENTOWN

Cathedral of Saint Catharine of Siena

ALLENTOWN, PENNSYLVANIA

Established April 11, 1961

Saint Catharine of Siena Parish in Allentown was established by Archbishop Dennis Cardinal Dougherty of Philadelphia on October 8, 1919. Father John Phelan was appointed as the first pastor. Property was acquired from Mrs. Leonard Sefring. The Sefring home was converted into a rectory and chapel. Father Phelan celebrated two Masses at the rectory on November 16, 1919. By the spring of 1920, parishioners began converting a stable and carriage house into a chapel. The chapel was completed by September 1920 and served Saint Catharine's parishioners until 1927. Funds were raised for the construction of a combination church, school, and convent in June 1926. They were completed in time for the celebration of Mass on December 25, 1927. The building still stands as Saint John Vianney Regional School's McShea Building on North 18th Street.

Saint Catharine of Siena School was opened by the Sisters of Saint Joseph on September 4, 1928. In 1937, the Sisters moved into a new convent, permitting the school to expand to the third floor. In 1944, extensive repairs were made to the building which served as the church and school. Plans for a new and larger church were begun in 1949. On June 9, 1952, ground was broken for the new church by Monsignor Leo Fink. The cornerstone was laid by the Most Reverend Joseph M. McShea on April 26, 1953

and the church was dedicated on April 25, 1954. In May 1957, the convent was expanded with the purchase of property on North 18th Street. The School Annex was built in 1958 at the corner of Eighteenth and Emmet Streets.

The Diocese of Allentown, carved from the Archdiocese of Philadelphia and consisting of five counties in eastern Pennsylvania (Berks, Lehigh, Northampton, Schuylkill, and Carbon) was established in 1961. A great honor was bestowed on Saint Catharine of Siena Parish and the church became the Cathedral Church of the new Diocese. The Most Reverend Joseph McShea, D.D. was installed as the first Bishop of Allentown on April 11, 1961 and Saint Catharine's became the Cathedral Church.

In 1964, the school Annex building was renovated. Bishop McShea concelebrated a Mass of Thanksgiving on October 5, 1969, marking the 50th Anniversary of the founding of the Cathedral Parish. In 1972, Bishop McShea began renovations of the Cathedral, modeling the sanctuary after Santa Maria in Piazza Campitelli in Rome. Changes were needed to the interior of the church in order for it to look more like a cathedral. In 1980, Bishop McShea commissioned Dana Van Horn to paint murals for the north and south sanctuary walls of the Cathedral depicting events in the life of Saint Catharine of Siena. The canvass paintings were installed and dedicated on November 14, 1982. The north wall painting depicts Saint Catharine leading Pope Gregory XI from Avignon to Rome and Blessed Raymond of Capua riding an ox. The south wall painting shows Saint Catharine addressing Pope Urban VI with Blessed Raymond behind the Pope serving as advisor and translator. In 1983, Most Reverend Thomas J. Welsh was installed as the second Bishop of Allentown. The early 1980s was also a time for new additions to the school. A new library was constructed in 1983. The Bishop Thompson Scholarship Fund was also established. In 1998, Most Reverend Edward P. Cullen was installed as the third Bishop of the Allentown Diocese.

In June 1999, Monsignor Alfred Ott began a renovation plan and announced the purchase of six properties. The Walson Center was built next to the McShea Building. The convent and Tribunal Office were torn down. The Parish Hall was renovated and is now known as the Parish Activity Center. Bishop Cullen led the way for more renovations and additions to the interior of the Cathedral in 2005. A "cathedra", the seat of the diocesan bishop, was positioned on the left hand side of the sanctuary. A huge white marble cross replaced the statue of the Virgin Mother holding the infant Messiah. Surrounding the crucifix, a large golden mosaic was installed. Statues of Mary with the Child Jesus and Saint Catharine of Siena were placed on the left and right front walls. A new Crawford ceiling with medallions of the image of Bishop Cullen's shield replaced the old ceiling. In 2009, a new pulpit was situated on the right side of the sanctuary. Monsignor Andrew Baker is the pastor since June 2009.

School

Immaculate Conception Of Blessed Virgin Mary Parish

ALLENTOWN, PENNSYLVANIA

Established 1857

A s the first Roman Catholic parish in Lehigh County, Immaculate Conception is historically significant in the Allentown Diocese. Immaculate Conception of the Blessed Virgin Mary Parish in Allentown was established in 1857. The first church was dedicated by Bishop John Neumann in 1857. The current magnificent Gothic church was completed in the early 1880s.

Immaculate Conception was a pioneer of formal Catholic education in Allentown. In October 1858, early classes were held for 30 children at the Ridge Avenue home of Peter Koehler. The parish grade school was opened by five Sisters of Saint Joseph in September 1907. From 1923 to 1943, the parish grade school also housed the Allentown Catholic High School. In 1975, the parish schools of Immaculate Conception, Saint John the Baptist and Saints Peter and Paul were combined to form Holy Spirit School. Immaculate Conception Church was chosen to house the National Shrine of Our Lady of Guadalupe, Patroness of the Americas in 1974. Monsignor Albert Byrne, M. Div. is the current pastor of Immaculate Conception Parish.

Our Lady of Mercy Catholic Mission traces its history to a group of Syriac families from Allentown. At their request, Bishop Joseph McShea visited them. Many years later it was decided there was a need for a Catholic Mission not only for the Syriac families but for all Catholic families with an Arabic background. With the support of Father Harold Dagle, pastor of Immaculate Conception, Bishop Younan sent Father Samer to establish Our Lady of Mercy Syriac Catholic Mission in October 2002. Father Bassim Shoni has been administrator of the mission since 2005. Our Lady of Mercy Mission serves about 150 families.

School

Our Lady Help of Christians Parish

ALLENTOWN, PENNSYLVANIA

Established June 16, 1927

Located in a section of Allentown then called Rittersville, Our Lady Help of Christians' original church held Mass in the old Bast School. In March 1927, Father Leo Fink asked Archbishop Dennis Cardinal Dougherty of Philadelphia for permission to buy property in Rittersville for a mission that would serve the patients at Allentown State Hospital. The Bast School property was purchased and converted into a chapel and a temporary classroom. On June 16, 1927, Our Lady of Good Help of Christians Parish was established by Archbishop Dougherty. He appointed Father Joseph Mathis to serve as both pastor and as chaplain for Catholics at the State Hospital.

On December 18, 1927, an annex for the church-school was erected on ground between the chapel and rectory. On April 29, 1928, ground was broken for a new church-school building and the building was completed on December 16, 1928. On December 25, 1928, Father Mathis offered the first Christmas Mass in the new building. The Sisters of Christian Charity were appointed by the Archbishop to operate the parish school. The students used kneelers as seats and pews as desks until December 3, 1928, when they were transferred to the 2nd and 3rd floors of the new church-school building.

In 1957, the first addition to the school was completed. A second addition to the school was completed in 1961. A new convent with a private chapel was completed in 1962, followed by a new rectory in 1963. The cornerstone for a new church was laid in 1963 and dedicated on December 12, 1964. By 2003, a major school renovation took place. Monsignor Ed Domin became pastor in 2006 and was responsible for the painting of the church interior. Father John Pendzick, M.A. has served as pastor since 2008.

School

Sacred Heart of Jesus Parish

ALLENTOWN, PENNSYLVANIA

Established September 12, 1869

Under orders from Bishop James Wood of Philadelphia, Father Ernest Hilterman purchased the present site of Sacred Heart Church and the property was immediately prepared for the erection of a brick church. On September 12, 1869, the cornerstone was laid by Bishop Wood. The parish school opened in the basement of the church by the Sisters of Saint Francis of Glen Riddle on October 2, 1870. The church was dedicated to the Sacred Heart of Jesus on November 6, 1870.

Father John Maus served as pastor from 1883 to 1899. During his pastorate, the parish was enlarged with a separate building in the rear of the church to provide meeting space and a hall in the church basement. Father Joseph Nerz served as pastor from 1899 to 1911. He dedicated much of his energy to building a three-story school. Monsignor Peter Masson served as pastor from 1911 to 1926 and founded Sacred Heart Hospital.

The next pastor was Monsignor Leo G. Fink, who for 38 years from 1926 to 1964, presided over a flurry of activity both within the parish and in the larger community. He was the first Vicar General of the Diocese of Allentown.

Until the 1960s the predominant ethnic identity at Sacred Heart was German, then Austrian. Today the Spanish-speaking immigrants of Central and South America and the Caribbean countries have necessitated adding more Masses and services in Spanish.

Monsignor Joseph Sobiesiak was appointed pastor in June 1992. He continued upgrading the parish buildings including remodeling the convent into a Religious Education Center. An extensive church renovation project was launched and the basement was converted into Pastors' Hall. Monsignor John Grabish has served as pastor since 2001.

Our Lady of Mount Carmel Parish in Allentown was established by Archbishop Prendergast on May 1, 1914 to serve the Italian families of Allentown. Father Carmine Cillo was appointed the first pastor. The parish purchased a house on Ridge Avenue for use as a chapel and rectory on November 24, 1914. The former Calvary Methodist Episcopal Church was purchased on April 24, 1921 and the church was dedicated by Monsignor Masson as Our Lady of Mount Carmel Church in 1921.

Father Francis Nave retired in 1995 as the last resident pastor of Our Lady of Mount Carmel. Monsignor Grabish was the administrator of the parish when it closed July 15, 2008 and was consolidated with Sacred Heart parish.

School

Saint Francis of Assisi Parish

ALLENTOWN, PENNSYLVANIA

Established 1928

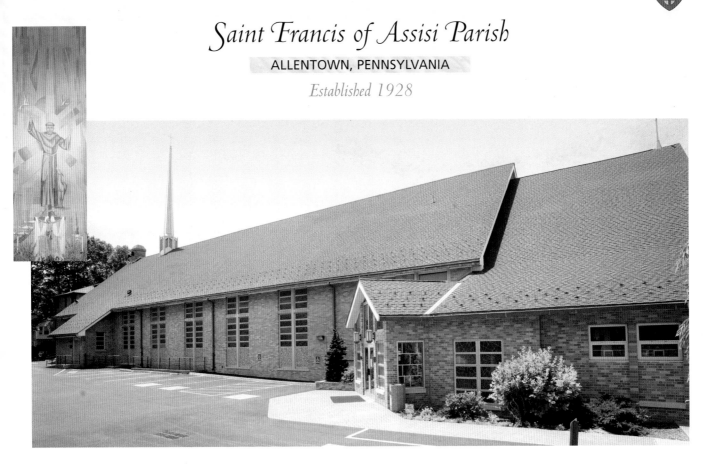

Saint Francis of Assisi Parish in Allentown was established in 1928. Father Francis W. Walters appointed as the first pastor. Mass was celebrated in the Hall above Levan's Garage and the New Allen Theatre. The parish purchased a house at 761 North Eleventh Street for use as a rectory. Construction of a combination church-school building began in 1930. The church-school building was dedicated by Auxiliary Bishop Gerald O'Hara of Philadelphia in May 1931.

Saint Francis of Assisi School was opened by the Sisters of Saint Francis in September 1931. In 1931, the rectory on North Eleventh Street was converted into a convent for the Sisters of Saint Francis and Father Walters set up residence at the school. A new rectory was built at 801 North Eleventh Street in 1938. A new convent for the Sisters was built at 1028 West Cedar Street in 1948. The Saint Francis of Assisi School Annex was built in 1952. Ground was broken for a new church in March 1962. On August 4, 1963, the new church was dedicated by Bishop McShea.

Our Lady of the Rosary Chapel was dedicated on December 8, 1987. In July 1992, the Saint Francis of Assisi Convent was closed and the Sisters of Saint Francis of Philadelphia were reassigned. The convent was converted into a parish center in 1993. Excavations began for a new parish addition to the church on September 15, 1997. On August 30, 1998, Bishop Welsh dedicated the new addition. Renovations of the church interior, new parish center and Heritage Hall were also completed. In 2006, the rectory meeting room was remodeled for use as a daily Mass chapel. In 2007, the Church Adoration Chapel was remodeled and the remodeled Early Learning Center was renamed the Franciscan Center. Monsignor David James was named pastor of Saint Francis of Assisi Parish in 2009.

Saint John The Baptist Parish

ALLENTOWN, PENNSYLVANIA

Established December 31, 1906

As the number of Slovak people increased in Allentown, they began to work towards founding a parish of their own. In 1906, Father Francis Vlossak was given the responsibility of organizing a parish and raising funds for a church. On December 31, 1906, a mansion house on 4.25 acres was purchased by Monsignor William Heinen and Father Vlossak from the Allentown Iron Company. Saint John the Baptist Parish in Allentown was officially established on December 31, 1906.

Beginning on November 3, 1906, Father Vlossak came every Sunday to Allentown and said Mass in the Church of the Immaculate Conception. He continued this until March 3, 1907, when the remodeling of the first floor of the mansion into a temporary chapel had been completed. Father Aloysius Vychodil was then appointed as the first pastor of the newly founded parish. After a short time, the number of parishioners continued to increase. A new church was soon needed when the chapel became too small to house the parishioners that came to Mass. Work on the new church was begun by Father Vychodil in 1911. The church building was completed in 1913. Father Joseph Novorolsky became pastor in 1915. During his short stay, three bells were installed in the belfry of the church.

In 1918, Reverend Doctor Petro was appointed pastor. In 1921, the church was

School

frescoed and the Stations of the Cross were put in the church. Father Petro also began plans for a new parish school. Work on the new school was begun in 1923 and completed in 1924. Saint John the Baptist School was opened by the Missionary Sisters of the Most Sacred Heart of Jesus in the fall of 1924. In 1928, a new rectory was built. The old rectory was immediately remodeled and turned into a convent for the Sisters. In 1949, a new facade and bell tower were added to original church. In 1968, the convent was renovated, followed by the construction of a new social hall in 1969. In 1975, Saint John the Baptist School was consolidated with Immaculate Conception School to form the new Holy Spirit School. Holy Spirit School was closed in 2010. Father Dominic Kalata is the current pastor of Saint John the Baptist Parish.

Saint Paul Parish

ALLENTOWN, PENNSYLVANIA

Established June 13, 1928

Saint Paul's Church was founded as a mission of Sacred Heart Parish in Allentown by Monsignor Fink on October 12, 1927. The old Aineyville Public School at 1110 South Front Street was purchased and required extensive renovations. For the next 20 years, the former school served as the center for all parish activities. The parish hall was on the first floor, the rectory on one wing of the second floor and the church on the other wing. The first Mass was held on November 6, 1927. On June 13, 1928, Saint Paul's was established as a parish by Archbishop Dougherty of Philadelphia. Father Frederick Fasig was appointed the first pastor.

In the summer of 1945, the six-acre former Edgemont Ball Park was purchased. Ground was broken for the basement church by Monsignor Fink on November 30, 1947. The laying of the cornerstone and dedication was held on August 22, 1948. The first Mass was held in the basement church on April 10, 1949. The rectory was completed in 1952. Work began on an addition to the church-school building in 1953. The new second and third floors ultimately would house eight classrooms, the convent, and administrative offices. The new school was opened in September 1954 with five Sisters of Mercy. A new convent was completed in the fall of 1957.

School

Ground was broken for the new church on July 4, 1970. Included in the project were the renovation of the basement church into an auditorium-gymnasium and an addition to the school. The first Mass was celebrated in the new church on September 11, 1971. Both the church and parochial school addition were formally dedicated on October 15, 1972. With the approaching Golden Jubilee in 1978, some of the parish buildings received a much needed renovation. Decorations were added to the new church's unfinished shrines and chapels. An addition was also made to the rectory. The old building in which the parish started, located at 1110 South Front Street, was sold in February 1978. Monsignor Joseph Sobiesiak, Th. M. is the current pastor of Saint Paul Parish.

Saints Peter and Paul Parish

ALLENTOWN, PENNSYLVANIA

Established November 1912

Towards the end of the 19th century, a small group of Polish families settled in Allentown. In time, arrangements were made by Father Alfred Wroblewski, pastor of Saint Stanislaus Parish in Bethlehem, to provide them with a local place in which to worship. Monsignor Masson, pastor of Sacred Heart of Jesus Church in Allentown and a staunch friend of the Poles, permitted Father Wroblewski to celebrate Mass in the basement of his church. In 1912, the Poles approached him with the idea of building a church of their own. Monsignor Masson presented the matter to the church authorities who agreed to establish a parish for the Polish inhabitants of Allentown. In November 1912, Saints Peter and Paul was established as a parish and Father Michael Strzemplewicz was appointed as the first pastor.

In January 1913, Father Strzemplewicz bought a plot of ground for the site of the new church. In late 1913, Monsignor Masson blessed the new church building. In 1915, Father Leon Pateracki became pastor. During his administration, the parish purchased a house to serve as the rectory. Father Peter Kucharski served as pastor from 1925 to 1930. During his pastorate, the church was decorated and the present rectory was built. Adjoining lots to the church and rectory were also purchased.

Father Theophilus Lewandowski became pastor in 1938. After World War II, he had the interior of the church decorated. Father Bruno Kucment became pastor on January 5, 1950. The church was completely renovated during 1962. On September 23, 1962, a Mass was celebrated by Bishop McShea to commemorate the 50th Anniversary of the parish. The church and rectory were both renovated in 1982. The rectory basement was converted into a social hall. Father Dominic Kalata is the administrator of Saints Peter and Paul Parish.

Saint Stephen of Hungary Parish

ALLENTOWN, PENNSYLVANIA

Established 1915

In 1913, the growing number of Hungarian Catholics of Allentown decided they needed their own church. While exploring options to build a church, the group held services in the basement of Sacred Heart of Jesus Church in Allentown. In 1915, Saint Stephen of Hungary Parish was established. On April 24, 1916, church members purchased the property at 502-506 Union Street with plans to build a formal church on the site. Construction of the church began and the cornerstone was laid on August 25, 1917. In August 1924, the parish purchased the property at 510 Union Street. On August 17, 1925, Father Ladislaus Nagy was appointed pastor. He was responsible for various upgrades and improvements to the then existing church building.

After World War II, more Hungarians immigrated to Allentown and the long postponed plans to expand the church began. In September 1948, work also began on the new rectory at 510 Union Street. In May 1950, Father Nagy started a building fund drive for a new church. On May 2, 1953, ground was broken for the new church and the cornerstone was laid on October 16, 1955. On December 23, 1956, the church was dedicated. Because of the Hungarian Revolution of 1956, many people fled their homeland and settled in Allentown; and many newly-arrived Hungarian families joined the parish. The new church soon filled with additional members. In 1982, the parish again purchased more land adjacent to the church property. With the onset of center-city redevelopment within the City of Allentown, the number of parish families dwindled as former parishioners joined churches in their new neighborhoods.

Following the death of Father Richard Ford, the pastoral care of Saint Stephen's was assigned to the Cathedral Church of Saint Catharine of Siena in Allentown in 2005. During that time, parish schedules were adjusted to allow the priests of the Cathedral to serve both parishes. The possibility of suppressing Saint Stephen's Parish and selling the facilities to establish a Syrian Rite Catholic parish in Allentown was raised and met with clear opposition. In September 2006, Bishop Cullen established Saint Stephen's as the diocesan site for the celebration of the Traditional Latin Mass. The first Traditional Latin Mass was celebrated at Saint Stephen's in October 2006. Father William Seifert has served as pastor since June 2006.

Saint Thomas More Parish

ALLENTOWN, PENNSYLVANIA

Established May 1966

Swain School to the gymnasium of the partially completed school building. Saint Thomas More School was opened by the Sisters of Saint Joseph of Chestnut Hill in September 1969.

Saint Thomas More Church was formally dedicated by Bishop McShea on October 17, 1971. In 1974, a new parish center was completed. A highlight in the parish's history was a visit by Mother Teresa in April 1976. She came to express appreciation to the community for its financial support through Operation Rice Bowl, the nationwide Lenten sacrificial program founded at Saint Thomas More in 1975. A two-story arts and science center was added to the school in 1977. In 1979, a new choir loft and organ were added to the church.

The Sisters of Saint Joseph continued to staff Saint Thomas More School until 1982. The Bernardine Sisters of Saint Francis agreed to staff the school in 1982. In 1982, the Saint Thomas More Family Center was constructed and dedicated in April 1983. This was followed by the renovation of the parish center. In 1989, the church was renovated with a new roof and a major refurbishing of the interior including a new sanctuary and baptismal font. A chapel for daily Mass was also added. Monsignor John P. Murphy is the current pastor of Saint Thomas More Parish.

School

Saint Thomas More Parish in Allentown was established in May 1966, when Bishop Joseph McShea announced its formation with a nucleus of 550 families and 17 acres of undeveloped land in Salisbury Township. Father Robert J. Coll was appointed the first pastor. During the summer of 1966, Sunday Masses were celebrated at Swain Country Day School and week-day services at Hope United Church of Christ. In November 1966, the parishioners endorsed a $1.4 million proposal to build an entire church complex that included a church, school and convent. Groundbreaking for the complex was held on December 24, 1967. As the church was being built, daily worship took place in a small construction shed on site and then in a chapel converted from a garage in the first rectory. In mid-1968, Mass was moved from the

Saint Joseph Parish

ASHLAND, PENNSYLVANIA

Established 1856

Saint Joseph Parish in Ashland was established by Bishop John Neumann in 1856. The first mass in Ashland was said by Father Lyndon, pastor of Saint Patrick Church in Pottsville, on June 14, 1856. The first church was a stone building on the corner where the present rectory now stands. The first Mass in the church was held on Saint Patrick's Day 1857. Father Michael Sheridan was appointed as the first pastor in 1857.

The cornerstone of the present church was laid on August 29, 1886. A rectory was also built. Construction of the school was begun in 1913. Saint Joseph's School was opened by the Immaculate Heart of Mary Sisters in 1914. A high school was added in 1915. Father Joseph McDermott became pastor in 1924. He remodeled and enlarged the school. Father Francis Hoey became pastor in 1930 and built Saint Anne's Mission Chapel in Big Mine Run.

Father John McPeak became pastor in 1964. Under his pastorate, the church and school were remodeled, Saint Anne's Chapel in Big Mine Run was closed and a new Chapel was built in the church basement. Father Maletz became pastor in 1982. He removed the confessionals from the rear of the church, removed the third floor of the school, remodeled the hall and installed the Saint Anne's Shrine. Saint Joseph's School was closed in the 1990s and the Sisters, Servants of the Immaculate Heart of Mary left the parish. Bishop Cullen celebrated the 150th anniversary of the parish with a Mass on June 11, 2006. Father Adam Sedar became pastor in 2006. He constructed the Grotto of the Holy Family and made improvements to Saint Anne's Chapel. Father John Bambrick has served as pastor of Saint Joseph Parish since July 15, 2008.

Saint Mauritius Parish

Established September 1856

The first German Catholics settled in Ashland about 1840. The first Mass was celebrated by Father Weggeman at the home of Ferdinand Loeper. Masses were also celebrated in a house owned by Adam Hornung and in the school house located at Tenth and Walnut Streets. Priests came to Ashland once a month from Saint Clair, Patterson and Minersville. Saint Mauritius Parish was organized in September 1856. On September 19, 1856, three lots located between Brock and Pine Streets were purchased from John Brock. The church foundation was laid in 1856. In March 1858, Father John Baptist Frisch was appointed as the first resident pastor. He began construction on the first rectory. Father J. B. Bach became pastor in 1861. In 1862, Father Bach enlarged the church. The first rectory was also completed.

Father Frederick W. Longinus became pastor in 1873. During his pastorate, the Sisters of Saint Francis came to Saint Mauritius and held classes in the basement of the church. A new roof and three new altars were also added to the church. Father Anthony Nathe became pastor in February 1878. He erected the Saint Mauritius Parochial School building in 1881. Father Aloysius Misteli was appointed pastor in October 1898. Upon his arrival, the stone church had deteriorated so badly due to bad mortar that it was razed. In 1900, a new church was erected. The old rectory was rebuilt in 1910. Saint Elizabeth's Mission Chapel in Lavelle was established in 1936.

Monsignor Joseph Marzen became pastor in 1969. During his pastorate, the inside of the church was renovated. The Sisters of Saint Francis left the parish in 1972, due to the consolidation of Saint Mauritius and Saint Joseph Schools as the new Immaculate Heart Elementary School.

Father Edwin Schwartz became pastor in 1974. Father Schwartz did further remodeling in the church and had the interior of the Chapel painted. Saint Elizabeth Mission Chapel in Lavelle was closed in 2002. Saint Mauritius Parish celebrated their 150th Anniversary with a Mass on September 17, 2006. Father John Bambrick has served as pastor since July 15, 2008.

Most Blessed Sacrament Parish

BALLY, PENNSYLVANIA

Established 1741

Most Blessed Sacrament Parish in Bally was originally established as the Chapel of Saint Paul in Goshenhoppen by a Jesuit priest named Father Theodore Schneider in 1741. Most Blessed Sacrament is the oldest parish in the Diocese of Allentown. The school is recognized as the oldest Catholic-public school in the Thirteen Original Colonies. Father Theodore Schneider was chosen to come to Goshenhoppen to establish a permanent Catholic mission. According to tradition, the Catholics and Mennonites built Saint Paul's Chapel together. The present parish church consists of the old Chapel of Saint Paul, to which the Church of the Most Blessed Sacrament was added. This structure was ultimately enlarged by an extension of the nave and by the addition of a Colonial facade and vestibule. The little schoolroom, known as Father Bally's School, forms a link or passage way from the church to the rectory, which is built of red bricks in the traditional homestead style.

The first Catholics settled in Goshenhoppen as early as 1741, when Father Schneider first arrived.

The earliest record of Jesuit missionary work in the vicinity was the first baptismal record dated August 23, 1741 at Falkner's Swamp, which was later known as Pottsgrove or Pottstown.

A total of 499 acres were purchased in 1742 and 1747. Father Schneider first said Mass in the homes of the people until he acquired a residence in a two-story frame house and made it his rectory and parish school. The first mention of Goshenhoppen was the baptism of George Melchoir on February 13, 1743. In 1743, he began building the Chapel of Saint Paul, which still stands in the apse of the present Church of the Most Blessed Sacrament. One of the great achievements of Father Schneider's pastorate was the founding of the first Catholic parish school in Pennsylvania. Father Schneider died on July 10, 1764. Father John Baptist de Ritter, S.J. served as pastor from 1764 to 1793. He led the parish during the Revolutionary War.

Father Augustin Bally, S.J. was appointed pastor on October 31, 1837. When he first came to Goshenhoppen, he found that the name had been changed to Churchville. Father Bally built a new schoolhouse. Father Bally died on January 20, 1882. The name of the village was subsequently changed to Bally in 1883. The Sisters of St. Francis from Glen Riddle arrived on August 1, 1889 and were the first religious community to teach at Bally. Their first home was the residence between the church and the priests' house where Father Bally had lived. The current Saint Francis Academy was opened on September 1, 1889. A new school was built in 1893. The Sisters convent was built in 1922.

On May 22, 1952, Father Charles L. Allwein was appointed pastor and his first concern was to build a new school. A plot of ground at the corner of Seventh and Pine Streets in Bally was obtained and ground was broken on March 1, 1953. The new school was opened for classes on September 10, 1953 and dedicated on April 9, 1954. Restoration and renovation of the parish church took place between 1984 and 1991. Most Blessed Sacrament Parish celebrated its 250th anniversary during 1991-1992. In May 1997, the church's historic Krauss organ was rededicated and the parish museum was dedicated. Monsignor Edward Coyle is the current pastor. Most Blessed Sacrament Parish in Bally serves 1000 families.

Our Lady of Good Counsel Parish

BANGOR, PENNSYLVANIA

Established 1915

Father Thomas O'Neill was the inspiration of the church, which was named for Saint Vincent de Paul as the founder of the Congregation of the Missions (Vincentians). The first Masses were celebrated about 1923 at Fulmer Hall, also known as the Red Hall, on what is now State Street. After the building was condemned, Masses were held at the Patti home until the following spring when they moved away. Mass was then celebrated in the Moreken home until the church was built in 1925. The land where the church was built was donated by Charles Munsch so a church could be built there. The church was struck by lightning twice and later renovated. The first Sunday school classes were held in Portland and Mount Bethel by lay teachers. In 1954, the Salesian Sisters took over the mission classes.

Father John Fitzgerald, C.M. was named pastor of Our Lady of Good Counsel in 1975. In 1988, an outdoor shrine was built in honor of Our Blessed Mother. As part of the parish's 75th anniversary, interior church renovations were completed in 1990. After two years of dedicated efforts, a new grotto was also dedicated during the 75th Jubilee of Saint Vincent de Paul Mission on May 7, 2000. Monsignor Thomas Derzack, M. Div. has served as pastor since 2009.

The Slate Belt was served from 1893 until 1915, by priests from Our Lady of Mount Carmel Parish in Roseto. Beginning in 1915, Father James Lavezzari staffed Our Lady of Mount Carmel with an American confrere. The confreres began the parish in Bangor to take care of Irish Catholics who had previously gone to Roseto. Father Joseph P. McKey of the Congregation of the Missions came to the Slate Belt area in 1915. He planned a Catholic Mission Center at Bangor. Soon, a solid brick church and rectory were constructed. On September 2, 1917, the church was dedicated to Our Lady of Good Counsel by Father Patrick McHale, head of the Order of Saint Vincent de Paul in Philadelphia. Father Jeremiah Tracy, C.M. was the first active pastor.

The roots of Saint Vincent de Paul Mission in Portland begin in 1921. Father Blake, pastor of Our Lady of Good Counsel, took a census of the Catholic families in the area. About 10-12 families lived in the Portland area. The people of this area first attended Mass at Our Lady of Mount Carmel in Roseto and later at Our Lady of Good Counsel. Because of the large area covered by Our Lady of Good Counsel, a mission church was built in Portland in 1925.

St Vincent de Paul Mission, Portland

Saint Richard of Chichester Parish

BARNESVILLE, PENNSYLVANIA

Established October 1, 1950

The Church of Saint Richard of Chichester in Barnesville was begun as a mission in 1946 by Father Joseph McCaffrey of Saint Canicus Church in Mahanoy City. Services were held first in the Ryan Township Fire Company, the Lakewood Ballroom and later, in the Lakewood Tennis Club Building.

On October 1, 1950, Archbishop Dennis Cardinal Dougherty of Philadelphia established the mission as a parish under the direction of Father Edwin Horn as pastor. Two acres of land with a house, for use as a rectory, was given by the Guinan family to the parish. Archbishop John F. O'Hara gave permission to build a new church and designate it as Saint Richard of Chichester. Ground was broken for the church in July of 1954. The first Mass was held in the church on Easter Sunday 1955. The dedication of the church and laying of the cornerstone by Auxiliary Bishop J. Carroll McCormick of Philadelphia took place on July 3, 1955.

Father Stephen Halabura became pastor in 2001. He participated in the reorganization of the area's parishes and actively argued for Saint Richard's Church to remain open based on its location and potential for growth. His argument succeeded and the parish remained open. Father Joseph Whalen, M. Div. became pastor in July 2008.

Sacred Heart of Jesus Parish

BATH, PENNSYLVANIA

Established 1920

Sacred Heart of Jesus Parish owes its beginning to Father Bernard Greifenberg, pastor of Holy Family Parish in Nazareth, who first saw the necessity of a mission church in Bath. In 1915, he rented an old motion picture theater located on the southwest corner of Northampton and Chestnut Streets and converted it for use as a church. Every second Sunday, Mass was said there for about two dozen Catholic families. A large black Crucifix was painted on the movie screen and beneath stood the improvised altar. The narrow theater benches served as pews and a high-backed pedal organ stood up near the front on the right side. Religious training was also offered in the building on Saturday afternoons and was conducted by the Nazareth Sisters of the Sacred Heart.

With the permission of the Archbishop Dennis Cardinal Dougherty of Philadelphia, land was purchased and a church erected in 1920. The church was dedicated to the Sacred Heart of Jesus by Monsignor Masson of Allentown in the fall of 1920. For two years, the parish was served by Father Greifenberg from Holy Family. Father Jacob William Post was appointed as the first resident pastor in June 1922. During his pastorate, the parish purchased ground for a cemetery in September 1922 and built the school, convent and rectory. The school was dedicated by Monsignor Masson when partially completed in the late spring of 1925. In September 1925, Sacred Heart School was opened by the Sisters of Mercy. A convent was constructed for the Sisters in late 1926.

Interior and exterior renovations of the church were accomplished in 1938 and 1953. The back of the church building was expanded to add a new sanctuary and sacristies in 1938. The church was again expanded by rebuilding the front in 1953. The cornerstone was laid and the new façade of the church was dedicated by Archbishop John Cardinal O'Hara of Philadelphia on September 11, 1955. The convent was completely remodeled with an addition added in 1964. Monsignor Francis Nave, M. Div. has been pastor of Sacred Heart Parish since 2007.

Assumption of The Blessed Virgin Mary Parish

BETHLEHEM, PENNSYLVANIA

Established October 16, 1952

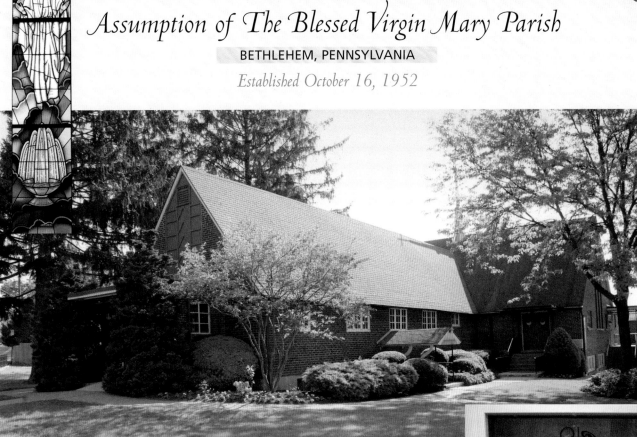

The historical roots of Assumption Parish began as a mission of Saint Ursula Parish. In 1927, a small structure was built to serve as a mission chapel. For the next twenty five years, Catholics in Colesville were served by the priests of Saint Joseph, in Limeport.

On October 16, 1952, Assumption of the Blessed Virgin Mary was named a parish of the Archdiocese of Philadelphia. Father William Drobel was appointed as the first pastor in October 1952. In 1955, an addition was incorporated into the original structure to accommodate the congregation. In 1962, Father James Hanlon was named pastor. His pastorate saw the formation of an elementary school and convent for the Sisters of Saint Joseph. In 1977, the school was merged with Saint Joseph's in Limeport to form Saint Michael the Archangel Elementary and Middle school.

Monsignor Robert J. Coll became pastor in 1987 and immediately focused his attention on repairing and updating the school. By 1990, plans were underway for the construction of the Hanlon Community Center. In order to defray the cost, the parish rectory sold as residential property. The convent, vacated by the Sisters of Saint Joseph, then became the new rectory.

Monsignor John J. Martin became pastor on June 1, 1996. The building of a new pre-school room and dining hall for the school was already underway upon Monsignor Martin's arrival. Once completed, plans were developed for a more ambitious addition to the school that included a parish religious education office and two beautifully designed gathering spaces. New construction continued with an addition to the rectory. The Church of the Assumption of the Blessed Virgin Mary celebrated its 50th anniversary as a parish in 2002.

Holy Ghost Parish

BETHLEHEM, PENNSYLVANIA

Established October 1871

A German-speaking Catholic congregation was first formed in 1854 on Bethlehem's North Side. Services were held only once a month. As the number of parishioners grew, Holy Ghost Parish was established in October 1871 to serve the German Catholics. Father John Joseph Albert was assigned to the parish as the first pastor in October 1871. By 1875, the rented space became too small and a church was constructed. Father Aloysius Fretz was appointed pastor on June 4, 1891. Ground was broken for the present church on June 21, 1895. The original church was a one-story structure which later became the parish social hall. On March 1, 1896, the basement of the church was blessed by Archbishop Ryan of Philadelphia.

On April 3, 1899, Father Fretz broke ground for the erection of a new school. It was completed and blessed on August 26, 1900. In September 1900, the school was opened by seven Franciscan Sisters. On Pentecost Sunday, 1906, the cornerstone of the present church was laid. The old rectory set back, with an addition was made to it in the front and a third story added in 1906. In 1909 and 1910, the interior of the church was outfitted with the main and side altars in the sanctuary, the Stations of the Cross, the communion rail and the rose window. The upper church was completed and dedicated by Archbishop Prendergast on September 25, 1910. On March 25, 1913, ground was broken for a new convent on property next to the church. The church interior was finally complete when, during 1918-1919, the magnificent stained glass windows and murals were installed in the church.

Father Reginald Billinger became pastor in December 1961. His first concern was the renovation of the interior of the church. Starting on February 2, 1962, interior renovation began with the painting of the walls, the Stations of the Cross, and the entire sanctuary with its altars. Bishop McShea approved a merger of Holy Ghost and Saint Ursula Schools effective September 1982. It was also decided that the Saint Ursula school building would be the site for the new Holy Child School. Holy Ghost School closed its doors in June 1982. Shortly after Father Scheaffer became pastor, he undertook a program of needed maintenance that included the rededication of the stained glass windows and renovation of the Monsignor Reginald Billinger Social Hall beneath the church. Father Wayne Killian is the current pastor of Holy Ghost Parish.

Currently the Parish has taken responsability for the Newman apostolate of Lehigh University. It is the Catholic Center of Lehigh University.

Holy Infancy Parish

BETHLEHEM, PENNSYLVANIA

Established 1861

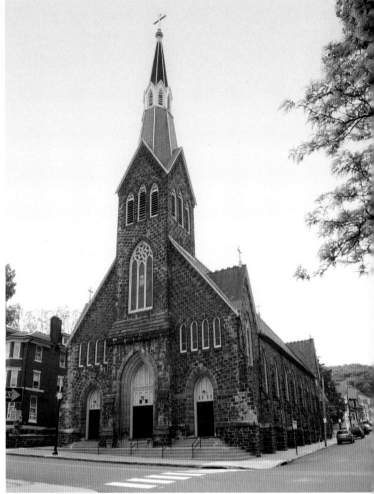

Holy Infancy Parish was the first Catholic Church to be established in South Bethlehem in 1861. Until 1855, Catholics of Bethlehem attended either Saint Bernard's or St. Joseph's Church in Easton. Beginning in 1855, they worshipped in the old Church of the Nativity on Union Street. Mass was celebrated there once a month by priests from Easton. By 1857, Mass was held twice a month by priests from Immaculate Conception Church in Allentown.

In 1861, Father Michael McEnroe established Holy Infancy Parish and built a church on property donated by the Moravians located at the southeast corner of Fourth and Taylor Streets. The cornerstone of the church was laid in 1863 by Archbishop Wood of Philadelphia. In 1865, Father McEnroe took up residence in Bethlehem at a house on the northwest corner of Fourth and Taylor Streets. Prior to that, he had traveled from Allentown to Bethlehem every Sunday.

On May 22, 1882, construction on a larger church was begun. The new church was built around the old building, which was torn down

Convent

after Easter 1883. From 1883 to 1886, services were conducted first at Saint Michael's Hall and later in the basement of the new church. In 1886, the present church was dedicated by Archbishop Ryan. In 1894, an elementary school and convent were built. Father J. J. O'Connell became pastor in 1910 and had erected a new rectory by 1912.

In 1925, the Catholic High School on Fourth and Webster Street was erected. The basement of the Church was outfitted as a chapel for the Spanish speaking people of Bethlehem in 1929.

During World War II, the steeple of the church was also lowered. In 1998, the parish began the "Be An Angel" fundraising campaign to restore the exterior of the church and adjoining rectory. Monsignor Robert Biszek is the current pastor of Holy Infancy Parish.

Incarnation of Our Lord Parish

BETHLEHEM, PENNSYLVANIA

Established July 15, 2008

Slovak fluently, the Slovaks had an opportunity of hearing a sermon in their native tongue for the first time since they arrived in Bethlehem. In early 1891, plans were made for the erection of a church building and an entire block of land was purchased from Lehigh University. Monsignor William Heinen aided in the establishment of this new parish and the cornerstone of the church was laid on May 24, 1891. The first church was built at Linden and Thomas Streets and dedicated by Monsignor Heinen on November 30, 1891. Father John Novacky was appointed as the first pastor and built the first rectory on Linden Street in 1892. Construction on a new church at Thomas and Buchanan Streets was begun in 1903 and completed in 1905. The first Mass was celebrated in the new church on Pentecost Sunday 1906. In 1909, the old church was converted into a school staffed by Missionary Sisters of the Sacred Heart. The completion of a new rectory, conversion of the old rectory into the convent and addition of four classrooms to the school all occurred in the summer of 1912. In 1948, the Missionary Sisters of the Sacred Heart withdrew from the school and were replaced by the School Sisters of Saint Francis. A new school was built in 1964 under Msgr. Felix Labuda. In 1989, an interior renovation of the church took place. The parish gathered to rededicate the church on February 10, 1990. Monsignor Michael Chaback, S.T.D. served as the last pastor of Saints Cyril and Methodius Parish.

Our Lady of Pompeii of the Most Holy Rosary Parish was established in 1902. The parish grew out of about 15 Italian immigrant families that petitioned Archbishop Patrick J. Ryan of Philadelphia to appoint a priest who could speak their native tongue in 1901. In response, Father Maggio was sent to them in the fall of 1901 and became the first Italian pastor of the Lehigh Valley. Masses were celebrated at Holy Infancy Church but plans were soon made to erect their own church. A plot of ground was donated and the cornerstone of the original brick church was laid on April 26, 1902. Father Ferdinando Gherardelli became pastor in 1911. In 1918, he oversaw the expansion of the church building. During March and April 1956, the old church was torn down and construction on the new church began. The church was completed and Mass held on April 27, 1957. A new rectory was built in 1963. Monsignor Paul della Picca, S.T.D. served as the last pastor of Our Lady of Pompeii of the Most Holy Rosary Parish.

Saint John Capistrano Parish was established in 1903, when Archbishop Patrick Ryan of Philadelphia appointed Father Alexander Varlaky to organize the first Hungarian parish of the Archdiocese of

Incarnation of Our Lord Parish in Bethlehem was established on July 15, 2008. Monsignor William T. Baker, S.T.L. was appointed as the first pastor and officially installed by Bishop Cullen on October 12, 2008. Incarnation was formed by the consolidation of five older neighboring Bethlehem parishes that included: Saints Cyril and Methodius Parish, Our Lady of Pompeii of the Most Holy Rosary Parish, Saint John Capistrano Parish, Saint Stanislaus Parish and Saint Joseph's Parish. The Solemn Opening of Incarnation Parish took place on July 18, 2008, with representatives from each of the closed parishes participating in the liturgy.

In January 1891, Saints Cyril and Methodius became a parish and was the first Slovak parish in what was then the Archdiocese of Philadelphia. The mission church was begun July 20, 1890, by a group of Slovak Catholic immigrants and Monsignor William Heinen of Mauch Chunk. During the years 1890-1891, the Slovaks worshipped at Saint Bernard's. In these two years, Monsignor Heinen visited the parish quite frequently. Because he was able to speak

Philadelphia. Early services were held in a stone basement church. In 1909, a school and convent were added to complete the building. Sisters of the Mission Workers of the Sacred Heart were placed in charge of the school. In 1918, Father Joseph Reseterics was appointed as pastor. The cornerstone of the new church was blessed on August 20, 1922. Formal dedication of the completed church took place on September 3, 1923. The Polish Sisters were replaced by the Hungarian Nuns, Sisters of Divine Charity in 1920. A major remodeling of the school and church began in 1969. Four frescos were painted in the sanctuary and changes were made to the pulpit and the main altar. Founders' Hall was built in the church basement in 1978. In June 1981, Saint John Capistrano School was closed, followed by the convent in 1985. After city inspectors condemned the school building, the structure was demolished in the fall of 1986. Father Edward Bolez, Th. F. served as the last pastor of Saint John Capistrano Parish.

Saint Stanislaus Parish in Bethlehem was established in 1906. In June 1905, Father Francis Wieszok was authorized to form a parish for Polish Catholics in Bethlehem. With the support of the pastors of the Hungarian parish of Saint John Capistrano, services were first held there. Saint Stanislaus Church was begun in 1905 and completed by 1906. Father Raymond Slezak, M.Div. served as the last pastor of Saint Stanislaus Parish.

Saint Joseph Parish in Bethlehem was established in July 1913 by Father Anselm Murn, a Franciscan Father. Services were first held in the basement of the Holy Infancy Church. The cornerstone of the church was blessed by Monsignor Masson on July 4, 1914. The first services were held on November 13, 1916. The parochial school was dedicated by Monsignor Joseph Whitaker on July 5, 1926. The school was staffed by the Sisters of Saint Francis of Christ the King, who arrived at the parish on August 24, 1926. The parish was served by the Franciscan Fathers from its inception until 2004. Although the original priests were Slovene, Croatian priests began ministering to the parish since a charter change in 1927. Saint Joseph's School was closed in 1977. Father Lawrence Frankovich became pastor in June 1985. During his four year tenure, the former baptistry was converted into a Reconciliation Chapel. Father Raymond P. Slezak, M.Div. served as the last pastor of Saint Joseph's Parish.

Saints Cyril and Methodius Parish, Our Lady of Pompeii of the Most Holy Rosary Parish, Saint John Capistrano Parish, Saint Stanislaus Parish, and Saint Joseph Parish were all closed on July 15, 2008. The new Incarnation Church now occupies the former Saints Cyril and Methodius Church building in Bethlehem.

Convent

Notre Dame of Bethlehem Parish

BETHLEHEM, PENNSYLVANIA

Established February 11, 1954

O n February 11, 1954, the Archdiocese of Philadelphia authorized the establishment of a new parish to be located at Catasauqua and Kelchner Roads in Bethlehem. The site was a five acre plot of land, part of the Werner estate, containing only a farmhouse and an old dairy barn. The new parish was named Notre Dame of Bethlehem. Archbishop John F. O'Hara appointed Father Thomas J. Doyle as Notre Dame's first pastor.

Father Doyle enlisted the aid of future members of the newly named parish and a contract was awarded to remodel the barn. The remodeled barn served as a temporary church while a refurbished farmhouse served as a temporary rectory. On April 4, 1954, the first Mass in the church was celebrated by Father Doyle. Construction of an elementary school was begun on September 26, 1954. The Sisters of Saint Joseph of Chestnut Hill were asked to staff the school

On September 12, 1956, a new rectory was completed. A second floor was added to the school in the summer of 1957. A convent building was also completed in April 1959. On July 1960, ground breaking for a new church was held and the first Sunday Mass was celebrated on June 25, 1961. The renovation of the main altar was completed in 1969. In October 18, 1975, a new shrine in honor of Our Lady was dedicated. In 1994, a capital campaign gave rise to an annex to the school and the renovation of the church. On October 1997, the new annex of the school was dedicated. Monsignor Thomas D. Baddick became pastor of Notre Dame Parish in 2007.

School

Our Lady of Perpetual Help Parish

BETHLEHEM, PENNSYLVANIA

Established May 21, 1963

The first Masses were celebrated there on June 3, 1963. In July 1963, Father Hynes presented his ideas for a U-shaped, one-story colonial style building consisting of a church, school and hall with a separate convent building. On August 1, 1963, permission to build was granted. In order to open the school as soon as possible, Father Hynes was granted permission to use four of the classrooms on the lower level of Notre Dame High School. Our Lady of Perpetual Help School was opened in September 1964 with an enrollment of 135 students. The beautiful new school was completed on March 1, 1965 and all classes were relocated to the new building. The Sisters of Saint Joseph from Chestnut Hill staffed the school. The Sisters convent was completed in 1967.

Three weeks after moving into the school, the parish began celebrating the first Masses in the new church on March 21, 1965. In August 1975, Father John Conte was appointed pastor. When the Sisters of Saint Joseph left the school in 1986, Father Conte replaced them with the Dominican Daughters of the Immaculate Mother. The Dominican Sisters remained at Our Lady of Perpetual Help until August 1988. The old convent building was renovated into the new Parish Center in November 1989. On November 23, 1991, a new church was dedicated by Bishop Welsh. Monsignor Edward Sacks, M. Ed. has served as pastor since June 1988.

On May 21, 1963, Bishop McShea formally established Our Lady of Perpetual Help as the first new parish in the new Diocese of Allentown. At the time of its establishment, the parish consisted of 450 families. Bishop McShea selected Father Harry Hynes as the first pastor. When the parish was established, a house on Santee Road was acquired by the Diocese as a temporary rectory and the basement was converted into a combination office/chapel. Father Hynes moved into the rectory on June 21, 1963.

A location for the celebration of Sunday Masses had to be secured for the new parish as soon as possible. Father Hynes obtained permission to use the gym at Notre Dame High School.

Sacred Heart Parish

BETHLEHEM, PENNSYLVANIA

Established June 11, 1936

Sacred Heart Parish, in the Miller Heights section of Bethlehem Township, was established on June 11, 1936. Prior to this, Mrs. Josephine Sakovics held Sunday school classes in her parents' home. She decided the 67 children needed larger quarters when the children were interested in presenting a Christmas program. An old blacksmith shop, located on Willow Park Road, was soon converted into a Sunday school. Sacred Heart was a direct result of this Sunday school.

In the summer of 1935, Monsignor Leo G. Fink noticed a large placard advertising a Sunday school picnic for the Sacred Heart Sunday school. He discovered this was a private undertaking in the Miller Heights area by two dedicated churchwomen, Mrs. Mary Klopach and Mrs. Josephine Sakovics. On October 20, 1935, Monsignor Fink celebrated the first Mass in the former blacksmith shop. Church officials soon organized a missionary chapel for the Miller Heights area. Built under the direction of Father Joseph May, a church was dedicated by Archbishop Dennis Cardinal Dougherty on September 20, 1936.

As the parish grew, there was a need for a school and a larger church. Construction of a parish school on Second Street began in 1953. The school was dedicated on June 27, 1954. The convent was blessed and opened in September 4, 1954. The Sisters of Saint Joseph were assigned to staff the Sacred Heart School from 1953 to 1985.

The rectory was moved to its present site in 1961 to utilize the ground for a new church. In 1964, the present church was erected. In 1974, Father William Bigos became pastor and converted the old church into a beautiful kindergarten. The old church later became the Monsignor May Memorial Hall. Father Robert J. George has served as pastor since July 2008. From its humble beginning of less than 200 families, Sacred Heart Parish now serves over 1100 families.

Saint Anne Parish

Established November 14, 1929

Saint Anne Parish in Bethlehem, originally a mission church of Saints Simon and Jude Parish, was established on November 14, 1929 with 80 families. Father Joseph Mooney was appointed as the first pastor in 1929. The first chapel was in the old Triangle Garage beginning December 1, 1929. In January 1930, land known as "The Cloverleaf Tract" was purchased for a permanent building. Although the combination church and school were not complete, the first Mass was offered on April 26, 1931.

On October 24, 1944, Father John J. Burns became pastor. Although not yet completed, Saint Anne's School opened in September 1949. The completed school building was dedicated by the Most Rev. J. Carroll McCormick on May 28, 1950. Ground was broken on November 5, 1950 for a convent to accommodate 18 sisters. Plans were soon drawn up for a new church, rectory and addition to the school. The cornerstone of the present church was laid on November 29, 1953. The first Mass in the new church was held on December 12, 1954 and Bishop O'Hara dedicated the building on April 17, 1955.

In October 1969, the church sanctuary was remodeled and an Italian marble altar replaced the temporary altar. In 1971, the vacated basement church became a community center which included a large hall, meeting rooms, stage, and school library. On November 3, 1972, Monsignor John McPeak was named pastor. In March 1974, an addition to the rectory was completed. In May 1984, the parish began a major campaign to raise funds for a Christian Education Building and second floor for the school. By 1986, all renovations and construction were completed. The parish completed construction on an athletic center in 2005. Father Anthony Mongiello is the current pastor. Saint Anne Parish serves over 1800 families.

School

Saints Simon & Jude Parish

BETHLEHEM, PENNSYLVANIA

Established 1917

On July 21, 1917 Archbishop Edmond F. Prendergast appointed the Rev. Elmer Stapleton founding pastor of SS. Simon and Jude. Fr. Stapleton was offered the use of a small chapel by Father Fretz, pastor of Holy Ghost Church in Bethlehem. For the first three years, the people of Saints Simon and Jude worshiped in the small chapel on Union Boulevard.

The first church of the parish, originally called the Church of the Nativity, was built in 1856. After more than a century, the building remains standing today on West Union Street, although recognized neither as a historical site nor as a church. In 1863, Holy Infancy Church in South Bethlehem was established. For many years, English-speaking Catholics from West Bethlehem walked to South Bethlehem to attend Mass. The German Catholics continued to use the Church of the Nativity in West Bethlehem, but in 1888 they dedicated the new larger Church of Saint Bernard in South Bethlehem. When Holy Ghost Church was completed, the Church of the Nativity in West Bethlehem became a mission church.

In July 1917, Father Stapleton began holding services at the old Church of the Nativity. Father Stapleton purchased a house on Union Boulevard as the first rectory. The historic Church of the Nativity became inadequate for parish needs, so a campaign to raise funds for a larger church was soon undertaken. The Olivet Evangelical Church on Broad Street was purchased in 1920. On September 25, 1920, the church was dedicated by Archbishop Dennis Dougherty. In 1922, construction of a school and a convent was begun. On

September 8, 1923, Saints Simon and Jude School was opened by the Sisters, Servants of the Immaculate Heart of Mary. In 1925, a new rectory was built. In 1930, the parish decided to build a new church. Dedication of the new church occurred October 2, 1932.

By 1964, the old school and convent were about to collapse with old age. The first step was the construction of the new school in the rear of the present school. On September 4, 1966, the groundbreaking ceremony was conducted. When the new school was completed, the old school was razed. A new convent was built on the same site. The new school opened on September 7, 1967. In September 1968, the new convent was completed and the old convent was demolished. Dedication of the new school and convent took place on October 28, 1968. On June 1, 1976, Monsignor Charles Moss was named pastor. He later transformed the rectory into a parish meeting room and the church basement into a parish hall. On June 14, 2005, Monsignor William F. Baver was appointed pastor. Saints Simon and Jude School was closed in June 2006 and a newly consolidated school, Seton Academy, opened at the same site in September 2006. The Sisters, Servants of the Immaculate Heart of Mary, vacated the Convent and School after 87 years of service in July 2010 to address additional needs of their community within our Diocese and the Archdiocese of Philadelphia.

School

Saint Columbkill Parish

BOYERTOWN, PENNSYLVANIA

Established June 9, 1921

Saint Columbkill Parish in Boyertown was established by Archbishop Dennis Cardinal Dougherty of Philadelphia on June 9, 1921. Father Bernard J. Creemers was appointed as the first pastor for the parish of 12 people. In 1921, a large home was purchased at 35 Chestnut Street and was used as the church until 1968 and as the rectory until 1971. The building underwent several renovations during that time.

By 1953, the original church proved to be too small and a major addition was made to the building. Stained glass windows were also added to the building at that time. Father David B. Morrison became pastor in 1966 and obtained the present parish property that year. A new church was dedicated on the property by Bishop McShea in 1967. In 1971, Father Auchter built the current rectory and the Chestnut Street property was sold to the Boyertown Area Historical Society.

In December 1986, Father Robert C. Quinn was appointed pastor. He established a building committee and built the Father Bernard Creemers Parish Center to provide space for the Religious Education Program. In 1997, the parish began plans for a new church. Construction began in May 2000. Bishop Edward P. Cullen consecrated the new church on April 23, 2001. Father Martin Kern is the current pastor of Saint Columbkill. Today, the parish serves over 2200 families.

Annunciation of Blessed Virgin Mary Parish

CATASAUQUA, PENNSYLVANIA

Established September 9, 1857

Annunciation of the Blessed Virgin Mary Parish was established by Bishop John Neumann on September 9, 1857. Prior to 1847, Jesuit Missionaries ministered to the spiritual needs of the German Catholics in Catasauqua. The first efforts towards establishing a congregation at Catasauqua were made in 1847. Mass was celebrated for the first time in the home of George Schneider at 300 Church Street. By 1856, the small struggling congregation had increased to eighteen families. The Schneider house had became too small. A small plot of ground was acquired where the church is now located.

From 1857 to 1869, the church was attended to by the pastor of Immaculate Conception Church in Allentown. In 1869, Annunciation Church was attended to by the pastor of Holy Ghost in Bethlehem. Father John Henry Badde built the first parochial school in 1878. The school was opened by the Sisters of Saint Francis of Glen Riddle with 64 students. Father Badde built the first brick church and it was dedicated on August 18, 1878. Father Badde was appointed as the first resident pastor in 1884. Father John Seimetz was appointed pastor on April 26, 1889. Father Seimetz began to renovate and enlarged the church in June 1896. The enlarged church was dedicated by Archbishop Ryan on November 26, 1896. In May 1904, the old school was razed. A new school building was dedicated in November 1904.

In 1927, construction on a basement church began and the cornerstone was laid on October 30, 1927. The new church was dedicated by Archbishop Dougherty on December 16, 1928. Father John Fries was appointed pastor on January 10, 1934. Upon arrival, he began to make much needed repairs and improvements to the church and school. He decorated the church interior and rebuilt the altar. In the school, he shifted the classrooms to the second floor to make room for social functions on the first floor.

Annunciation School was merged with Saint Elizabeth School in Whitehall to form Saint Elizabeth Regional School in 1984. The entire church was renovated and modernized in the early 1980s. Monsignor Joseph Kurtz, now the Archbishop of Louisville, completed an addition to the church vestibule area with a rear sacristy off the main vestibule and a new stained glass window. Father Edward Domin later presided over the renovation of the main sanctuary area. Monsignor Victor Finelli is the current administrator of Annunciation of the Blessed Virgin Mary Parish.

Saint Andrew Parish

CATASAUQUA, PENNSYLVANIA

Established November 30, 1902

Saint Andrew Parish in North Catasauqua was founded by Archbishop Patrick John Ryan of Philadelphia on November 30, 1902, from what was originally known as the Mauch Chunk Mission. The parish was established to serve the needs of Slovak immigrants in Upper Lehigh and Northampton Counties. This was largely due to the efforts of Reverend William Heinen, pastor of Saint Joseph's Church in East Mauch Chunk (now Jim Thorpe). During his ministry from 1894 to 1910, he came into contact with many Slovaks. Sensing a great need, Father Heinen took it upon himself to reach out to those early immigrants and to learn their language. He became known as the "Apostle to the Slovaks" in Eastern Pennsylvania. He was later assisted in this ministry by three men: Fathers Paul Lisicky, Joseph Kasparek and Francis Vlossak.

In 1902, Father Heinen began to organize the people of Saint Andrew's. Father Heinen and his assistant, Father Peter Schaaf, began celebrating the Sacraments for the original 64 members during the first 5 months. Father Paul Lisicky arrived at Saint Andrew's in March 1903 and was appointed as the first pastor. The cornerstone for the church was laid in 1903.

Father Michael Stone was appointed administrator of Saint Andrew's in June 1989. The rectory soon became a convent for the Sisters of Saint Francis (Glen Riddle). Because of the heavy weekend Mass schedule covering both parishes, Father Stone sought the assistance of the Barnabite Fathers. In March 1992, Father Stone was appointed as pastor of both Saint Andrew's and Blessed Virgin Mary Parish. The parish completed a program of restoration and renovation in 1998. The baptismal font was moved to the rear entrance and the chancel was elevated. Most of the work was centered on the restoration of the church building with statues repainted, the floor redone, marble added to the chancel area, gold leafing added to the walls and ceiling. In June 2002, Father William Baker was appointed pastor of both Saint Andrew and Saint Lawrence Parishes by Bishop Cullen. Father Eric Gruber has served as administrator of both parishes since 2008.

Saint Lawrence Parish

CATASAUQUA, PENNSYLVANIA

Established July 12, 1858

He was assigned the task of getting the Catasauqua parish organized and the church built. In June 1857, groundbreaking for the church took place. By late December 1857, the church was complete and Christmas Mass was celebrated in the church. On May 16, 1858, Bishop Neumann blessed and dedicated the new church. Father Brennan was appointed as the first pastor. In 1863, the church was expanded and the rectory was built.

Father Peter Quinn was appointed pastor in 1896. During his pastorate, he realized the need for a parish school. In 1905, the parish school was opened by the Sisters of Saint Francis (Glen Riddle). A convent was also completed in 1905. Father Henry Connor was appointed pastor in June 1907. Under his direction, the gothic structures of the church and rectory were remodeled according to the lines of Spanish Mission architecture. Church renovations took place in 1924 that included the removal of the spire from the church tower, the removal of the original stained glass windows, the installation of manufactured glass windows, and the plastering of the red brick exteriors. These renovations were completed in 1925. In 1945, the parish school and part of the convent were destroyed by fire. Both buildings were repaired and renovated. In June 2002, Father William Baker was appointed pastor of both Saint Lawrence and Saint Andrew Parishes by Bishop Cullen. Father Eric Gruber has served as administrator of both parishes since 2008.

B y 1840, a number of Catholic families had begun to settle in the Catasauqua area. They were tended to by the priests from Saint Bernard's in Easton. Mass was usually celebrated in private homes or spacious buildings. By 1850, Bartholomew Murtaugh and Edward Crampsey were working with the priests from Saint Bernard's to organize the Catholic population and show the need for establishing a parish. In 1851, Bishop John Neumann began working towards the establishment of a parish.

In the spring of 1856, Bishop Neumann gave instructions for the purchase of land to be used as the site for the new parish. On July 19, 1856, Bishop Neumann purchased one-half acre of land from the Faust family for a church and burial ground at 2nd and Chapel Streets. Father Lawrence Brennan arrived at Saint Bernard's in 1856.

Saint Peter Parish

COPLAY, PENNSYLVANIA

Established June 16, 1927

Saint Peter Parish in Coplay was established on June 16, 1927. Cardinal Dougherty of Philadelphia appointed Father Joseph Ostheimer as pastor previously on June 6, 1927. Father Ostheimer immediately procured land, even before the official establishment of the parish, located at Fifth and Coplay Streets. On July 4, 1927, the first Mass on the property purchased for the parish buildings was held. The cornerstone of the church was laid by Cardinal Dougherty on October 30, 1927. The combination church and school building was dedicated on July 1, 1928. A house on North Fifth Street was rented as a rectory on May 15, 1928.

Saint Peter's School was opened by the Missionary Sisters of the Most Sacred Heart of Jesus on September 4, 1928. Ground was broken for the rectory on July 26, 1939. The rectory was opened on January 24, 1940. A new convent was dedicated on June 28, 1953. Ground was broken for a new church building on March 24, 1963. The first Mass in the new church was held on June 28, 1964. The cornerstone was laid and the church was dedicated by Bishop McShea on August 2, 1964. On July 3, 1983, a renovation of the church was begun. The altar server sacristy was converted into an enclosed chapel and the choir loft was enlarged.

Saint Peter's School was closed in June 1983. The school was consolidated along with Holy Trinity School in Egypt and Saint John the Baptist School in Whitehall to form the new Christ the King Regional School. Following the withdrawal of the Missionary Sisters of the Sacred Heart from the parish on June 13, 1993, Saint Peter's convent was later converted into the Christ the King/Saint Peter Pre-School Center. A renovation of the entire church interior and chapel took place in October and November of 1993. Monsignor William Handges has served as pastor of Saint Peter Parish since 2005.

Christ the King School

Immaculate Conception of Blessed Virgin Mary Parish

DOUGLASSVILLE, PENNSYLVANIA

Established December 25, 1915

Immaculate Conception of the Blessed Virgin Mary Parish was established by Archbishop Edmond Prendergast of Philadelphia in 1915. The E. & G. Land Company agreed to provide a former dance hall building on West Main Street to use free of charge as long as it was used as a church. Father Victor Strumia was appointed the first pastor and about 50 families made up the parish when the first Mass was celebrated on December 25, 1915. By spring 1916, a permanent altar had been installed and Holy Mass was celebrated. In the 1920s, the church building was enlarged and a rectory was also built in 1926.

After a major fund drive, ground was broken for the new church on November 18, 1951. Due to materials being rationed during the Korean War, construction was slow. The first Mass in the new church was celebrated in February 1953. The old church reverted to the Land Company, which had it demolished. About 1960, the "white" house was purchased at the corner of Spruce and Main Streets and was used for meetings and CCD classes for the next 20 years. As the parish grew, a parish center was erected onto the existing church on Main Street. Groundbreaking was held on June 24, 1979, and the parish center was dedicated on December 7, 1980.

In 1998, it was determined that a new home for the parish was needed. In 2001, a 60-acre site just south of Birdsboro was selected. Groundbreaking at the new location was held on September 28, 2002. The new parish church was consecrated on December 17, 2003. Immaculate Conception Academy opened its doors for the first time in September 2003. Monsignor John McCann, S.T.L. is the current pastor. Immaculate Conception BVM Parish now serves over 1400 families.

School

Our Lady of Mercy Parish

EASTON, PENNSYLVANIA

Established July 15, 2008

Our Lady of Mercy Parish in Easton was established on July 15, 2008. Father Deogratias Rwegasira, A.J. was appointed as the first pastor. Our Lady of Mercy was formed by the consolidation of three older neighboring parishes that include: Saint Bernard Parish, Saint Joseph Parish and Saint Michael Parish.

Saint Bernard Parish was established in 1829. In the early 1800s, Father John Fitzpatrick traveled on horseback from Milton to Easton to minister to the Catholics of the Lehigh Valley. In 1829, he purchased land for a church on South Fifth Street and Saint Bernard Parish was founded. In 1836, the church was dedicated by Bishop Kenrick. Father James Maloney was appointed as the first resident pastor. Father Thomas Reardon became pastor in 1847. Under his pastorate, a rectory was constructed next to the church, improvements were made to the church interior and a school was begun in the church basement. In 1867, Father Reardon decided to expand the size of the church. On April 9, 1867, a workman's torch ignited the new tower and destroyed the church. The church was rebuilt and rededicated on June 14, 1868. Father James McGeveran became pastor in 1887. He enlarged the church and installed new marble altars, pews and stained glass windows in 1898. In 1912, a third floor was added to the rectory and the church hall was remodeled. Property for a new school was purchased on South Sixth Street in 1909. The school was opened by the Sisters, Servants of the Immaculate Heart of Mary. In 1916, the only Catholic High School in Easton opened in the building next to the elementary school on South Sixth Street.

The high school was closed when Notre Dame High School opened in 1957. The elementary school was closed in 1970. The Sisters, Servants of the Immaculate Heart of Mary left the parish in June 1990. In late 1998, construction on a new parish center was begun. The building was blessed by Bishop Edward Cullen on September 25, 1999. Monsignor John Campbell was the last pastor of Saint Bernard Parish.

Saint Joseph Parish in Easton was established in 1852. The German Catholics had organized the Saint Joseph's Aid Society of South Easton on January 1, 1848. Members of this society discussed establishing a church of their own. In the spring of 1852, Bishop John Neumann sent Father Rudolph Etthofer to South Easton to organize a new parish. On October 3, 1852, Bishop Neumann laid the cornerstone of the new church. A school was also

set up in the basement of the church. In 1871, Father Hubert Schick became pastor. He immediately set to work repairing the church and building a school. The second floor of the school was the home of the Benedictine Sisters who had come to staff the school. Father Maurice Graetzer became pastor in 1878. He built a new rectory and brought the Sisters of Saint Francis to take charge of the school. A new school building was dedicated on September 7, 1890. The old school was converted into a convent. A new brick church was begun in 1890, on the spot of the old church. The new church was dedicated by Archbishop Ryan on April 15, 1894. On March 10, 1911, a fire destroyed both the church and school. A school building was dedicated on May 12, 1912. The school auditorium was converted into a temporary chapel. The new church was begun in the spring of 1915 and the cornerstone was laid on June 27, 1915. The church was dedicated on May 19, 1918. In 1952, the basement chapel was refurnished and the main church was redecorated. An extensive renovation of the twin towers, roof and church interior was begun in 1990. The renovations were completed in time for the 150th anniversary of the parish in 2002. Monsignor John Campbell was the last pastor of Saint Joseph Parish.

Saint Michael Parish was established in 1916. Saint Michael's first organized in 1907, when Father Kaulakis of Philadelphia was assigned by Archbishop Patrick Ryan to visit the Lithuanian people of Easton. With the help of Father Gudaitis of Tamaqua, the Lithuanians began holding meetings and raising funds for their own church on August 7, 1912. Saint Michael Parish was established in 1916. On May 31, 1916, the former Heptasoph Hall on Spring Garden Street was purchased and remodeled by Father Gudaitis. After the renovations, the church was dedicated by Monsignor Peter Masson on August 5, 1917. Father Rastutis was appointed as the first resident pastor in 1917. The church was refurbished in 1950 and a new rectory was purchased in 1954. The steeple was destroyed by lightning and replaced with a bronze fleche in 1958. Father Thomas Benestad became pastor in 1980. In 1985, he began renovations to emphasize the historical character of the church. Following the departure of the Sisters of Saint Joseph, Father Benestad converted the convent into the Holy Family Residence which was later sold. Monsignor John Campbell was the last pastor of Saint Michael Parish.

Saint Bernard Parish, Saint Joseph Parish and Saint Michael Parish were all closed on July 15, 2008. The new Our Lady of Mercy Church now occupies the former Saint Joseph Church building in Easton. St. Bernard is now an Oratory.

Saint Anthony of Padua Parish

EASTON, PENNSYLVANIA

Established October 1909

The Archdiocese of Philadelphia sent Father Amalio Landolfi to establish Saint Anthony of Padua Parish in Easton. Father Landolfi set up a temporary chapel known as the Italian National Church of Saint Anthony of Padua in October 1909. This chapel was established on the second floor of Gazzetta's garage on South Bank Street near Lehigh Street. The chapel was dedicated by Father Joseph M. Corrigan on November 20, 1910. In 1914, Father Landolfi purchased property at 323 Lehigh Street. On February 20, 1914, a cornerstone was laid for a church building. Father Giovanni Daraio oversaw the completion of the church. The church was on the first floor and the rectory was on the second floor.

Father J. William Herron became pastor in 1926. He purchased land at Ninth and Lehigh Streets and groundbreaking for a three-story building took place on May 17, 1928. The building was dedicated by Bishop O'Hara on September 3, 1929. Due to the Depression, the parish decided to place an altar on the third floor for use as a chapel. In September 1936, the old rectory was sold. The priests then moved to a home one block from the new building. The third floor chapel was moved to the first floor and the congregation began to increase. Two thirds of the second floor of the new building was converted into a rectory in February 1937. The third floor, the former chapel, was converted to a social hall. On September 29, 1938 the Salesian Sisters came to Easton and opened a Nursery-Kindergarten in the remaining one third area of the second floor. On January 3, 1943, Saint Mary's Mission Chapel was blessed and the Sisters of Saint Anthony began a school there. In 1950, Archbishop Dougherty gave his approval for the establishment of a school. Work began to convert the second floor of the church into a school in April 1951. Saint Anthony's School was opened by the Salesian Sisters in September 1951.

Father Anthony Ricapito became pastor in 1970. Saint Anthony's School was consolidated with Saint Bernard's School and Saint Joseph's School to form the Easton Catholic Elementary School in 1971. The classrooms at Saint Anthony's continued to house grades 5-8 and became Easton Catholic Middle School. In the spring of 1974, the Congregation of the Angelic Sisters of Saint Paul came to the parish. The Salesian Sisters left the parish in June 1976. In August 1976, the Daughters of Divine Zeal came to the parish and remained until 1979. In 1984, the church underwent a major renovation. A parish center was dedicated by Bishop Welsh on June 4, 1994. Saint Mary's Chapel was closed in 2008. On June 5, 2009, Easton Catholic School was closed. Monsignor Edward Zemanik has served as pastor since 2008.

Saint Jane Frances de Chantal Parish

EASTON, PENNSYLVANIA

Established January 19, 1920

A small tract of land in Wilson Borough was destined to become the new home of Saint Jane's Church. Saint Jane Frances de Chantal Parish was established on January 19, 1920 to serve 200 families. Father Michael Bennett was appointed the first pastor. The new parish celebrated its first Mass in Bondon Hall, a former feed store located at 15th and Washington Streets. Later, the fledgling parish purchased a home at 19th Street and Hay Terrace for use as a rectory. A workshop in the rear of the home was converted by the men of the parish into a small chapel. Mass was celebrated in the small chapel until 1926.

On March 15, 1924, groundbreaking ceremonies were held to begin construction on a combination church/school building. The cornerstone was laid by Monsignor Thomas McNally on June 21, 1925. The new building was dedicated on December 20, 1925. The addition of the basement auditorium added a new dimension to parish life. After years of attending class at Saint Bernard's School, 176 pupils entered the doors of Saint Jane's School on September 8, 1926. The school was staffed by the Sisters Servants of the Immaculate Heart of Mary. The Sisters convent was opened in October 1926.

In July 1955, Father Donnelly saw the need for expansion. He purchased two homes on Washington Boulevard, which were converted into a combined convent and chapel. Major renovations to the old school building were completed in 1959. The old school quickly became too small. Ground was broken for the new church/school combination on January 23, 1960. The building was dedicated by Bishop McShea on October 2, 1960. When more room was needed for the school, the intended location of the church on the upper floors was used for classrooms. The church's location in the basement was intended only as a temporary location.

In the 1980s, Father Sheehan had the interior of the church renovated. In the 1990s, he successfully completed the first capital campaign called "Challenge of Faith" for a new church. In the late 1990s, Monsignor Gerald Gobitas initiated a second building campaign called "A Time to Build" and property was purchased. The new church was dedicated by Bishop Cullen on February 3, 2002. The Immaculate Heart of Mary Sisters continued to staff the school until 2002. Monsignor Stephen Radocha is the current pastor of Saint Jane Frances de Chantal Parish.

Saint Ann Parish

EMMAUS, PENNSYLVANIA

Established June 8, 1931

The first Catholic services in the Emmaus area took place in 1763. Father Theodore Schneider, S.J., from Goshenhoppen (Bally) performed a marriage in a house in Macunshie. For more than a century, missionary priests traveled throughout the developing country and cared for the spiritual needs of Catholics in the region. In 1923, the Catholic families of Emmaus built a temporary basement church for services. A permanent church was completed in 1929. During this period, the church was a mission of Saint John the Baptist Parish in Allentown.

On June 8, 1931, Archbishop Dougherty of Philadelphia established Saint Ann Parish in Emmaus and appointed Father Paul Pekarik as the first pastor. In 1938, a rectory was constructed. Saint Ann's School was begun in 1949 with classes conducted by the Sisters of Saint Francis in the basement of the church. In 1951, a convent was built for the eleven Sisters who staffed the school. The new school was built in 1954.

Upon the retirement of Father Pekarik in 1975, Father James E. Sweeney was appointed pastor. A new church was constructed in 1982. After 45 years of service, the Sisters of Saint Francis decided to leave Saint Ann's. Monsignor Thomas Hoban was appointed pastor in 1986. A new convent was constructed in 1988, to house the Benedictine Sisters who had come to Saint Ann's. The convent later became "Transfiguration Priory" for the Benedictine Sisters in 1998. Additions were made to the school in 2000 and 2004. Renovations were also made to the church in 2001. Monsignor John Mraz has served as pastor since July 2008.

Saint Ursula Parish

FOUNTAIN HILL, PENNSYLVANIA

Established October 1919

On October 21, 1919, Archbishop Dennis Dougherty of Philadelphia assigned Father John Greene to organize a parish adjacent to South Bethlehem in the Borough of Fountain Hill. Saint Ursula Parish had a humble beginning and was established in October 1919. On November 30, 1919, the first Mass ever celebrated in the borough was by Father Greene in a private dwelling. In December 1919, a large garage was leased and made into a chapel where parishioners worshiped until the church was built. In May 1922, the parish purchased a plot of ground to build a church and school. Shortly thereafter, workers began construction on a combination church-school building.

On June 3, 1923, the church was dedicated with a Solemn High Mass. Saint Ursula's School opened in September 1923. In December 1926, Father Charles McGinley became the second pastor. During his pastorate, a convent was built in 1927 and followed by a rectory in 1928. In June 1931, Father Joseph McPeak became the third pastor. Over the next 26 years, he had the difficult task of paying off the parish debt during the Great Depression. Father James Sullivan was appointed pastor in 1957. He began the fundraising necessary to eventually build a new church.

Father Patrick Foley was appointed pastor in 1961. In 1966, he began construction on the new church located next to the old church building. The new church was dedicated by Bishop Joseph McShea on May 30, 1967. Bishop McShea consecrated the church on April 10, 1976. In 1982, Saint Ursula and Holy Ghost Schools were merged to form Holy Child School in Fountain Hill. Holy Child School, Saints Simon and Jude School and Saints Cyril and Methodius School all merged in 2006 to form Seton Academy in Bethlehem. Father Robert Potts is the current pastor of Saint Ursula Parish.

Annunciation of Blessed Virgin Mary Parish

FRACKVILLE, PENNSYLVANIA

Established 1917

The beginning of Annunciation of the Blessed Virgin Mary Parish was slow due to language barriers and factions among the early Lithuanians. In 1917, there were two groups with opposite opinions on where the intended parish should be located. One group felt the new parish should be located on Broad Mountain Avenue and the other wanted to purchase a vacant church structure on North Balliet Street. The Archbishop of Philadelphia directed Father M. Durickas of Saint Casimir in Saint Clair to hold Sunday Mass wherever a temporary hall could be obtained and until a proper location could be found. This situation continued for several months until Saint Joseph Parish relocated to their present site on North Nice Street. The Archbishop then permitted Annunciation Parish to be established on Broad Mountain Avenue later in 1917. This small church building, formerly a mission of Holy Rosary Parish in Mahanoy Plane, was slightly remodeled. Father Durickas held the first Mass there on December 25, 1917.

Father A.E. Bakunas was appointed pastor in June 1920 and immediately began to build a rectory. The rectory was completed in 1921. In January 1927, Father Stanley J. Norbutas was appointed pastor. He enlarged and remodeled the little church in 1934. Two small homes on Broad Mountain Avenue were purchased next to the rectory and converted into a school and convent. Annunciation School was opened in the early 1940s by the Sisters of Jesus Crucified. A new school and auditorium were built from 1953 to 1957. A church hall was completed in 1957.

In 1965, the new school auditorium was expanded and the rectory remodeled into a convent. A new rectory was dedicated on May 23, 1965. In the late 1960s, the parochial schools of the Annunciation and Saint Joseph's in Frackville were consolidated and staffed by the Sisters of Jesus Crucified. The two schools remained

separate with two convents. Annunciation and Saint Joseph's Schools were merged and renamed the Holy Family School in August 1981. The church was renovated in 1983. On September 11, 1983, the church was rededicated by Monsignor Anthony Muntone. In the summer of 1991, an addition was built onto the school building at Annunciation. Holy Family School was closed in June 2006 when it merged with other local Catholic schools. Father Edward J. Essig was named as pastor on July 15, 2008.

Saint Ann Parish

FRACKVILLE, PENNSYLVANIA

Established June 14, 1924

Through the intercession of Father Mioduszewski and Father James Graham, pastor of Saint Joseph's in Frackville, Archbishop Dougherty of Philadelphia deemed it advisable to establish a separate parish for the Polish Catholics in Frackville.

Saint Ann Parish in Frackville was established by Archbishop Dougherty on June 14, 1924. Father Stanislaus Garstka was appointed as the first pastor. A plot of ground situated on North Line Street in Frackville was purchased. The blessing and groundbreaking for the church took place June 21, 1925. The cornerstone was laid on September 7, 1925. The first Mass was celebrated in the new church on December 21, 1925. In 1926, the congregation painted the interior and installed new pews. The new church was dedicated by Archbishop Dougherty in May 1926. At the rear of the church, a rectory and two classrooms were added in 1931.

Prior to 1920, the spiritual needs of Polish Catholics in Frackville were taken care of by Saint Joseph's and Annunciation BVM Parishes in Frackville. A mission was organized for the Polish families of Frackville in 1920, which was attended first by Father Peter Kucharski and then Father John Mioduszewski, both pastors of Saints Peter and Paul in Saint Clair.

During the summer of 1937, the parish added a garden and statue of Saint Ann and the Blessed Virgin to the grounds adjoining the church. Dedication

of the shrine took place in October 1937. The sanctuary was renovated and a new main altar erected. The blessing of the main altar took place on July 14, 1940. In 1961, the church building was extensively remodeled and beautified. A new rectory was constructed in 1968.

Saint Ann's established the Holy Family Preschool located in the hall off the rear of the church in 1986. The preschool was renovated in the late 1990s. In 2003, parish renovations included a new roof on the rectory, painting of the church interior and the restoration of the church statues. The preschool changed its name to Saint Ann's Preschool in June 2006. Father Edward Essig, M. Div. has served as pastor since July 15, 2008.

Saint Joseph Parish

FRACKVILLE, PENNSYLVANIA

Established 1909

The history of Saint Joseph Parish goes back before 1870, when the first Sunday school was started in an old school building on Nice Street in Frackville. At the time, Catholics attended Holy Rosary Church in Mahanoy Plane. In 1878, the Sunday school moved to Houghton's Hall on South Balliet Street. Catholics residing in Frackville attended Holy Rosary Parish in Mahanoy City. As membership grew, Saint Joseph's Mission was established at the present site of Annunciation BVM Church on Broad Mountain Avenue. The first Mass was celebrated in Frackville on August 15, 1893.

Within a short time, a committee was formed to request that Archbishop Ryan of Philadelphia establish a church for the Catholics of Frackville. Archbishop Ryan granted permission for part of a school building to be purchased, remodeled and converted into a church. The new mission church was served by Father John Loughran, pastor of Holy Rosary. In 1897, Father James A. Hogan became pastor of Holy Rosary and continued to serve the mission. The church building was expanded during the time Father Hogan was pastor. On April 25, 1903, property between Nice and Center Streets was purchased from Francis Haupt and included a mansion-type house that became the rectory.

Father Thomas Hurton was appointed the first pastor in April 1909. A parish cemetery was established in 1912 on West Pine Street in Frackville. A special meeting of the parish was held on June 10, 1912 to decide if a larger church and a parochial school should be built. The decision was made to build on the site of the present church building. The foundation of the church was dug and set by parishioners. The cornerstone was laid in September 1912. The new church was dedicated by Archbishop Edmund Prendergast of Philadelphia on May 18, 1913. The combination church, school and hall were all completed by the fall of 1913.

Saint Joseph's School was opened by the Sisters of the Immaculate Heart of Jesus in September 1914. This was the first parochial school in Frackville. Temporary living quarters for the sisters were in the classrooms until the convent was purchased. The Sisters remained at the school until 1972. The Sisters of Jesus Crucified arrived to staff the school in 1972. Saint Joseph's School was merged with Annunciation BVM School to form Holy Family School in 1981. The Sisters of Christ Crucified continued to teach at Holy Family School until it was closed in 2007. Father John Michael Beers has served as pastor of Saint Joseph Parish since 2008.

Saint Joseph Parish

GIRARDVILLE, PENNSYLVANIA

Established August 10, 1870

The parish school was established in 1921 and has been continuously served by the Sisters, Servants of the Immaculate Heart of Mary. In 1981, Saint Joseph School became Immaculate Heart Elementary School through a joint venture with Saint Vincent de Paul in Girardville; Saint Joseph and Saint Mauritius in Ashland; and Our Lady of Good Counsel in Gordon. With the establishment of the Allentown Diocese in 1961, Saint Joseph Parish became the diocesan headquarters for the Society of the Propagation of the Faith under the direction of Monsignor Francis King. Father Edward Connolly, M. Div. is the current pastor of Saint Joseph Parish.

Saint Joseph Parish in Girardville was established on August 10, 1870 as a territorial parish with Father Joseph A. Bridgman as the founding pastor. The parish was previously served through the missionary efforts of Father Michael Sheridan, who traveled an area from Pottsville to Danville.

The cornerstone of the present church was laid on October 21, 1872. Major problems with the building's structure followed and the church was considered architecturally unsafe. Father Bridgman refused to pay the contractor. The church was then seized by the county and sold at sheriff's sale. Father Bridgman's successor was Father Daniel O'Connor. He purchased the building for $12,000 and had the structure modified with buttresses for support. The church was finally dedicated by Archbishop Frederic Wood of Philadelphia on October 19, 1879.

Saint Vincent de Paul Parish

GIRARDVILLE, PENNSYLVANIA

Established 1907

Lithuanian people began settling in Girardville as early as 1904. Father Anthony Milukas came to Girardville from Shenandoah to take care of the spiritual needs of the Lithuanians. In the beginning, Masses were held in an Opera House and a store room. Saint Vincent de Paul Parish was founded by Father Milukas in Girardville during the fall of 1907. In October 1907, Father Milukas purchased the old Armory Hall from the Girard Estate and the building was converted into a church. The church was blessed by Archbishop Ryan of Philadelphia in November 1907. A rectory was also established on Main Street.

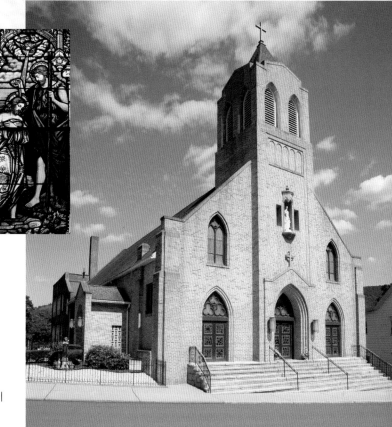

Father Jerome Augustaitis became pastor on November 22, 1913. During his pastorate, a new rectory was built beside the church. Father Ignatius Valanciunas became pastor on June 15, 1920 and found the church in poor condition. During the next few years, there was talk of building a new church. In 1923, the old building was torn down to make way for a new church structure.

The building of the new church-school combination building took about two years. During that time, services were conducted in the basement of Saint Joseph's Church. The cornerstone of the new church was blessed by Dennis Cardinal Dougherty in November 1925. On May 30, 1926, the church was blessed by Dennis Cardinal Dougherty. Father Michael Daumantas became pastor in August 1933. During his pastorate, many improvements took place. A new marble altar was imported from Italy and erected in 1935 and the church was repainted in 1939.

A parochial school was opened by the Sisters of Jesus Crucified in September 1939. From 1939 to 1945, the Sisters of Jesus Crucified were housed on the third floor of the school. A large convent was obtained for the Sisters from the Girard Estate and a beautiful chapel was constructed for them. The convent was blessed by Archbishop Dougherty on October 13, 1945.

The new rectory was purchased from the Girard Estate in 1952. Father J. Pascal Sabas was appointed pastor in 1970. Under his pastorate, the convent and rectory were sold. A new rectory was built next to the church. Father James J. Lofton became pastor in August 1977. He was responsible for having the church completely renovated. Father Edward B. Connolly is the current pastor of Saint Vincent de Paul Parish.

Our Lady of Good Counsel Parish

GORDON, PENNSYLVANIA

Established June 1922

Prior to 1902, Catholics from Gordon worshipped at Saint Joseph's Church in Ashland. From time to time, Mass was celebrated in the home of Michael Sullivan in Gordon. In 1902, the Catholics leased the Band Hall on Hobart Street and began holding services there. In the summer of 1903, the men of the church began to dig a foundation for the church on land donated by Michael Sullivan. The cornerstone for the church was laid in 1905. Our Lady of Good Counsel Church was dedicated by Auxiliary Bishop Prendergast of Philadelphia on October 22, 1906.

The church remained a mission of Ashland under the care of Father Hugh McGettigan until 1913. Father Daniel McGinley cared for the mission until 1922. In June 1922, Archbishop Dougherty of Philadelphia established 12 new parishes including Our Lady of Good Counsel in Gordon. Father John V. Brogan was appointed the first pastor on June 19, 1922. His first task was to build a rectory. Shortly afterwards, Saint Helen's Mission Chapel was built in Fountain Springs. In 1931, the church was repaired and the interior renovated.

Father Raymond Manning became pastor in 1955. During his pastorate, Our Lady of Fatima Shrine was dedicated next to the rectory on May 11, 1958. In the fall of 1972, a bad leak in the church roof caused several decorative plaster casts to fall from the walls and the church interior was renovated. In recent years, the interior of Saint Helen's Chapel was painted and the church hall was painted and remodeled. Father John Bambrick has served as pastor of Our Lady of Good Counsel since 2008.

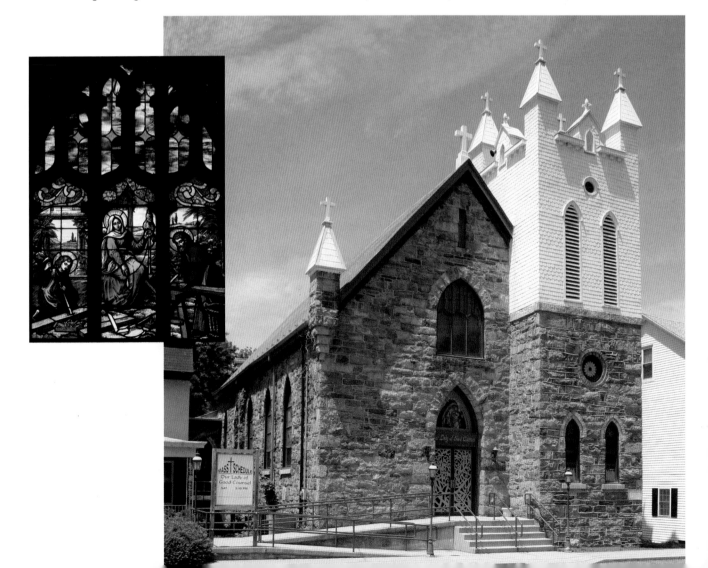

Saint Mary Parish

HAMBURG, PENNSYLVANIA

Established 1854

Saint Mary Parish in Hamburg traces its existence back to 1853, when Bishop John Neumann granted permission for the establishment of a new parish. On June 19th, Father Peter Carbon blessed the cornerstone which marked the beginning of the construction of a new red brick and stone church. Bishop Neumann, who referred to the new parish as "Rosary BVM" in his diary, dedicated the new church on September 24, 1854. No priest was initially assigned to the new parish and, for the first several years, priests served St. Mary as a mission church. In those years, the Catholics of northern Berks County were served by "circuit rider" priests who traversed the area on horseback, usually coming from Most Blessed Sacrament in Bally, St. Peter in Reading, or St. Ambrose in Schuylkill Haven.

In 1886, records indicate that "difficulties" forced the closing of the church until it was rededicated with Monsignor Scott Fasig as pastor on August 29, 1915. Monsignor George Bornemann, pastor of Saint Paul Parish in Reading, engaged the services of an architect to repair and renovate the original structure. Monsignor Bornemann paid for all expenses of the restoration. In 1928, property was purchased at 508 Island Street in Hamburg to serve as the rectory for priests assigned to the parish. Prior to having a rectory, priests roomed in local hotels or later resided in a tenant house on State Street. Under the guidance of Father

Aloysius Schmid, the parish embarked on a series of building projects. In 1955, land was purchased at the corner of State and North Fifth Street with plans to erect a parish hall. A sacristy and new exit were added on the east side of the church in 1955. Bishop McShea dedicated the parish hall on August 4, 1963.

On November 27, 1999, ground was broken for a new church on 10 acres in Tilden Township. The church was dedicated by Bishop Cullen on December 8, 2000. A new rectory was constructed in the fall of 2003 and blessed by Bishop Welsh on December 8, 2003. On that same day, Bishop Welsh also officially opened the 150th Jubilee year of the parish. On August 15, 2008, the new religious education center was dedicated. The new facility is connected to the church and serves as a bridge wing to the new Ave Maria Social Hall, which was blessed and first opened on September 6, 2008. Father Donald Cieniewicz, M. Div. is the current pastor.

The picturesque parish campus includes almost 30 acres of beautiful rural land at the base of the Blue Mountain and Appalachian Trail.

Saint Theresa of The Child Jesus Parish

HELLERTOWN, PENNSYLVANIA

Established November 12, 1925

The first Catholic Mass in Hellertown was celebrated at a private residence in 1854. It was not until 1921 that a mission parish was established in Hellertown. Saints Nereus and Achilleus was established as a mission church of Saints Cyril and Methodius Parish in 1921. Father John H. Trescak was assigned to lead the mission congregation of 13 families. Father George Check was appointed as mission administrator in 1923.

On November 12, 1925, Saints Nereus and Achilleus Mission was given full Canonical status as parish and the name was changed to Saint Theresa of the Child Jesus Parish. Father George Check was appointed as the first pastor. The Sisters of Saint Francis arrived in 1938. Saint Theresa of the Child Jesus School was opened by the Sisters of Saint Francis in 1939. The school was officially dedicated in 1941. A new church and rectory were dedicated by Auxiliary Bishop McCormick of Philadelphia in 1956. Father

Stephen Daday became pastor in 1965. He immediately began renovations that included moving the church altar, additions to the school and construction of a new convent. In 1975, the Saint Theresa Shrine was erected.

Monsignor Raymond Merman became pastor in 1984. Under his pastorate, many improvements were made to the parish including the renovation of the church interior, installation of new church windows and the renovation of Friendship Hall in the school. The Sisters of Saint Francis remained at the parish until 1997. The Sisters, Servants of the Immaculate Heart of Mary arrived to assist in the church and school in 1997. The rectory was renovated in 2009. Father Jerome A. Tauber is the current pastor of Saint Theresa of the Child Jesus Parish.

Immaculate Conception of The Blessed Virgin Mary Parish

JIM THORPE, PENNSYLVANIA

Established 1848

In November 1848, Father Patrick J. Hennegan was sent to minister to the Catholics of Mauch Chunk and established a parish dedicated to Saint Mary of the Immaculate Conception. Mass was first celebrated on a regular basis in the local school on West Broadway. The principal place of worship in the early days was the house of Michael McGeady at 130 Susquehanna Street. Mass was also said on occasion in the homes of John Mulhem and John Tree. As the congregation grew and could not be accommodated in a private dwelling, Mass was celebrated on a regular basis in the Old School House on West Broadway.

The first parish property was the plot of ground acquired on West Broadway for the building of the church. Work on the church building began in 1850 and the cornerstone was laid on October 12, 1851. The church was completed by January 1852 and dedicated in 1853. Father Michael J. Blacker became pastor in November 1861. He completed the extensive alterations of the church and began to make arrangements for the erection of a rectory. In 1865, Father Blacker established the first parochial school in the basement of the church. The school was discontinued in 1868. A rectory was completed in 1870.

A parochial school was opened by the Sisters, Servants of the Immaculate Heart of Mary in September 1884 with an enrollment of 140 students. Classes were held in the basement of the

church. The ground was purchased to build a school and convent in the summer and early fall of 1884. Construction on the school and convent began in 1885. The school was dedicated on September 4, 1887. Father Thomas Larkin became pastor in October 1903.

Ground was broken for the present church on April 23, 1906 and the cornerstone was laid on June 24, 1906. The dedication of the church took place on October 4, 1908.

Father Larkin continued making improvements in the school and a lot on the lower side of the school was purchased in 1914. Construction on a new school was begun in 1924. The new school was completed in 1925. The parish school was closed in 1982 because of building deterioration and a decline in enrollment and religious staff. A new rectory was built adjacent to the church in 1972. The former school building was razed in June 1991. Father James J. Ward, M. Div. is the current pastor of Immaculate Conception.

Saint Joseph Parish

JIM THORPE, PENNSYLVANIA

Established 1871

In 1871, Father John Gerhard Freude was the first priest to say Mass for the group of German speaking Catholics in East Mauch Chunk. Saint Joseph Parish in Mauch Chunk was established the same year. Father Freude was appointed as the first pastor. He continued to reside at Saints Peter and Paul Parish in Lehighton while performing his pastoral duties at Saint Joseph's. Later in 1871, Father Freude began to celebrate Mass twice a month in East Mauch Chunk. A small dilapidated old schoolhouse at the northeast corner of Fourth and North Streets was rented for this purpose. Later, a new school building at 616 North Street was used for Mass and instruction.

A meeting was called for the purpose of procuring ground and building a church. A suitable plot was soon purchased from Charles Skeer, located on the corner of North and Sixth Streets in East Mauch Chunk. A frame church with a small bell tower was constructed in 1872 and named in honor of Saint Joseph the Worker. One of the first buildings erected was a parochial school in 1874. The school was staffed by the Sisters of Christian Charity. The frame church building eventually became too small and the present church was started. The new church was completed and dedicated on November 28, 1901. A new school was built in 1913-1914.

In 1941, the parish undertook an extensive renovation of the church. In 1942, the outdoor shrines honoring Saint Joseph and Our Lady of Fatima were erected. In the years following World War II, a tract of land in the Germantown area was donated and developed as a site for outdoor parish functions. A bungalow type building was constructed and a shrine in honor of the Blessed Mother of Jesus was built. The site was named Our Lady of the Hills Camp. Our Lady of the Hills campsite was sold in 1965.

In 1975, the front platform and church steps were replaced. In December 1977, a renovation of the church interior began. The work was completed by Easter 1978. Immaculate Conception School was closed in June 1980. In 1994, the tower roof needed replacement and was completed later that year. In conjunction with the 125th anniversary, the church interior was renovated. The church was closed from April 15, 1996 to June 30, 1996, while the renovation work was being completed. The weekend Masses were held at the Penn Forest Fire Company Hall and Rimsky's Social Hall. On June 30, 1996, the church was rededicated by Bishop Welsh. Father Francis Baransky, M. Div. is the current pastor.

Saint Mary Parish

Established October 8, 1919

Saint Mary Parish in Kutztown was established on October 8, 1919. Father John Lorenz was appointed as the first pastor. On December 25, 1919, the first Mass in the parish was celebrated by Father Lorenz at the home of Miss Mary Miller. On April 3, 1920, Father Lorenz purchased property in Kutztown. A house on the property was converted into a rectory. Masses were then held in the rectory. Father John Tunner was appointed pastor in April 1928. On June 7, 1928, plans were announced to construct the church on the lot next to the rectory. Saint Mary's Chapel in Evansville was opened on October 5, 1928. Saint Mary's Church was dedicated by Bishop Gerald O'Hara of Philadelphia on June 9, 1929. Father Charles Keller was appointed pastor on June 1, 1930. In 1930, the Missionary Sisters of the Sacred Heart of Jesus began teaching religion classes at the Evansville chapel. The Sisters continued teaching in Evansville until 1969.

Father Francis Adolf was appointed as pastor on April 30, 1942. Groundbreaking on an extension to Saint Mary's Church was held on November 17, 1947. The church extension was dedicated on October 31, 1948. Construction of an outdoor shrine dedicated to the Blessed Mother was begun on May 15, 1954. The shrine was dedicated on August 15, 1954. Father Francis Glunz was appointed as pastor in May 1963. Ground was broken for a new religious education and social hall on October 16, 1977 and completed on November 26, 1978. This building is now known as the parish center.

Ground was broken for a new church on May 22, 1993. The dedication by Bishop Welsh took place on October 8, 1994. At that time, Saint Mary's Chapel in Evansville was closed and the parishioners were consolidated into Saint Mary's Parish. Groundbreaking for a new parish center took place on October 6, 1996. Saint Mary's new parish center was completed and dedicated by Bishop Welsh on June 28, 1997. Groundbreaking for Saint Mary's Pavilion Project was held on July 19, 1997. The Pavilion Project was completed on May 23, 1999. This was followed by the groundbreaking for Saint Mary's Religious Education Center on October 17, 2000. Monsignor James Treston presided at the dedication of the new religious education center on August 26, 2001. Monsignor Walter Scheaffer, M. Ed. has served as pastor since April 29, 1986.

Saint Peter the Fisherman Parish

LAKE HARMONY, PENNSYLVANIA

Established June 15, 1989

Mass was first celebrated at Lake Harmony in 1936. For 47 years, Mass was celebrated in various locations including private homes, Split Rock Lodge, and the Fire Hall. Bishop McShea eventually gave Monsignor Joseph Dooley permission to build a mission church and the Mission was founded on December 7, 1982. The first Mass in this beautiful church was offered on July 4, 1983. The name for the church came from a painting of Saint Peter holding a fisherman's net that was given to Monsignor Dooley by Bishop McShea. The mission church was named Saint Peter the Fisherman. The painting, by Dana Van Horn, hangs in the Choir area of the church.

Saint Peter's remained a mission church of Immaculate Conception Parish in Jim Thorpe under Father Robert Quinn. The church was dedicated by Bishop Welsh on September 7, 1986. Under Father John Chizmar, the mission church continued to grow. He began the necessary steps to prepare the mission for parish status. Bishop Welsh, now believing that the Mission

church could support itself, established Saint Peter the Fisherman Parish in Lake Harmony on June 15, 1989. Father John Auchter was appointed as the first pastor.

The immediate need of the new parish was a parish center to be used for parish gatherings, socials and religious education classes. A campaign was organized and the parish center was soon built. Bishop Welsh dedicated the new parish center on October 6, 1991. A parish rectory with living quarters and office space was finally built under Father Auchter's guidance. The rectory was dedicated by Bishop Welsh on December 8, 1995. In 2001, Monsignor Auchter retired and was replaced by Father Joseph Campion. Father Anthony Drouncheck became pastor in June 2003 and was later succeeded by Monsignor John Chizmar as pastor. In 2006, Saint Peter took his prominent spot in the center circle and was dedicated on September 11, 2006. Saint Peter the Fisherman Parish currently serves over 425 families.

Saint Katharine Drexel Parish

LANSFORD, PENNSYLVANIA

Established July 15, 2008

Saint Katharine Drexel Parish in Lansford was established on July 15, 2008. Father Kenneth Medve was appointed the first pastor. Saint Katharine Drexel Parish was formed by the consolidation of six older neighboring parishes that including: Saint Michael the Archangel Parish in Lansford, Saint Mary of the Assumption Parish in Coaldale, Saint Ann Parish in Lansford, Saints Peter and Paul Parish in Lansford, Saint John the Baptist Parish in Coaldale, and Saints Cyril and Methodius Parish in Coaldale.

Saint Michael the Archangel Parish in Lansford was established in June 1891 to serve the area Slovak Catholics. On September 21, 1890, the Slovaks of the Lansford area first organized a fraternal society under the protection of the Sacred Heart. In June 1891, Father William Heinen, pastor of Saint Joseph's in East Mauch Chunk, called a meeting at the Lansford Opera House to discuss founding a Slovak parish. The parish was established and placed under the patronage of Saint Michael the Archangel. On July 28, 1891, Father Heinen purchased a plot of ground and immediately the men of the parish began preparing the foundation of the church. The cornerstone was laid on August 30, 1891. While the church was being completed, services were held at Saint Joseph's in Summit Hill. On December 20, 1891, the new church was completed. Due to the scarcity of Slovak priests, Saint Michael's became a mission chapel of Saint Joseph's and Father Heinen traveled to Saint Michael's each Sunday to celebrate Mass. Two side chapels and a steeple were added to the church in 1893. In December 1894, Father Joseph Kasparek was appointed pastor. After only nine months, he was transferred and Saint Michael's again became a mission-chapel administered by Father Heinen. Father Peter Schaaf became pastor in May 1903. The church was painted and plans for a parochial school were begun. The cornerstone of the school was laid on July 1, 1906. On September 1, 1907, the school was blessed by Monsignor Fisher of Philadelphia. Since the original Saint Michael Church was destroyed by fire earlier in 1907, two of the classrooms were used for Mass. The school was opened by the Missionary Sisters of the Sacred Heart on September 5, 1908. Attention then turned to the erection of a new church. On Memorial Day 1908, the cornerstone was laid and the church was dedicated by Archbishop Prendergast on November 30, 1911. In 1968, a tunnel connecting the church and school was built. Bishop Welsh celebrated the parish's 100th anniversary on September 29, 1991. The rededication of the church cornerstone took place on Thanksgiving Day, 1991. Father Lawrence

Bukaty was the last pastor of Saint Michael the Archangel Parish.

Saint Mary of the Assumption Parish in Coaldale can trace its roots to 1826, when Father William Fitzpatrick was the first priest to minister to Catholics in the Panther Valley. He journeyed from far distant Sunbury to Summit Hill. In the early days, the people of Coaldale walked to Summit Hill to attend Mass. On August 6, 1892, the parish of Saint Joseph in Summit Hill donated $1,000 to the people of Coaldale for the construction of the church. Mass was offered for the first time in Coaldale on August 14, 1892, in the Phillips Street School Building. Father Francis Brady officiated at the first service held. On May 21, 1893, the cornerstone of the new church was laid. On November 1, 1893, Father Daniel Murphy arrived as the first pastor. The church was dedicated on November 19, 1893. Father Robert Hayes became pastor in 1911 and was

responsible for the building of the school. Saint Mary's School was closed during the Depression. Father Cornelius Devitt was appointed pastor in June 1960. He was responsible for the modernizing of the church. Father John Pavlosky, M. Div. was the last pastor of Saint Mary of the Assumption Parish.

Saint Ann Parish in Lansford was established in June 1907. The church was built at East Bertsch and Tunnel Streets. Bishop Thomas J. Welsh blessed the newly remodeled Saint Ann's Church in Lansford on July 26, 1992. The renovations were begun on September 1, 1991. Father Lawrence Bukaty, M. Psy. was the last pastor of Saint Ann's Parish.

Saints Peter and Paul Church in Lansford was established in October 1907 and a church was soon built. The most recent renovations began with the closing of the church on April 6, 1992. The first Mass after the renovations was on July 4, 1992. During the renovations, parishioners worshiped at Saint Ann's in Lansford. Extensive plaster repairs, painting, and refinishing were part of the major interior restoration. The church was rededicated by Bishop Thomas Welsh on October 31, 1992. Father Lawrence Bukaty, M. Psy. was the last pastor of Saints Peter and Paul Parish.

Saint John the Baptist Parish in Coaldale was established in 1914 to serve the Lithuanian Catholics. In 1907, Mass was celebrated in the basement of the Public School on East Phillips Street. In 1908, a Lithuanian priest named Father Durickas began celebrating Mass in the little Red School House behind the Public School. In September 1911, Father Peter Gudaitis arrived in Coaldale with the intention of formally organizing a parish and building a church. Saint John's first wood frame church building was dedicated on May 10, 1914. Father Gudaitis took up residence at Tamaqua in 1913 and continued to serve as pastor of Saint John's until January 1922. During Easter Mass on April 1, 1920, the wood frame church caught fire. Efforts to save the building were unsuccessful and it was completely destroyed. The new church was dedicated on July 4, 1921. Father Joseph Shelonis became pastor on January 15, 1977. He refurbished the social hall and completed

the facade and east wall of the church. Father John J. Pavlosky, M. Div. was the last pastor of Saint John the Baptist Parish.

Saints Cyril and Methodius Parish in Coaldale was established on June 10, 1920, due to the efforts of Slovaks who petitioned Archbishop Dougherty of Philadelphia to establish a church for the Slovak people in Coaldale. Father Nicholas Terna was appointed the first pastor and the new parish was placed under the patronage of Saints Cyril and Methodius. Initially, the people gathered to worship at the former Welsh Congregational Church on the corner of Ridge and Fourth Streets. By 1922, the men of the parish excavated the ground for the foundation of a new church on the corner of Ruddle and Third Streets. Mass was first celebrated in the church on December 25, 1924. In September 1928, an elementary school was opened in the lower level of the church building and staffed by the Missionary Sisters of the Sacred Heart until 1969. Father John J. Pavlosky, M. Div. was the last pastor of Saints Cyril and Methodius Parish.

Saint Michael the Archangel Parish, Saint Mary of the Assumption Parish, Saint Ann Parish, Saints Peter and Paul Parish, Saint John the Baptist Parish, and Saints Cyril and Methodius Parish were all closed on July 15, 2008. The new Saint Katharine Drexel Church now occupies the former Saint Michael the Archangel Church building in Lansford.

Saints Peter & Paul Parish

LEHIGHTON, PENNSYLVANIA

Established 1885

Catholicism in Lehighton dates back to 1850, when there were seven Catholic families in the area. During the latter part of the nineteenth century, these Catholic families were cared for by Father Freude. He visited the Lehighton area only once a month, celebrating Mass at the Schwartz home on First Street. Father William Heinen built a small church to accommodate the Catholics of the town and gave them their own place of worship. This church was dedicated by Bishop Wood. The exact date of the founding of the church is unknown.

The Catholics of Lehighton were first attended by a priest from Saint Joseph's in East Mauch Chunk. Saints Peter and Paul in Lehighton became a parish in 1885. Father Hubert H. Hammeke was the first resident pastor from 1885 to 1890. In 1885, the Sisters of Charity were brought to the parish from Saint Joseph's in East Mauch Chunk to instruct the Catholic youth of Lehighton. The parish school was opened by three Sisters of Saint Francis (Glen Riddle) in 1886. The old church was remodeled to serve both as a school and church.

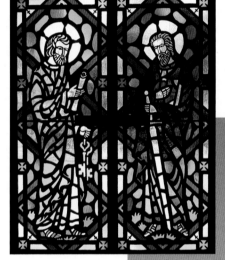

On August 21, 1906, ground was broken for a new church. The cornerstone was laid on October 7, 1906 and the church was dedicated by Archbishop Prendergast on September 1, 1907. The old church was then remodeled for use as a full-time parochial school. An early morning fire struck the church in 1910. The fire originated in the sacristy adjoining the altar. Due to the fire, the new church was renovated, including being frescoed and beautifully decorated. The church was reopened on December 25, 1910. The cornerstone for the new

school was laid on August 17, 1924 and classes were held for the first time on February 9, 1925.

Father George Fenzil became pastor on March 27, 1953. In 1954, he built an addition onto the school. In 1975, Father Fenzil began renovating the exterior of the church when the church steeple was lowered and brick exterior were replaced. Father William Handges became pastor in 1976. On July 9, 1979, he began renovations to the interior and exterior of the church. The renovations were completed on September 21, 1979. The Sisters of Saint Francis left the parish in 1985. At that time, the Grey Nuns of the Sacred Heart agreed to teach at the school. A major renovation of the church, parish center and rectory was begun in 2007. Father Michael Ahrensfield has served as pastor of Saints Peter and Paul Parish since 2008.

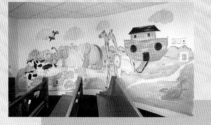

Saint Joseph Parish

LIMEPORT, PENNSYLVANIA

Established November 21, 1927

In 1926, the Catholics of Limeport attended services at Sacred Heart Parish in Allentown. Through the efforts of Father John Fries and the blessing of Monsignor Leo Fink of Sacred Heart, the first Mass was celebrated in Limeport by Monsignor Fink in a large service room at the Limeport Hotel on March 26, 1926. In 1927, Monsignor Fink wrote to Archbishop Dougherty requesting permission to purchase property along with several buildings for a parish in Limeport. Plans were made to convert a two-story stone building into a rectory. A large two-story stone barn would be converted into a convent with a school below and a church above. Saint Joseph Parish in Limeport was established on November 21, 1927.

In September 1961, Saint Joseph's School was opened. In need of a new church building, ground was broken for the church in early 1970. The first Mass was celebrated on December 25, 1970. In September 1977, Saint Joseph School and Assumption B.V.M. School consolidated their resources to become one school with the new name of Saint Michael the Archangel. In August 1991, a Parish Center building was completed on the site of the original church building.

On June 13, 1997, as the student population continued to grow, ground was broken for the addition of four classrooms to the school. The school addition was completed by September 1997.

On December 1, 2002, the parish's 75th Anniversary Mass was celebrated by Bishop Edward P. Cullen. Following the Anniversary Mass, Bishop Cullen blessed the four new classrooms of Saint Michael the Archangel School Limeport Campus that were completed in September 1997. Father Thomas Buckley, M. Div. is the current pastor of Saint Joseph Parish.

Saint Mary Magdalen Parish

LOST CREEK, PENNSYLVANIA

Established 1879

Saint Mary Magdalen Parish in Lost Creek was established in 1879. Father Martin P. Walsh was appointed the first pastor. Father Walsh carried out services in various school houses in the area, traveling from place to place by horse and buggy. The first frame church building was dedicated on December 25, 1879, situated next to the site of the current church. In 1880, Father Walsh erected a rectory on the lot adjoining the church property. In 1892, Father R. P. Daggert became pastor. He was responsible for the remodeling of Temperance Hall.

Father Vincent Corcoran became pastor in 1908. He began to remodel the rectory and during the repair work, the rectory was destroyed by fire in 1908. Father William T. Kelly became pastor on July 10, 1915. He began plans for a new church, rectory, school and convent. The church was started in March 1916. Mass was celebrated for the first time in the new church on December 25, 1918. The school and convent were completed in 1925. Classes were previously conducted in the basement of the church by the Sisters of Saint Francis. Father Henry Kiggins became pastor in 1937. In February 1938, the Pennsylvania Department of Labor and Industry forced the closing of the church. Father Kiggins set up a temporary chapel in the rectory where Mass was celebrated until 1940. A new church was completed on June 16, 1940. A new auditorium was completed on September 19, 1940. In 1963, Saint Mary Magdalen School and convent were closed.

A tragic fire destroyed the church on January 19, 1984. After considering the decline in parishioners, Bishop Welsh announced that the church would not be rebuilt but that the rectory chapel would be renovated and enlarged to hold 75 people. Father Joseph Whalen, pastor of Annunciation BVM Parish in Shenandoah, became pastor of Saint Mary Magdalen Parish in 1988. This was the beginning of a sisterhood of these two parishes.

In 2003, Father Charles Dene became a full time resident of Saint Mary Magdalen rectory and celebrated all the weekday Masses there. A decline in parish membership and a steep rise in fuel costs caused the discontinuation of services at Saint Mary Magdalen Church in the winter of 2008. Parishioners of Saint Mary Magdalen were welcomed to hold services at Annunciation BVM Church, where they participate fully in the spiritual life of the parish.

Blessed Teresa of Calcutta Parish

MAHANOY CITY, PENNSYLVANIA

Established July 15, 2008

Blessed Teresa of Calcutta Parish in Mahanoy City was established on July 15, 2008. Father Kevin P. Gallagher, M. A. was appointed as the first pastor. Blessed Teresa of Calcutta Parish was formed by the consolidation of seven older neighboring parishes that included: Saint Canicus Parish in Mahanoy City, Saint Fidelis Parish in Mahanoy City, Saint Joseph Parish in Mahanoy City, Assumption BVM Parish in Mahanoy City, Saint Casimir Parish in Mahanoy City, Sacred Heart Parish in Mahanoy City, and Our Lady of Siluva Parish in Maizeville.

Saint Canicus Parish in Mahanoy City was established in 1862. Archbishop Wood decided to purchase a lot at the northwest corner of Catawissa and Pine Streets for the parish on March 19, 1862. Father Michael McAvoy was appointed as the first pastor. Mass was first celebrated in "Blind Ryan's House" until it was destroyed by fire, after which the congregation attended Mass in a tent erected on the southwest corner of Catawissa and Pine Streets. In 1863, two adjoining lots were purchased and construction of the church began. On October 19, 1864, a severe wind storm blew down the entire rear wall of the church building still under construction. The church was dedicated by Archbishop Wood in July 1867. A new rectory was built in 1924. The old rectory was torn down and replaced by a combination church-school building in 1925. The first floor of the church was renovated in 1987. Monsignor William Glosser, M.A. was the last pastor of Saint Canicus Parish.

Saint Fidelis Parish in Mahanoy City was founded in 1863 by Archbishop Wood of Philadelphia for the area German families. Father Buenig was appointed the first pastor and built the church on East Mahanoy Street soon after the parish was established. In 1992, the parishioners were surprised to learn that, due to the weight of the church's six ton bells, the steeple had became structurally unsound. Bishop Welsh decided to temporarily close the church. Work on the steeple began and the bells were secured with steel beams. The church was reopened on August 16, 1992. Monsignor William Glosser, M.A. was the last pastor of Saint Fidelis Parish.

Saint Joseph Parish in Mahanoy City was established in 1888 by Archbishop Ryan. Father Peter Abromaitis was appointed the first pastor in August 1888. The cornerstone of the church was blessed by Archbishop Ryan on September 30, 1888. After a short time, four lots were purchased at the corner of West Mahanoy and C Streets with plans for a new brick church with a steeple. The church was completed and dedicated by

Archbishop Ryan on June 8, 1893. A brick rectory was built beside the church in 1894. A parish school was built near the church in 1907, but was unable to open for 18 years due to legal issues that were later settled in court. In 1925, Saint Joseph's School was opened by the Sisters of Saint Francis of Pittsburgh. The school closed in September 1971. In the 1970s, the church and hall were renovated. A new rectory was built in 1978. Monsignor Anthony Wassel was the last pastor of Saint Joseph Parish.

Assumption of the Blessed Virgin Mary ("Saint Mary's") originally existed as a mission church for the Slovaks by about 1890. In 1892, Father Francis Vlossak and the Slovaks gathered together to form a parish. Saint Mary Parish in Mahanoy City was established in early 1892. Masses were celebrated in German's Hall on Linden and Market Streets. Land off West Centre Street was purchased and a church was constructed. Father Vlossak celebrated the first Mass in the church in the summer of 1892 and was appointed as the first pastor in September 1892. On June 9, 1893, the new church was dedicated by Archbishop Ryan. The famous "bells of St Mary's" were most likely blessed at the dedication and installed in the steeple. Father Joseph Kasparek became pastor in September 1898. He built a rectory and school behind the church before 1905. In 1928, the old church was razed. The cornerstone of the new church was laid on September 23, 1928. The dedication took place on November 12, 1928. In the fall of 1929, Saint Mary's School was opened by the Bernardine Sisters of Saint Francis. The school was closed in 1955. The newly decorated church was rededicated in 1977. Around this time, Assumption of the Blessed Virgin Mary became the official name of the parish. An arsonist set fire to the church and severely damaged the sacristy on March 9, 1992. The first Mass in the newly renovated church was on June 7, 1992. Monsignor Anthony Wassel was the last pastor of Assumption BVM Parish.

Saint Casimir Parish in Mahanoy City was established to serve 35 Polish families in 1893. Father Martin Tarnowski was appointed the first pastor. Mass was conducted in the basement of Saint Mary's Slovak Church. On October 20, 1893, Father Tarnowski purchased the Welsh Baptist Church at South Catawissa Street. The church was dedicated in late 1893. Father Januszkiewicz became pastor in 1894. He erected a rectory and added a church tower. In 1902, Father Joseph Biela was appointed pastor. A new wooden church was soon erected. In 1906, a new parish school was opened by the Bernardine Sisters. On January 10, 1927, fire completely destroyed the church. A new brick church with two steeples was dedicated on May 28, 1928. In 1971, the parish school was closed. A new rectory was built in 1984 and the new parish center was dedicated in November 1984. The interior and exterior of the church were renovated in 1988. Monsignor William Glosser, M.A. was the last pastor of Saint Casimir Parish.

Sacred Heart Parish in Mahanoy City was established in 1907 to serve the Italian Catholics in the vicinity. Land was purchased on East Pine Street and the church was soon built. Monsignor Anthony F. Wassel was the last pastor of Sacred Heart Parish.

Our Lady of Siluva Parish in Maizeville was originally established as Saint Louis' Parish in 1907 to serve the Lithuanians of Maizeville. The parish first purchased the former Primitive Methodist Church building. After minor renovations, the building was dedicated as Saint Louis' Church. Father A.M. Milakas was appointed as the first pastor. On September 26, 1914, the church was destroyed by fire and was rebuilt in 1915. In 1967, Saint Louis' Church was again destroyed by fire. A new church was erected and renamed as Our Lady of Siluva Parish. The parish was put under the care of Saint Joseph's Parish in Frackville in recent years. Father David W. Karns, M. Div. was the last pastor of Our Lady of Siluva Parish.

Saint Canicus Parish, Saint Fidelis Parish, Saint Joseph Parish, Assumption BVM Parish, Saint Casimir Parish, Sacred Heart Parish, and Our Lady of Siluva Parish were all closed on July 15, 2008. The new Blessed Teresa of Calcutta Church occupies the former Saint Joseph Church building in Mahanoy City.

Saint Rocco Parish

MARTINS CREEK, PENNSYLVANIA

Established 1929

Following World War I, Italian immigrants were drawn to Martins Creek by the availability of work at the Alpha Portland Cement Company. On November 22, 1913, the Alpha Company donated an old barn and property located on Pennsylvania Avenue and Locust Street that formerly housed the horses used in quarry operations. Father A. Landolfi, pastor of Saint Anthony's in Easton, was asked by Archbishop Edmund Prendergast to visit Martins Creek and determine if the Catholics of the area were interested in having their own parish.

After his visit, Father Landolfi petitioned the Archdiocese of Philadelphia for $850 with which to convert the Alpha barn for services. This structure became the Mission's first church building. Outfitted with wooden floors and a choir loft, the church could accommodate between 50 to 70 parishioners. At that time, Saint Rocco's was attended by priests from Saint Anthony's in Easton and Our Lady of Good Counsel in Bangor.

At a meeting of the Philadelphia Archdiocesan Consultors on April 25, 1927, it was decided to establish a parish in Martins Creek as soon as a priest was available. Saint Rocco Parish was established in 1929 and Father Alfred Procopio was appointed as the first pastor. During his pastorate, construction on the present church began in May 1937. The church took 4 months to complete and was dedicated on September 26, 1937. With the increased membership and activities of the church, an addition was made to the church rectory in 2004. Monsignor James Reichert has served as pastor of Saint Rocco Parish since June 2003.

All Saints Parish

MCADOO, PENNSYLVANIA

Established July 15, 2008

All Saints Parish in McAdoo was established on July 15, 2008. Father Richard Brensinger, M.Div. was appointed as the interim pastor. The first pastor is Rev. Father Ronnald J. Minner. All Saints Parish was formed by the consolidation of six older neighboring parishes that included: Saint Patrick Parish in McAdoo, Saint Mary of the Assumption Parish in McAdoo, Saint Kunegunda Parish in McAdoo, Immaculate Conception Parish in Keylares, Saint Michael Parish in Tresckow and Saint Bartholomew Parish in Tresckow.

Saint Patrick Parish in McAdoo was established in 1869. Father Marron was appointed as the first pastor. The first parish buildings were in Beaver Brook. In 1873, the parish moved to Audenried and a church was begun. The church was dedicated in 1875. The church was torn down and the parish was relocated to McAdoo in 1898. The new church in McAdoo was completed by Father Peter Malloy by the autumn of 1900. Saint Patrick's School was opened by six Sisters of the Immaculate Heart Order from Philadelphia in 1925. A tornado damaged the church on July 15, 1992. The tornado severely damaged part of the church tower, roof and support beams. Monsignor Edward Zemanik was the last pastor of All Saints Parish.

Saint Mary of the Assumption Parish in McAdoo was established in 1893. A group of Slovaks, Poles and Hungarians met with Monsignor Heinen from Mauch Chunk in 1891. On January 3, 1892, Father Francis Vlossak officiated at the first mission Mass at Saint Patrick's in Audenreid. The parish was established in 1893 and Masses were celebrated at the West Grant Street School in McAdoo. Two lots were acquired for a church and construction began in the fall of 1893. The cornerstone was laid in November 1893. Father Vlossak celebrated the first Mass in the new church on Pentecost Sunday 1894. The church was dedicated on August 15, 1894. Father Joseph Kasparek became pastor on May 15, 1895 and a rectory was soon built. A new rectory was built in 1902. The first school in McAdoo was opened by the Missionary Sisters of the Most Sacred Heart of Jesus in 1910. In 1912, the original rectory and church were destroyed by fire. A new brick church, school and convent were erected in 1913. The second church, school and convent burned down again in 1922. The cornerstone of the third church was laid in 1923 and dedicated in 1924. Bishop Welsh celebrated the 100th anniversary of the parish on June 6, 1993. Monsignor Edward Zemanik was the last pastor of Saint Mary of the Assumption Parish.

Saint Kunegunda Parish in McAdoo was established in 1893. Polish immigrants first worshipped at Saint Mary's in Audenried. In 1891, local Poles formed the Casimir Pulaski Guards. They arranged to have Father Anthony Klawitter preached to the Poles in their native language at Saint Mary's. The Casimir Pulaski Guards also sent a delegation to Archbishop Ryan to petition for the formation of a parish for the Polish-speaking people. In 1893, Archbishop Ryan authorized the formation of Saint Casimir's in Mahanoy City

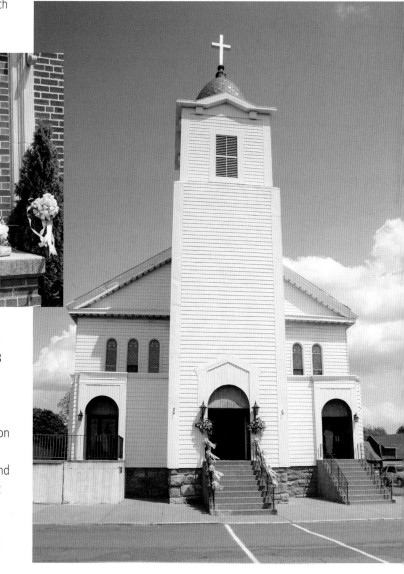

to serve the Polish people there. Father Maciej Tarnowski was appointed pastor and directed to minister to the Poles in McAdoo. The first mass for the Saint Kunegunda Mission was celebrated by Father Tarnowski in the Grant Street School on August 1, 1893. During those years, the pastors of Saint Casimir's celebrated an early Mass each Sunday in McAdoo. A small chapel at Tamaqua and Sherman Streets was constructed and used until 1905. Between 1894 and 1896, the local Polish congregation was granted a land parcel on Washington Street. Father Jan Dabrowski became the first resident pastor in January 1904 and built a new church at Washington and Cleveland Streets beginning in 1904. The church was dedicated on November 19, 1905. A parish school was opened in the church basement by the Bernadine Sisters from Reading in 1916. This school was closed in 1923. In May 1926, ground was broken for a new school. The school was opened by the Sisters of the Holy Family of Nazareth in September 1928. In 1954, the parish began razing the old frame church to make way for a new church. During the construction, Masses were conducted in the school auditorium. Ground was broken on June 16, 1962 and the first Mass was celebrated in the new church on October 13, 1963. The church was dedicated on April 12, 1964. Saint Kunegunda's School merged with St. Patrick's School in 1969. A new rectory was built in 1975. The Sisters of the Holy Family of Nazareth left the parish in 1980 and the Sisters, Servants of the Immaculate Heart staffed both schools. Saint Kunegunda's School closed in 1985. Bishop Welsh celebrated the parish's 100th anniversary on July 31, 1994. Monsignor Edward Zemanik was the last pastor of Saint Kunegunda Parish.

Immaculate Conception Parish in Kelayres was established in 1899. Prior to 1895, there was no Catholic congregation in Kelayres. Immaculate Conception began as a Chapel of Mission for the Italian speaking people of Keylares in 1897. The land on which the church stands was donated to the Archdiocese of Philadelphia on July 30, 1898. At this time, Father Lambertics Travi began renting a home in Kelayres. Prior to this, he made the long trek from Jim Thorpe to tend to the spiritual needs of the people on Sundays. In 1898, the church was completed. Immaculate Conception was elevated to parish status in 1899 and Father Travi became the first pastor. A steeple was added to the church in 1900. Father Ernest Amati became pastor in 1915 and undertook the first remodeling of the church. A church hall was erected in 1932. A renovation of the church took place in 1955. Bishop Cullen celebrated the 100th anniversary of the parish on July 25, 1999. Monsignor Edward Zemanik was the last pastor of Immaculate Conception Parish.

Saint Michael Parish in Tresckow was established by Archbishop Patrick Ryan of Philadelphia in 1908. The church was built in 1909. Father Thomas Shanfelt, M.A. was the last pastor of Saint Michael Parish. Saint Bartholomew Parish in Tresckow was established by Archbishop Edmond Prendergast of Philadelphia in 1917. The original church was built about 1917 and was replaced by a new church building in 1959. Father Thomas Shanfelt, M.A. was the last pastor of Saint Bartholomew Parish.

Saint Patrick Parish, Saint Mary of the Assumption Parish, Saint Kunegunda Parish, Immaculate Conception Parish, Saint Michael Parish and Saint Bartholomew Parish were all closed on July 15, 2008. The new All Saints Church now occupies the former Saint Patrick Church building in McAdoo.

St Matthew the Evangelist

MINERSVILLE, PENNSYLVANIA

Established July 15, 2008

Saint Matthew Parish in Minersville was established on July 15, 2008. Father Leo Maletz, M. Div. was appointed as the first pastor. Saint Matthew Parish was formed by the consolidation of four older neighboring parishes that included: Saint Francis of Assisi Parish in Minersville, Saint Mary Star of the Sea Parish in Branchdale, Saint Stanislaus Kostka Parish in Minersville and Saint Barbara Parish in Minersville.

Saint Francis of Assisi Parish in Minersville was established in 1895. The first Lithuanians came to Minersville in 1889. As their numbers increased, the Saint Anthony's Society was organized on May 12, 1892. During the first few years, Father Peter Abromaitis came from Shenandoah to care for the spiritual needs of the Lithuanians in Minersville. Services were held in Saint Vincent de Paul Church. As the congregation grew, they began to look for a more suitable place to conduct Mass. Saint Francis of Assisi Parish was founded in 1895 and Father Matulaitis was appointed pastor. The congregation began to hold Sunday services in a classroom at Our Lady of Mount Carmel School. Since the Germans were also conducting Sunday Masses in the same room, difficulties developed and plans for their own church began. Father Albinas Kaminskas became pastor in 1898. On May 18, 1900, the Archbishop of Philadelphia gave permission for the purchase of the old English Evangelical Lutheran Church on Third Street. The church was then dedicated as a temporary place of worship. In 1909, the new church was built on land purchased in New Minersville. Only the basement of the church was completed with plans for a larger church later. Father Joseph Karalius became pastor in 1923. He built the parochial school and a convent for the Sisters of Saint Casimir. In 1938, a shrine dedicated to Our

Lady of Lourdes was erected. The church was renovated in 1950. Two bell towers were constructed and the inside of the church was redecorated. Father John Luksys became pastor in 1973. In 1974, he remodeled both the interior and exterior of the church. The interior of the church was renovated again in 1988-1989. Father David Liebner, M. Div. was the last pastor of Saint Francis of Assisi Parish.

Saint Mary, Star of the Sea Parish in Branchdale was established in 1902. It began as a mission chapel of Saint Vincent Parish in Minersville and was located on State Road in Branchdale in 1886. The cornerstone for the church was laid on May 30, 1886 and church bell arrived on January 11, 1887. The beautiful little church was dedicated by Archbishop Patrick Ryan of Philadelphia in May 1892. Prior to 1886, area Catholics had been attending Mass at the Ancient Order of Hibernians Hall in Branchdale and had originally walked a few miles to attend Saint Vincent's Church in Minersville. Father Philip Beresford served as pastor of Saint

Vincent's in Minersville and administrator of the mission from 1886 to 1895. St. Mary, Star of the Sea in Branchdale became a parish in 1902. The first resident pastor was Father Vincent Corcoran. A rectory was soon built adjacent to the church. In 1925, under the direction of Father Cornelius O'Brien, an elementary school was built and a convent erected. The Sisters of St. Joseph from Chestnut Hill staffed the school. In 1936, Father A. Paul Lambert oversaw a renovation of the church. The closing Mass at Saint Mary, Star of the Sea was celebrated on July 13, 2008. Father Leo Maletz, M. Div. was the last pastor of Saint Mary, Star of the Sea Parish.

Saint Stanislaus Kostka Parish in Minersville was established in November 1905. In 1903, Father Vincent Dargis, pastor of Saint Francis of Assisi, agreed to conduct services in the Polish language every second Sunday of the month in 1903. Archbishop Patrick Ryan established a new parish in Minersville for the Polish Catholics. The parish was established in November 1905. Masses were first held in Our Lady of Mt. Carmel Church on Third Street. The first Mass was celebrated on November 15, 1905. The church and rectory were built in 1906 and located on the old Kear Estate. Construction on a new church was begun in 1913 and completed by Christmas 1913.

In 1929, the interior of the church was decorated and 22 beautiful stained glass windows were installed. On December 3, 1936, the newly decorated church was dedicated. The church was renovated from 1961 to 1965. A shrine dedicated to Our Lady was dedicated on October 2, 1962. The church was rededicated by

Bishop McShea on May 9, 1965. The church was again renovated in 1986. Father Leo Maletz, M. Div. was the last pastor.

Saint Barbara Parish in Minersville was established on July 23, 1913 to serve over 100 Italian families. The parish was established thanks to the efforts of Father John DeStefano, pastor of Saint Joseph in Pottsville. The parish was dedicated to the Virgin Martyr Saint Barbara, special Patroness of miners. On October 23, 1913, the congregation bought the old church of the Schismatic Russians and began renovations. The first Mass was celebrated in the church on December 25, 1913. The church was dedicated in October 1914. Archbishop Dougherty of Philadelphia established the mission as a parish in July 1924. Father Joseph Landolfi was appointed the first pastor on July 13, 1924. He built the rectory in May 1925. Father Landolfi began an enlargement and renovation of the church. The rededication was held on October 18, 1953. On February 4, 1956, a fire destroyed a major portion of the church nave, sanctuary and rectory. During the reconstruction, services were held in Saint Vincent's School Hall. The first Mass in the reconstructed church was held on December 24, 1956. During the 1970s, the church was again renovated. Father David Liebner, M. Div. was the last pastor of Saint Barbara Parish.

Saint Francis of Assisi Parish, Saint Mary Star of the Sea Parish, Saint Stanislaus Kostka Parish and Saint Barbara Parish were all closed on July 15, 2008. The new Saint Matthew Church now occupies the old Saint Stanislaus Kostka Church building in Minersville.

Saint Michael the Archangel Parish

Established July 15, 2008

Saint Michael the Archangel Parish in Minersville was established on July 15, 2008. Father Adam Sedar was appointed as the first pastor. Saint Michael the Archangel Parish was formed by the consolidation of three older neighboring parishes that included: Saint Vincent de Paul Parish in Minersville, Our Lady of Mount Carmel Parish in Minersville, and Saint Kieran Parish in Heckscherville.

Saint Vincent de Paul Parish in Minersville was established by Bishop John Neumann in 1842.

Father Nicholas Cantwell was the first priest to offer Holy Mass in the Minersville area. Father Hugh Fitzsimmons was appointed the first pastor by Bishop Peter Kendrick of Philadelphia in 1846. The original church was dedicated by Bishop Kendrick on December 6, 1846. Father Michael Malone became pastor in 1848 and the present rectory was built in 1852. He completed work on the church interior and added the bell tower in August 1860. Father Lawrence Fahey began work on a parish

school in 1919. The new parish school was dedicated by Archbishop Dougherty in 1920 and staffed by the Sisters of Saint Joseph. Saint Vincent's School was closed in the 1970s, following a school merger that created Saint Elizabeth Ann Seton School. Father William Jones became pastor on November 7, 1978. Within a few months, Father Jones decided it was necessary to build a new church. The last Mass in the original church was offered on November 2, 1980 and the building was demolished on February 2, 1981. The first Mass was offered by Father Jones in the new church on Thanksgiving Day 1981. Bishop McShea dedicated the new church on July 11, 1982. Father Eric Gruber, M. Div. was the last pastor of Saint Vincent de Paul Parish.

Our Lady of Mount Carmel Parish was established in 1855 by Bishop John Neumann for the German Catholics of Minersville. Prior to 1855, the local German Catholics had to walk to Saint John's Church in Pottsville to attend Mass. The first pastor of the parish was Father Mathias

Meurer. The cornerstone of the original church was laid on July 15, 1855. On June 29, 1856, Bishop Neumann dedicated the church. Father Joseph Nerz purchased the ground next to the church for the original parish school building in 1889. In September 1889, the Sisters of Saint Francis from Glen Riddle came to staff the school. The Sisters lived in the school on the second floor until 1915. Father John Vitt became pastor in 1911 and provided the Sisters with a convent in 1915. Father Aloysius Hammeke became pastor in May 1928. The present church was erected in 1936 and the new school in 1954. Father Hammeke served as pastor until May 1972. Father Eric Gruber, M. Div. was the last pastor of Our Lady of Mount Carmel Parish.

Saint Kieran (originally Saint Kyran) Parish in Heckscherville was established by Bishop John Neumann in 1857. As early as 1845, the local Catholic residents had to walk to Saint Patrick's Church in Pottsville to attend Mass. In 1847, Bishop Neumann had erected Saint Vincent's Church in Minersville which shortened the

distance considerably for the next 11 years. Bishop Neumann began construction of the church in Heckscherville in April 1857. He instructed Father Malone, pastor of Saint Vincent's in Minersville, to visit every Catholic family in Heckscherville and solicit aid from each Catholic family for the erection of the new church. The cornerstone was laid by Father Nicholas Cantwell on September 16, 1857. The oldest available records of the church give August 1, 1858, as the day when Sunday Mass began to be regularly celebrated. The first baptism was performed by Father John Scanlon. Subsequent years saw the construction of a rectory next to the church. The two stone buildings were situated beautifully on the hillside. In 1900, Father P.J. Tierney undertook improvements to the church interior. The walls and ceiling were refinished and repainted. Work on the church interior was continued by Father William Motley in 1904. He had the stained glass windows installed. By October 1916, the school building and auditorium were complete. The church was remodeled in 1917 and included a new floor, pews, and altars. The sanctuary was also enlarged by the removal of the two sacristies. The church's original name, Saint Kyran, was changed to Saint Kieran in 1919. In 1938, a new chapel was erected in Greenbury by Father McMahon. Our Lady of Lourdes Grotto was completed and dedicated in 1938. Bishop Thomas Welsh dedicated the new church murals in 1983 and the altar in 1988. The last pastor of Saint Kieran Parish in Heckscherville was Father William Nahn.

Saint Vincent de Paul Parish, Our Lady of Mount Carmel Parish and Saint Kieran Parish were all closed on July 15, 2008. The new Saint Michael the Archangel Church now occupies the former Saint Vincent de Paul Church building in Minersville.

Saint Benedict Parish

MOHNTON, PENNSYLVANIA

Established February 10, 1955

In 1952, Mary and Caroline Archer donated 600-acres of land to the Benedictine Monks. On March 3, 1952, Archbishop John O'Hara of Philadelphia granted permission for the Benedictine Fathers of Saint Benedict's Abbey in Benet Lake, Wisconsin, to accept the Archer Estate in Berks County for the purpose of establishing a monastery there. The first Mass was celebrated by Father Leonard van Ackeren, the Prior of Saint Benedict's Monastery, in a farm building on October 26, 1952 with seating capacity of 35. On February 10, 1955, Archbishop O'Hara established Saint Benedict's Parish and entrusted the care of this parish to the Benedictine Fathers.

The parish was suppressed by Bishop Joseph McShea in August 1972, after the Benedictine Fathers decided to retire from Saint Benedict's and return to Benet Lake in Wisconsin. The last Mass at the monastery was celebrated by Father Albert Meyer OSB on October 29, 1972 and the parish was closed.

On November 13, 1972 Bishop McShea permitted Saint Benedicts to operate as a mission under the direction of Fr. David Soderland with Masses being celebrated at Robeson Lutheran Church, Plowville until a new church was built. Daily Masses were offered in the quaint Gates candy factory that had been converted into a chapel.

Ground was chosen for a new church on July 2, 1973 and the fourteen acre property was purchased on November 23, 1973. Saint Benedict Parish was re-established by the Diocese of Allentown on January 1, 1974. Ground breaking for the new church took place on February 23, 1975. The church was completed in November 1975. The first Mass at the New Saint Benedict's Church, Mohnton (Plowville) was held on November 9, 1975. St. Benedicts continued to grow in members as a vibrant faith community. Quickly the parish out grew the 1975 church and plans were underway for expansion under the direction of Fr. Dennis T. Hartgen and completed by Fr. Albert J. Byrne. The current church was dedicated by Bishop Edward Cullen on March 5, 2000 with seating capacity of 520. Fr. Philip F. Rodgers is the current pastor of Saint Benedict Parish.

Holy Family Parish

NAZARETH, PENNSYLVANIA

Established 1908

Holy Family Parish in Nazareth was established by Archbishop Patrick Ryan of Philadelphia in 1908. Father Peter Fuengerlings was appointed the first pastor. Groundbreaking for the church, with a school on the second floor, was begun in early May 1908. Father Fuengerlings celebrated the first Mass in the church on November 18, 1908. The hardships encountered in the first two years of the parish caused the first pastor to request an early transfer. In 1913, Archbishop Pendergast of Philadelphia was ready to put the entire property on the auction block. With the arrival of Father Bernard Greifenberg, MSC as pastor in December 1913, Archbishop Pendergast was willing to give Holy Family Parish a second chance.

new gymnasium was built. Ground was broken for the new church in 1964. In 1977, a new rectory was built on Forest Drive by Father Michael Camilli, MSC. Father Daniel Cipar, MSC became pastor in 1982. Under his guidance the school was expanded in 1985. Father Joseph F. Tobias, MSC has served as pastor since 2005. Holy Family Parish in Nazareth currently serves over 2,600 families.

The Missionary Sisters of the Most Sacred Heart served the parish from 1910 until 1991. Initially, the Sisters lived in two rooms next to the classrooms on the second floor of the church building. A convent was eventually built for the Sisters in 1928. Father Frederick Struchholz,

MSC served as pastor from 1939 to 1946. He made improvements to the church that included new altars, pews and the remodeling of the convent.

Father Michael Walsh, MSC served as pastor from 1947 to 1952. He began a building fund to construct a new church and school. In November 1954, the new school on Convent Avenue was completed. Soon after a

Saint Francis of Assisi Parish

NESQUEHONING, PENNSYLVANIA

Established July 15, 2008

Saint Francis of Assisi Parish in Nesquehoning was established on July 15, 2008. Father Anthony Drouncheck, M. Div. was appointed as the first pastor. Saint Francis of Assisi Parish was formed by the consolidation of three older neighboring parishes that included: Sacred Heart Parish in Nesquehoning, Our Lady of Mount Carmel Parish in Nesquehoning and Immaculate Conception Parish in Nesquehoning.

Sacred Heart Parish in Nesquehoning was established originally as Saint Patrick Parish in 1839.

Saint Patrick's Church was built on West Catawissa Street and Mill Street in 1839. Father James Maloney was the founder of Saint Patrick's. He resided in Beaver Meadows and said Mass once a month in Nesquehoning prior to 1848. Decades later, Father Michael Bunce said Mass every other Sunday in Nesquehoning. In 1883, he purchased property on West High Street for the new Sacred Heart Church and the cornerstone was laid on September 4, 1887. The old Saint Patrick's was torn down in 1889. Saint Patrick's Church site became a parish cemetery. Sacred Heart School was built in 1925 and taught by the Sisters of Mercy of Merion. The convent was erected in 1925. In January 1929, the school was damaged by a disastrous fire. Students attended classes in Saint Mary's church hall, during rebuilding of the school. The school closed on June 8, 1973. In 1975, the church was completely renovated and the basement excavated for use as a social hall. Sacred Heart celebrated their 100th anniversary with a Jubilee Mass on August 30, 1987. Father Clifton Bishop, M. Div. was the last pastor of Sacred Heart Parish.

Our Lady of Mount Carmel Parish in New Columbus was established in November 1913. The parish began in a town named Little Italy. Italian immigrants founded Little Italy in 1884. Numbering approximately 120 families, these early settlers worshipped at Sacred Heart in Nesquehoning. In 1904, Father Paolo Gentile came to Little Italy to say Mass on Sundays in a dilapidated building. He built the first church in 1905. In 1906, the church in Little Italy became a mission church of Saint Joseph's in Pottsville. In November 1913, Archbishop Prendergast elevated the mission to a parish and appointed Father Luigi LaBella as the first resident pastor. A rectory was built in 1914. In 1918, Little Italy was abandoned due to mining operations, making it necessary for the residents to relocate to the new town of New Columbus. By 1920, the entire population of Little Italy had moved to New Columbus. The new church in New Columbus was rebuilt and dedicated by 1920. On October 15, 1945, the Grotto Shrine was dedicated. A parish hall was completed in 1950. Ground was broken for a new church on February 26, 1950. The cornerstone was laid on July 16, 1951 and the dedication took place on May 29, 1955. A new rectory was added in 1967. Father Clifton Bishop, M. Div. was the last pastor of Our Lady of Mount Carmel Parish.

Immaculate Conception Parish in Nesquehoning was established in 1914. Corby's Hall on West Catawissa Street was rented to a group of Slovak immigrants for the purpose of conducting Sunday services in 1912. Father John Ludwig, pastor of Saint Joseph's in East Mauch Chunk, was appointed to administer services in Nesquehoning. The rented hall soon became overcrowded and a larger place was rented on West Railroad Street.

On April 12, 1914, Father Ludwig held the first Mass on West Railroad Street. Membership increased rapidly and he proposed that a larger church be erected on a suitable parcel of land to be purchased. A house and lot were purchased on West Mill Street. The cornerstone for the new church was laid in 1920. Father John Neverosky was appointed the first resident pastor in 1923. In 1940, building of the new church was begun. The church was dedicated by Bishop Lamb of Philadelphia on June 1, 1941. In 1950, additional land was purchased and a new rectory was built. Later, the rectory was transformed into a Religious Education Center. Father Clifton Bishop, M. Div. was the last pastor of Immaculate Conception Parish.

Sacred Heart Parish, Our Lady of Mount Carmel Parish and Immaculate Conception Parish were all closed on July 15, 2008. The new Saint Francis of Assisi Church now occupies the former Immaculate Conception Church building.

Holy Cross Parish

NEW PHILADELPHIA, PENNSYLVANIA

Established July 15, 2008

Holy Cross Parish in New Philadelphia was established on July 15, 2008. Father Joseph Kweder, M. Div. was appointed as the first pastor. Holy Cross Parish was formed by the consolidation of three older neighboring parishes that included: Holy Family Parish in New Philadelphia, Sacred Heart Parish in New Philadelphia and Saint Anthony of Padua Parish in Cumbola.

Holy Family Parish in New Philadelphia was established on November 1, 1866 to serve the growing number of Catholics in the Schuylkill Valley. Father John Loughran was appointed as the first pastor. When Father Loughran arrived, he procured a temporary building for use as a church. The old structure was renovated and improved. In 1880, the church was destroyed by fire. The parish then erected a large church and rectory on the old site. By 1890, a parish school was deemed necessary. A parochial school and convent were built in 1902. Archbishop Patrick Ryan of Philadelphia dedicated the school in summer 1902. Holy Family School was opened by the Sisters of Mercy of Dallas in September 1902. During the pastorate of Father A. Bennett Conway, the church interior was renovated and the grotto in honor of Our Blessed Mother was built on the side of the rectory. The Sisters served the parish until 1972, when Holy Family School merged with Sacred Heart School to form Holy Cross School. The Sisters of Saint Casimir arrived to staff Holy Cross School in 1972. A renovation and redecoration of the church took place in the spring of 1991. Father Joseph Kweder, M. Div. was the last pastor of Holy Family Parish.

Sacred Heart Parish in New Philadelphia was established in 1895. The Sacred Heart Lithuanian Society of New Philadelphia was organized around 1892. Twice a year it was customary for the

pastor of Holy Family Church to invite Father Simon Pautientius from Mahanoy City to administer to the Lithuanians in their native language. Father Pautientius realized that the people deserved more than just two brief visits a year. He encouraged them to organize and establish their own Lithuanian church. In the autumn of 1895, two delegates traveled to Philadelphia to petition Archbishop Ryan for permission to establish a Lithuanian church in New Philadelphia. The parish was established and Father Vincent Matulaitis of Minersville was appointed as the first pastor. Each Sunday, he commuted to New Philadelphia to hold services. Until their church was erected, the parishioners met in the public schoolhouse. In the spring of 1901, ground was broken for a church. The church was completed by Father Albin Kaminskas in 1901 and also housed the parish school. The Sisters of Saint Casimir served the parish from

1926 until 1994. Bishop Welsh celebrated the 100th anniversary of the parish with a Mass on September 17, 1995. Father Joseph Kweder, M. Div. was the last pastor of Sacred Heart Parish.

Saint Anthony of Padua Parish in Cumbola was established in November 1907 to serve the Polish speaking Catholics. The parish was organized by a priest from Minersville, who held services in the public school building. In 1908, Father Anthony Ziebura came from Minersville and organized the Saint Anthony's Society. With the help of this group, a small wooden frame church was built. Father Ziebura became the first pastor. Saint Anthony School was opened by the Bernardine Sisters of Reading in 1922. A rectory was also built in 1922.

Father S. S. Krystyniak became pastor on February 21, 1923. He supervised the building of the present church which also had a school and convent. This was built on the same spot where the old church was located. The old church was moved in back and used as a parish hall. The cornerstone was laid in May 1924. The new church was dedicated by Archbishop Dougherty in 1925. Saint Anthony's School was closed in 1955, due to a decline in enrollment. The interior of the church and rectory were renovated during the 1970s. Father Joseph Kweder, M. Div. was the last pastor of Saint Anthony of Padua.

Holy Family Parish, Sacred Heart Parish and Saint Anthony of Padua Parish were all closed on July 15, 2008. The new Holy Cross Church now occupies the former Holy Family Church building in New Philadelphia.

Assumption of The Blessed Virgin Mary Parish

NORTHAMPTON, PENNSYLVANIA

Established June 19, 1922

The first Catholic Mass with Slovak sermon and hymns was celebrated in Northampton at Laubach's Hall by Father Gaza in 1921. As the number of Catholic Slovaks in Northampton grew, so did the desire for their own church. Soon after, Archbishop Dennis Cardinal Dougherty began plans to establish a Slovak parish in Northampton. Land was purchased at 22nd Street and Washington Avenue. Father Andrew Fekety arrived in Northampton to help organize the parish on June 10, 1922.

Assumption of the Blessed Virgin Mary Parish in Northampton was established by Archbishop Dougherty on June 19, 1922 and Father Fekety was appointed as the first pastor. Work on the church began and the cornerstone for the church was laid in 1923. A rectory was completed in 1924. In 1926 land was purchased for a parish cemetery. The upper part of the main church was completed and dedicated by Bishop Gerald O'Hara in 1929. Father Michael Begany was appointed pastor in 1929. Assumption BVM School was opened in 1938, followed by the completion of a new rectory in 1939.

Father Michael Messaros became pastor in 1962. In celebration of the 50th Anniversary of the parish, he directed the renovations of the church interior in 1972. Father Michael Stone became pastor in 1980. In 1982, Assumption BVM School was consolidated with other parish schools to form the new Our Lady of Hungary Regional School in Northampton.

In 1992 Father Stephen Radocha was appointed pastor. In 1997, as part of the 75th Anniversary, an elevator was added and the entrance lobby, cry room, choir, and confessional were renovated. Father John Mraz was appointed pastor of Assumption BVM Parish in 2002. He continued improvements to the church. Father Francis Straka has served as pastor of Assumption BVM Parish since July 2008.

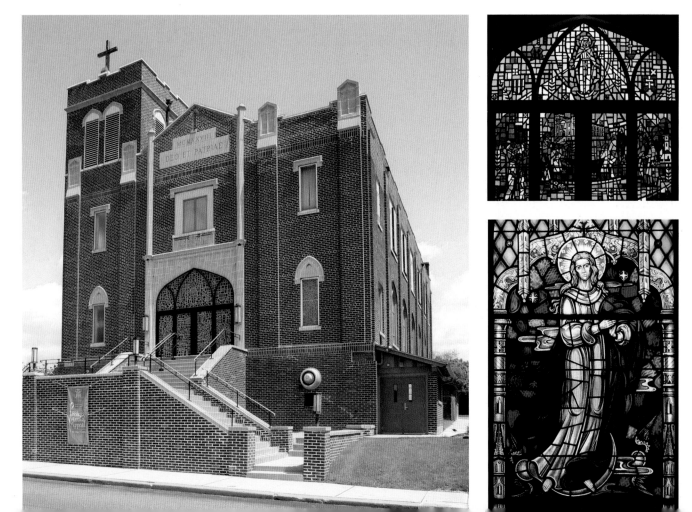

Queenship of Mary Parish

NORTHAMPTON, PENNSYLVANIA

Established July 15, 2008

Queenship of Mary Parish in Northampton was established on July 15, 2008. Monsignor John Campbell was appointed as the first pastor. Queenship of Mary was formed by the consolidation of two older neighboring parishes that included: Our Lady of Hungary Parish in Northampton and Saint Michael the Archangel Parish in Northampton.

Our Lady of Hungary Parish in Northampton was established in September 1906. Archbishop Ryan of Philadelphia saw the need to establish a church in Northampton and he asked Father Alexander Varlaky to make the necessary arrangements for the founding of the parish in 1906.

Father Varlaky established the parish on Labor Day 1906. In the early spring of 1907, building activity began with erection of the basement of the church where Mass was said temporarily.

Father Oscar Solymos became pastor on September 6, 1907. He saw the completion of the church and was instrumental in annexing the property adjacent to the church for use as a convent.

Our Lady of Hungary School was opened by the Missionary Sisters of the Most Sacred Heart of Jesus in September 1917. Father Paul Repchick became pastor in June 1923. Under his guidance, the parish house was purchased, and the church and school were remodeled. Father Edwin Schwartz was the last pastor of Our Lady of Hungary Parish.

Saint Michael the Archangel Parish in Northampton was established in February 1914. It was originally established as a Polish mission on March 23, 1913. They were cared for by Father Michael Strzemplewicz from Allentown and religious services were held in the basement of Our Lady of Hungary Church. The Poles of Northampton were not satisfied with only a mission as their congregation grew. A committee was formed in December 1913 to appeal to Monsignor Peter Masson, then Vicar Forane for the Philadelphia Archdiocese, that a Polish parish be established in Northampton. In February 1914, Father Adalbert Sulek arrived as the first pastor of Saint Michael the Archangel Parish. A public hall, known as Czapp's hall, was rented at the corner of 13th and Stewart Streets. Between 1914 and 1916, services were conducted in this hall. Father Martin Maciejewski became pastor in June 1916. He purchased the estate of George Stem at 829 Main Street. The large house was immediately converted into a chapel and rectory. Blessing of the new chapel took place on September 10, 1916. Father August Kuczynski became pastor in 1924. In November 1925, the cornerstone for the new church was laid. The building was completed in June 1926. The dedication and the blessing of the new church by Monsignor Marian Kopytkiewicz took place on July 4, 1926. Father John Sielecki became pastor in 1934. He was responsible for renovating the unfinished basement. Father Joseph Klosinski became pastor in 1939. Under his guidance, the interior of the church was painted and repairs were made to the rectory. A new rectory was completed on August 23, 1985. Father Edwin Schwartz was the last pastor of Saint Michael Parish.

Our Lady of Hungary Parish and Saint Michael the Archangel Parish were both closed on July 15, 2008. The new Queenship of Mary Church now occupies the former Our Lady of Hungary Church building in Northampton.

Saint Joseph The Worker Parish

OREFIELD, PENNSYLVANIA

Established June 7, 1948

By 1915, the growing number of Catholics in Fogelsville resulted in the need for Mass and religious instruction. Three Catholic families eventually shared their vision of a church for the area with Father Hugh McMullen, pastor of Saint Catharine of Siena in Allentown. On Easter Sunday 1936, the first Mass was celebrated in the mission church of Saint Joseph the Worker for 36 Catholic families. The church building was a little red school house known to two generations as the Clover Dell School, at the corner of Snowdrift Road and Second Street in East Fogelsville. In early 1947, more renovations were begun and the congregation held services in the Upper Macungie Township School in East Fogelsville. The work was completed by December 25, 1947. Archbishop Dennis Cardinal Dougherty officially established Saint Joseph the Worker in Fogelsville as a parish on June 7, 1948. The church was dedicated by Monsignor Leo G. Fink of Allentown on June 27, 1948.

In 1964, the parish acquired 15 acres of land at Applewood Drive and Clauser Road in Orefield with the intention of eventually constructing a new and larger church. Groundbreaking for the new church took place on June 1, 1975. Mass was celebrated for the first time in the new church on May 1, 1976. The parish was moved to Orefield in 1977 and a new rectory was built. A parish center was added in 1981. The Allentown Diocese retained the old church property in Fogelsville, with one or two Masses celebrated monthly until it was sold in March 1985. On Feb. 23, 1985, the parish held the closing service at the old Fogelsville church.

Monsignor Robert J. Wargo, M. Div. has been pastor of Saint Joseph the Worker since the early 1990s. He saw the necessity to expand the church building and construct a parish educational center. Funding was secured through a major capital campaign launched in June 1995. The generosity of Frederick Jaindl allowed the parish to acquire a tract of land across the street on Applewood Drive to build the educational center. Saint Joseph the Worker Center of Learning was opened to 315 students in grades one through eight on September 2, 1997. With the completion of the school, the expansion of the church was begun. The church expansion was completed on March 8, 1998. Saint Joseph the Worker Parish currently serves over 2400 families.

School

Sacred Heart Parish

PALMERTON, PENNSYLVANIA

Established 1908

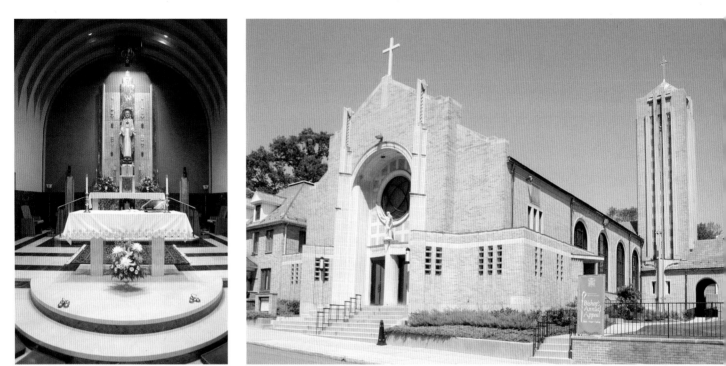

The roots of Catholicism in Palmerton began with the old Fireline Church, which stood where Dairy Road and Fireline Road are today. The church served the people of the area long before 1908. The Fireline Church was built in 1856 by a German Catholic congregation. Fire later destroyed the Fireline Church and a temporary place of worship was made on Third Street.

In 1906, Father John Clemens Vitt, pastor of Assumption BVM in Slatington, began ministering to the Catholic community of Palmerton. Sacred Heart Parish was established by Archbishop Patrick Ryan of Philadelphia in 1908. Four lots were purchased on the northwest corner of Lafayette and Third Street. On June 28, 1908, Father Vitt laid the cornerstone for the church. The structure was a small frame building that accommodated both church and school. Father Vitt continued serving Sacred Heart as a mission of Assumption BVM Parish in Slatington until 1911 when Father Joseph I. Plappert took charge. In 1913, Father Wladislaus Rakowski was appointed the first resident pastor.

In 1909, the Missionary Sisters of the Sacred Heart began visiting from Slatington and took charge of the parish school in the church basement each Saturday. Sacred Heart School was opened with an enrollment of 140 students in September 1909. Father John P. Vlossak was appointed pastor in March 1917. He immediately sought to enlarge the church property and acquired

the home adjacent to the church as a rectory. Shortly afterward, the double brick home opposite the church was purchased as a convent for the Sisters.

The original frame structure of the church was remodeled in 1928. The construction of the parochial school was begun in 1929 and dedicated by Bishop O'Hara in 1930. An addition was made to the parochial school in 1953. In June 1955, construction on the new church was begun and the cornerstone was laid in 1956. The first Mass was celebrated at Christmas Midnight 1957 by Father Matlos. The new Sacred Heart Church was dedicated on July 20, 1958. Sacred Heart Parish in Palmerton celebrated their 100th Anniversary Mass on June 1, 2008. Father William T. Campion is the current pastor.

Saint Elizabeth of Hungary Parish

PEN ARGYL, PENNSYLVANIA

Established November 14, 1929

Under the guidance of Father Lavazzari, a group of Catholics in the Wind Gap area first rented an abandoned schoolhouse for use as a church in 1915. In 1916, Mass was held in the Palace Theater on Main Street by Father Joseph McKee of the Vincentian Fathers. Saint Elizabeth's Church on Lobb Avenue was constructed in 1918 on land given by Richard Jackson III. In 1921, another group of Wind Gap Catholics purchased land from Henry Male on Lehigh Avenue for a church. The cornerstone of Saint Joseph's Church was laid on September 16, 1923, and the first Mass was said early in the winter of 1924.

Saint Elizabeth's Church and Saint Joseph's Church were both served as mission churches of Our Lady of Good Counsel Parish in Bangor until 1929. On November 14, 1929, Saint Elizabeth's and Saint Joseph's were combined with Saint Roch's in West Bangor to become Saint Elizabeth of Hungary Parish in Pen Argyl. Father

Theodore Wagner was appointed as the first pastor. Saint Roch's Church was established as a separate parish in 1937.

Through the efforts of Father Melley, Immaculate Conception School was given to the parish as a gift of the Archdiocese of Philadelphia in 1954. On September 11, 1955, Archbishop John Cardinal O'Hara of Philadelphia laid the cornerstone and blessed the new school. Father Melley secured the Sisters of Saint Joseph to staff the school. The parish rectory has been located at three sites in Pen Argyl over the past 50 years; first on Bell Avenue, then on Lobb Avenue, and now on Babbitt Avenue since 1968.

Saint Elizabeth of Hungary in Pen Argyl and Saint Joseph in Wind Gap were combined into the new church of Saint Elizabeth of Hungary in Pen Argyl. In the spring of 1999, ground breaking for the new church took place and the first Mass was held the week of November 5, 2000. The basement of the church was renovated for use as a social hall in 2004. The rectory basement was converted into classroom space in September 2008. Monsignor Vincent York, M. Ed. is the current pastor.

Saint Stephen Parish

PORT CARBON, PENNSYLVANIA

Established July 14, 1847

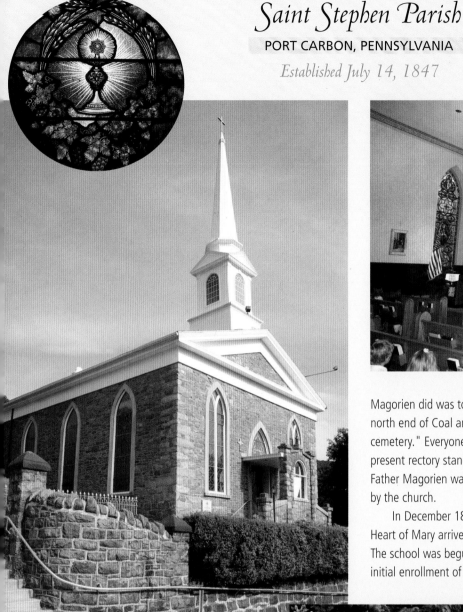

Magorien did was to buy land for a parish cemetery located at the north end of Coal and First Streets and known as the "old cemetery." Everyone buried beside the Mission House, where the present rectory stands, was moved and interred at the new location. Father Magorien was also responsible for the erection of a rectory by the church.

In December 1886, five Sisters, Servants of the Immaculate Heart of Mary arrived in Port Carbon to establish a parochial school. The school was begun in some spare rooms in the rectory with an initial enrollment of 99 students. In 1896, a new four room frame school building was erected. In 1901, the church was renovated and the present stained glass windows were installed. In 1920, three classrooms were added to the main school building. An addition to the school was also built to accommodate high school students in 1923.

A fire destroyed the sacristy of the church on February 23, 1947. After a successful financial campaign, a renovation of the church soon followed. In 1964, Father John McNamara became pastor. During his pastorate, the school and church were extensively renovated. In 1997, the church was renovated again in honor of Saint Stephen's 150th anniversary. Father David Karns, M. Div. is the current pastor.

Before Saint Stephen Parish existed, the Catholics of the village of Port Carbon built a log cabin mission house at the site where the present church stands. Jesuit missionary priests rode through these sections, once a month, to tend to the spiritual needs of the people. Saint Stephen Parish in Port Carbon was established by Bishop John Neumann on July 17, 1847. The Mission House was replaced by a new church on the same site in the area called "Irish Town." Several years after the church was completed, the front section of the church and the steeple were added. The first pastor was Father Daniel Magorien. When the church was complete, one of the first things Father

Saint John The Baptist Parish

POTTSVILLE, PENNSYLVANIA

Established 1841

Prior to 1840, German-speaking Catholics in Pottsville had monthly Mass said by Father Nicholas Steinbacher. He was a Jesuit priest who rode on horseback from Reading to hold services in the basement of Saint Patrick's Church prior. On August 19, 1840, a group of 12 laymen gathered to form their own German parish in Pottsville. The Philadelphia Diocese accepted a deed from the fledgling congregation of 27 families and formally recognized their intentions January 20, 1841. The first church was located at Fourth and Howard Streets and the cornerstone was laid in June 1842. Services were first held in the unfinished building in November 1842. Parishioners petitioned Bishop Francis Kenrick for a German-speaking priest. Father Joseph Burg was appointed the first pastor on November 10, 1842.

Due to a dissident group within the parish, Bishop Neumann closed the church for 7 months in 1858, before the matter was resolved and the church reopened. Father Francis Wachter became pastor on December 15, 1862. At this time, the old church at Fourth Street and Howard Avenue had become much too small for the growing congregation. The one-story stone school building could no longer accommodate the numerous children of the parish. The present church site was chosen and bought in 1865. Work on the new church was not begun until 1868. Father Bernard Baumeister became pastor in August 1869. Upon his arrival, the building of the new church had advanced to the lowest brown stone course just above the basement walls. Father Baumeister worked untiringly for the rapid completion of the church. The new church was dedicated by Bishop Wood on December 1, 1872.

In September, 1873, the parochial school was transferred from the one-story stone building on Howard Avenue to the basement of the new church. Lay women were employed as teachers until 1875, when Father Depman engaged the Sisters of Christian Charity to take over the school.

Father Frederick Longinus was appointed pastor on February 7, 1878. He had the church walls frescoed and stained glass windows installed. A rectory was purchased in 1883. The site for a new school on the corner of Tenth Street and Howard Avenue was purchased in 1893. Construction began in 1894 and the school was opened in September 1895. In 1950, the church was renovated and a grotto to the Blessed Mother was erected. Saint John's School closed in 1983, when it was consolidated with Saint Patrick's into the new All Saints School. The Sisters of Christian Charity bid farewell to the parish in 1984. The parish celebrated their 150th anniversary in 1991. Church renovations were begun in 1992 and the church basement was converted into the parish hall. Father David Loeper, M. Div. is the current pastor.

Saint Patrick Parish

POTTSVILLE, PENNSYLVANIA

Established 1827

From 1766 to 1785, the baptismal records of Father John Baptist de Ritter from Goshenhoppen (Bally) were entered under the caption of Sharp Mountain (Pottsville) and indicate that many Catholics lived in the immediate vicinity. Itinerant preachers traveled by horseback from Philadelphia to Pottsville. Father Boehm was one of those preachers. He held the first religious services in the forge of the Greenwood Furnace (built in 1806). This led the founder of Pottsville, John Pott, to donate the ground for a log house to be used as a school and church. The early settlers united and built the first non-sectarian church in Pottsville.

Saint Patrick Parish in Pottsville was established in 1827. A lone priest rode on horseback every two weeks to Mauch Chunk, Tamaqua and Pottsville. While attending Mass in a private home, a small group of Catholics decided to build a church on October 27, 1827. With the help of Father John Fitzpatrick, a plot of ground on Mahantongo Road was purchased from John Pott and the first log church was built. The first resident pastor was Father Arthur Wainwright. The log church became too small by 1837. A new church was built to surround it and so it remained until the time came when the new church was almost completed. The log church was then razed. Father Hugh Fitzsimmons became pastor in 1845. He completed the erection of the school. Father A.J. Gallagher became pastor in 1877. During his pastorate, a three-story school was built. Father William Duffy became pastor in 1889. He began the construction of a new church, following the laying of the cornerstone in 1891. Father Francis McGovern became pastor in 1892 and continued the work of building the church. A new rectory was erected in 1908.

Saint Theresa of Avila Mission Chapel was established in 1950 and was later renamed as Saint John Neumann Chapel. Saint Patrick's School was merged into the new All Saints Elementary School in 1983. In June 2008, the Sisters of Saint Joseph left the parish. Saint John Neumann Chapel also closed in June 2008. On July 15, 2008, three parishes were consolidated into Saint Patrick Parish. Saint Joseph Parish in Pottsville was established in 1906 to serve the area Italian families. Father Edward Connolly was the last pastor of Saint Joseph Parish. Mary, Queen of Peace Parish in Pottsville was established in 1920. Father John Bambrick was the last pastor of Mary, Queen of Peace Parish. Saint Francis de Sales Parish in Mount Carbon was established on January 19, 1922. Father Edward Connolly was the last pastor of Saint Francis de Sales Parish. All three parishes were closed on July 15, 2008. Monsignor Edward O'Connor has served as pastor of Saint Patrick Parish since May 2002.

Holy Guardian Angels Parish

READING, PENNSYLVANIA

Established November 1929

The formation of Holy Guardian Angels Parish can be traced to a determined group of Italian immigrant families who settled in Temple in the early 1920s. The Archdiocese approved their request for a church in Temple to be built by the parishioners in 1925. Initial plans for a church were developed at a Temple grocery store. Construction of a small chapel dedicated to Saint Anthony, began in 1925. The chapel was completed in 1926. Priests from Saint Joseph Hospital, the Missionaries of the Sacred Heart in Hyde Park and Father Eugene Marchetti from Holy Rosary celebrated Mass at the chapel.

Saint Anthony's Chapel was established as Holy Guardian Angels Parish in November 1929. Father Frederic Lanshe was appointed as the first pastor. He celebrated his first Mass at Saint Anthony's Chapel in Temple on November 23, 1929. A home at 3120 Kutztown Road in Hyde Park was donated to serve as the rectory and an additional chapel. The first Mass at the Hyde Park chapel was celebrated on December 8, 1929. In 1931, plans for a new church in Hyde Park were announced. Groundbreaking took place on June 7, 1931. The three-story church building also included a rectory, classrooms and social hall. The cornerstone was laid on August 30, 1931 and the church was dedicated by Archbishop Dougherty on November 8, 1931. In 1933, Holy Guardian Angels School was opened by the Missionary Sisters of the Most Sacred Heart of Jesus.

In 1962, additional land was purchased for a new church. Groundbreaking took place on June 17, 1962 and the new church was dedicated by Bishop McShea on August 18, 1963. The original church building was converted for school use in 1963. The present rectory was completed in 1979. In the fall of 1985, the old school was expanded with an addition at the front of the building. The new wing was completed in April 1986. In December 1998, the parish decided to build a new school on the existing site.

Groundbreaking for the new education center and chapel was held on March 26, 2000. The first day of classes at the new school took place on May 2, 2001. In June 2001, just before the old church and school was demolished, parishioners assembled in the building for a special decommissioning ceremony. Holy Guardian Angels Regional School opened on August 28, 2001 and was dedicated by Bishop Cullen on September 16, 2001. In August 2004, a beautiful church redecorating project was completed. Monsignor Dennis Hartgen has served as pastor since July 1998.

School

Holy Rosary Parish

READING, PENNSYLVANIA

Established October 2, 1904

School

At the turn of the century, many Italian immigrants came to Reading. Monsignor George Bornemann appealed to the Archbishop of Philadelphia to send an Italian priest to Reading. Monsignor Bornemann managed to acquire the former Saint Mark's Reformed Congregational Church at Schuylkill Avenue and Green Street in 1904. The Church of the Holy Rosary was dedicated by Archbishop Diomede Falconio, Apostolic Delegate to the United States on October 2, 1904. Father Gesualdo Paonessa was appointed the first pastor.

Monsignor Bornemann purchased an old public school building at Third and Franklin Streets for use as a parochial school. Holy Rosary School was blessed by Archbishop John Bonzano, Apostolic Delegate to the United States on November 2, 1914. The school opened under the direction of the Sisters of Saint Dorothy. Father Leonard T. Miconi became pastor in 1938. Upon his arrival, he inspected the church properties. The school and the Holy Rosary Chapel were

remodeled. The church was renovated and rededicated on May 21, 1939.

In 1940, the parish decided to relocate to the chapel at Third and Franklin Streets. Property located at 46 South Third Street was purchased and converted into a modern rectory on September 12, 1940. The chapel at 240 Franklin Street became the main church and a new altar dedicated to Saint Joseph was erected to enhance the sanctuary. The Daughters of Mary Help of Christians, known as the Salesian Sisters, came to the parish on August 15, 1942. In the summer of 1943, four properties on Franklin and South Third Streets were purchased on which the new church and rectory were to be built. The new rectory was built in 1950. The new church was built and dedicated in 1953. The old church was remodeled for use as a chapel in 1955.

Chapel

Holy Rosary School was closed in 1968. The Holy Rosary Chapel was remodeled in 1969. In 1972, Tropical Storm Agnes caused flood damage to the church hall and it was renovated. A remodeling of the main church sanctuary followed in 1975. Cabrini Academy was founded in 1976 and the Daughters of Divine Zeal arrived at the parish in 1979. The installation and consecration of Our Lady of the Most Blessed Sacrament Chapel in the Holy Rosary rectory took place in 1992. In 2004, the parish celebrated its 100th anniversary. Monsignor Felix Losito has served as pastor of Holy Rosary Parish since 1968.

Saint Anthony of Padua Parish

READING, PENNSYLVANIA

Established April 12, 1914

Saint Anthony of Padua Parish in Reading was established on April 12, 1914. In April 1914, the church building had been offered to a group of Polish speaking people living in the Millmont area of Reading. Father Peter Kucharski was appointed as the first pastor. Two classrooms were also added in the basement of the church in 1914. A rectory was established in 1916. Father John Dunajski was appointed as pastor in 1939. Under his pastorate, the church was repainted and decorated.

Groundbreaking for a parish school and auditorium took place in April 1957. Saint Anthony of Padua School was completed and dedicated by Archbishop John O'Hara of Philadelphia in May 1958. The school was opened by the Bernardine Sisters in September 1958. An addition to the parish rectory was built in 1962 and Saint Anthony's Convent was erected for the Bernardine Sisters in 1966.

Father Stephen J. Halabura was appointed as pastor in 1971. In 1974, he decided to build a larger church on the site of the existing church. The old church was razed in August 1974 and groundbreaking for the new church immediately followed. Bishop McShea dedicated the new church building in October 1975. Construction on a new parish center was begun in 1981 and completed in 1982. Father Raymond Slezak was appointed as pastor in 1984. Under his pastorate, additions were made to the church exterior and the church interior was renovated. Father Larry Hess was appointed pastor of Saint Anthony of Padua Parish in 2009.

Saint Catharine of Siena Parish

READING, PENNSYLVANIA

Established December 16, 1925

Archbishop Dougherty of Philadelphia authorized the establishment of a new parish in Mount Penn for 75 local Catholic families in 1925. In November 1925, a site on Perkiomen Avenue was purchased. Two small homes existed on the property. One of the homes was converted into a church and the other served as the rectory. Saint Catharine of Siena Parish in Mount Penn was established on December 16, 1925. Father Joseph Hayes was appointed the first pastor. The first Mass was offered by Father Hayes in the basement of the Mount Penn Fire Company on December 20, 1925. On Palm Sunday, 1926, Mass was held for the first time in the house on Perkiomen Avenue. The second floor of the house was used as an all-purpose room. Father Hayes also erected an addition to the church building. He later invited the Sisters of the Immaculate Heart of Mary to teach Catechism twice a week.

In 1937, the need for a parochial school became imperative and a large residence on Perkiomen Avenue was purchased. Saint Catharine's School was opened by the Sisters of the Immaculate Heart of Mary on September 1, 1938. In 1950, Archbishop Dougherty gave permission for the building of a new basement church. On October 2, 1950, the ground breaking ceremony took place. In

December 1951, the new church was privately blessed by Father Sullivan and the first Mass was held on December 25, 1951. The dedication of the church was held on April 30, 1952. On August 19, 1953, Father Sullivan broke ground for a new parish school. The first classes were held on January 3, 1955. The cornerstone was laid by Archbishop O'Hara of Philadelphia on January 23, 1955. Renovations to transform the former school into a convent were begun.

On April 27, 1962, ground was broken for a four classroom addition to the school and the erection of an auditorium building. In 1972, a renovation of the church included a redesigned sanctuary and moving the altar from the back wall. During renovations, Mass was held in the parish auditorium. Masses in the church resumed in October 1973. A new parish center was completed by 1979. A new school wing was completed in 1987. In 1988, Saint Catharine of Siena School and Immaculate Conception School in Birdsboro formed a Regional School. In 1989, the parish decided to build a new church on a 27-acre site in Reading. Ground was broken in October 1993. Bishop Welsh dedicated the new church in April 1995. Monsignor Edward Domin, M.A. is the current pastor.

Chapel

Saint Joseph Parish

READING, PENNSYLVANIA

Established 1891

Father Gerald Coghlan, pastor of Saint Peter Parish, founded the mission of Saint Joseph's in 1888. Archbishop Patrick Ryan of Philadelphia established Saint Joseph's as a parish in early 1891. Father P.J. Mellon was appointed as the first pastor by April 1891. Father Joseph Flanagan became pastor in 1897 and the old red brick church was built. By 1905, the construction of Saint Joseph's School had begun. The school was opened by the Sisters, Servants of the Immaculate Heart of Mary in the fall of 1906.

Father Thomas Harron served as pastor from 1925 until 1949. He was responsible for giving Saint Joseph's Church its Spanish Mission appearance. In addition to new exterior stucco appearance, the large circular stained glass window was installed behind the main altar. The church was totally refurbished inside including new stained glass windows, new ceiling frescoes, a new floor, and the chapel was added to the north side of the church. During the renovations, Masses were held in the Strand Theatre at 9th and Spring Streets. The church renovations were completed by Christmas 1926.

Father Joseph McGrenra became pastor in 1953. He refurbished the church sanctuary. Father William Ferry became pastor in October 1957. Under his pastorate, the inside of the school was painted and new stairways were installed. In the church, the cork floor was removed and replaced by the Terrazzo floor. The walls of the church were painted with scenes from the Lives of Jesus, Mary and Joseph.

Father Richard Loeper became pastor in August 1967. Monsignor Loeper later redesigned the church sanctuary. Father Thomas L. Edwards became pastor in August 1977 and was responsible for considerable improvements in the church and school. In 1990, Father Edwards did an in depth study of the future needs of the parish. A High School Gymnasium was built and attached to the Social Hall, which was named "The Cloister at Saint Joseph's". The Cloister at Saint Joseph's and the gymnasium were dedicated by Bishop Welsh on September 8, 1990.

Saint Margaret Parish

READING, PENNSYLVANIA

Established February 8, 1920

S aint Margaret Parish in Reading was established by Archbishop Dougherty of Philadelphia on February 8, 1920. Father Edward Curran was appointed as the first pastor. The parish's first Mass was celebrated by Father Curran in a movie theater in Reading. Soon after, construction began on a combination church and school building. On April 16, 1922, Father Curran celebrated the first Mass in the new basement church.

Saint Margaret's School was opened by the Sisters, Servants of the Immaculate Heart of Mary in September 1922. From the very beginning the Sisters, Servants of the Immaculate Heart of Mary were a dominant presence and constant help in the parish. In the earliest days of the parish, the Sisters lived at the school until a small row house was purchased for them four blocks away. A small convent was eventually built and the Sisters were later moved to the former rectory.

Father Edward Devine was appointed pastor in 1930. In 1931, an anonymous donor financed the building of the Our Lady of the Miraculous Medal Shrine on church grounds. The Shrine was dedicated on August 14, 1938. Father Andrew Lenahan was appointed pastor in 1964 and began construction on a new church

School

building. The new church was completed in 1970. Father Francis Schoenauer began refurbishing the church in 1997. The refurbishing project was completed by Father John Gibbons and the church was consecrated by Bishop Cullen in 2002. Father John Gibbon has served as pastor of Saint Margaret Parish since 2002.

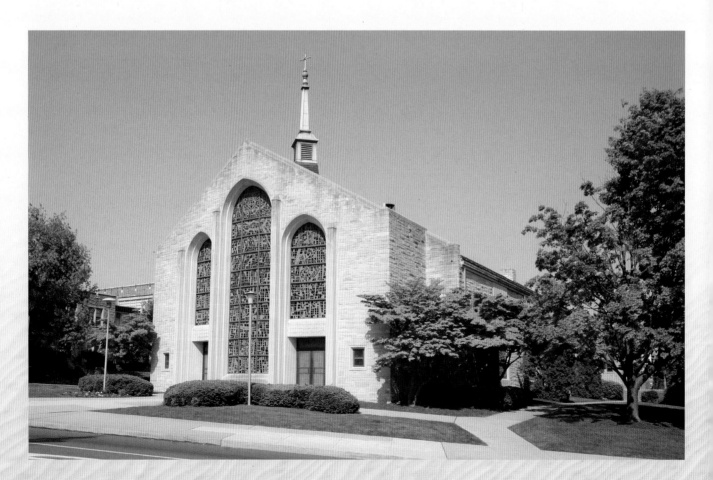

Saint Mary Parish (Church of the Blessed Virgin Mary)

READING, PENNSYLVANIA

Established 1888

The first Polish immigrants came to Reading in the mid-1800s. Father George Bornemann became pastor of Saint Paul's in Reading in 1867. He sought to bring in Polish-speaking priests to serve the needs of the small Polish community of Reading. In 1878, Father Emil Kattein was assigned to assist at Saint Paul's. Father Kattein ministered to the Polish families until 1882. In 1885, a committee was formed to organize a parish. Father Bornemann secured land for the Polish community in 1885 and 1886. The construction of the church basement was begun in 1888 and completed later that year.

Saint Mary Parish in Reading was established in 1888 and Father Mark Januszkiewicz was appointed as the first resident pastor in November 1888. He built a rectory to the right of the basement church. Upon its completion, he lived on the second floor, and the first floor became the parish school. The church was dedicated by Archbishop Patrick Ryan on April 28, 1889. Father Adalbert Malusecki became pastor in 1895. He soon began building classrooms in the church basement to relieve overcrowding at the 1st floor school. He also secured the Bernardine Sisters of Saint Francis to staff the parish school. The Sisters left the parish in 1898. In 1899, Father Malusecki began to plan the building of a church over the existing basement. The new church was dedicated in June 1900. A new school, adjoining the church at the back, was completed in 1904 and staffed

by the Felician Sisters. In 1908, a new rectory was built and the original rectory became the convent. A new convent was completed in 1924. In 1928, a new school was also completed.

Father John Mickun became pastor in 1938. His first project was to paint the interior of the church. Stained glassed windows were installed in the church during the 1950s. In 1963, the church was renovated and two steeples were rebuilt. During the 1970s, the original rectory, old school and 1908 rectory were razed. A new rectory was built. In 1978, the Felician Sisters left the parish and the Bernardine Sisters returned to staff the school. The Bernadine Sisters withdrew from the parish in 1991. Their convent became "Mary's Shelter" in 1995. Dwindling enrollment caused the closing of Saint Mary's School in 2001. Renovations to the front entrance of the church and the installation of a new roof were made by 2003. Father Leo Stajkowski has served as pastor of Saint Mary Parish since October 2, 1984.

Saint Paul Parish

READING, PENNSYLVANIA

Established 1860

Prior to 1860, the Catholic population of Reading attended services at Saint Peter's Church. Bishop John Neumann decided to establish a second Catholic parish in Reading and Saint Paul Parish became a reality in 1860. Bishop Neumann died before he could appoint a pastor for the parish. On May 3, 1860, Father Charles Schrader, pastor of Immaculate Conception in Allentown, began plans for a church. Construction on the church began in August 1860, on a lot donated by Anthony Felix Sr. at the corner of Ninth and Walnut Streets. The cornerstone was laid on September 8, 1860. The church was dedicated by Bishop Wood in 1861. Father Gerhard Wallmeyer became pastor in 1865. He opened a small boys' school in the basement of the church.

Father George Bornemann was appointed as pastor in February 1867. During 1869, a 200 foot spire was erected on top of the church and the cornerstone of new school building was laid. Saint Paul School was opened by the Sisters, Servant of the Immaculate Heart of Mary in 1870. A rectory was built beside the church in 1871. Father Bornemann was responsible for bringing the Sisters of Christian Charity to Reading in 1875. A new convent was built for the Sisters of Christian Charity in 1882. Extensive renovations to the church took place in 1886. Saint Cecelia's Chapel was built in 1895. In 1915, a new steeple was erected to replace the previous steeple which was destroyed by lightning. A two-story annex to St. Paul's School was completed in 1916.

Father Theodore Hammeke became pastor in 1924. He began the remodeling of the interior of church in 1927. Father William Hammeke became pastor in 1928. He was faced with completing the church renovations. The first Mass in the renovated church took place in 1929. Father Hammeke established Central Catholic High School in 1939. An annex to the school was built in 1941. In 1943, Father Hammeke received permission to set up a chapel at the rectory. Father Henry Huesman became pastor on November 1, 1955. He renovated the church including the sacristy and side chapels in 1956. In 1959, a new convent for the Sisters of Christian Charity was built on Eckert Avenue. In 1961, construction was begun on a new school building. In 1974, Saint Paul's School was closed due to decreased enrollment.

Monsignor William Handges served as pastor from 1980 to 1985. He was responsible for the razing of the convent and the erection of a new chapel on the site. Monsignor Seitzinger served as pastor from 1985 to 1997. During his pastorate, the church interior was painted and Saint Cecelia's Chapel was closed. The stained glass windows in the church were restored in 1991. Father Andrew Ulincy served as pastor of St. Paul parish between 1997 and 2010.

Saint Peter The Apostle Parish

READING, PENNSYLVANIA

Established 1752

Ten years after his arrival in Goshenhoppen, Father Theodore Schneider came to Reading in 1752. The few Catholics who settled in Reading shortly after its founding received ministrations from the priests from Goshenhoppen who came on horseback at regular intervals to serve their spiritual needs. Jesuit Fathers Schneider and Farmer served the Catholics in the town. The missionaries came regularly and the church grew slowly but surely. The first "meeting house" was a log cabin where Mass was said and where the first chapel was built on the East side of Duke Street (now 7th Street) prior to 1756. About 1790, the old building was demolished and the cornerstone for a small brick church was laid on August 17, 1791. Jesuit missionaries continued to come at regular intervals.

In 1818, Saint Peter the Apostle Church was incorporated and became an independent parish. Father George Schoenfelder was appointed as the first resident pastor. For a quarter of a century, the parish grew and prospered. By 1844, the congregation had outgrown the little church and a lot was purchased at 326 South Fifth Street. A brick church was erected and dedicated on May 24, 1846. Because of the scarcity of priests or difficulty with the board of trustees, Saint Peter's Parish was left without a pastor at times. During these times, Father Augustine Bally came to Reading to celebrate Mass.

Bishop John Neumann of Philadelphia was personally interested in establishing a parochial school for the parish. He purchased a property at 225-227 South Fifth Street for that purpose and proposed to the Sisters, Servants of the Immaculate Heart of Mary from Monroe, Michigan, that they come to Reading and staff the parish school. This request was accepted and the development of a parish school was completed with their arrival in July 1859. On September 2, 1859, Bishop Neumann celebrated the first Mass in the chapel and blessed the building. A Select School for Girls was opened on September 5, 1859; later on September 12th, a School for Boys was opened in the basement of the Church.

St. Peter's Church, as it stands today, is largely due to the untiring efforts of a man whose remains now rest beneath the church's south tower. This man was Father James E. Cleary, pastor from 1889 until his death in 1904. The work of rebuilding the church was begun by Father Cleary in 1900. The church was completely rebuilt and refurbished by 1905. Only the brick walls of the old church were left standing and served as the backing for the outer walls of granite. The congregation dedicated the main altar to Father Cleary's memory. Saint Peter's Church was dedicated by Archbishop James Cardinal Gibbons of Baltimore on July 2, 1905. Saint Peter the Apostle Parish celebrated its 250th anniversary in 2002. Father Charles Marciano served as pastor until his death in 2003. The rectory was renamed the Parish House in December, 2008. It contains St. Anthony Chapel named such to honor the Lithuanian parish located at 8th and Bingaman Streets which was consolidated with St. Peter Parish in 2004. St. Peter School celebrated its 150th anniversary on April, 25, 2009. Msgr. Thomas J. Orsulak has served as pastor since 2005.

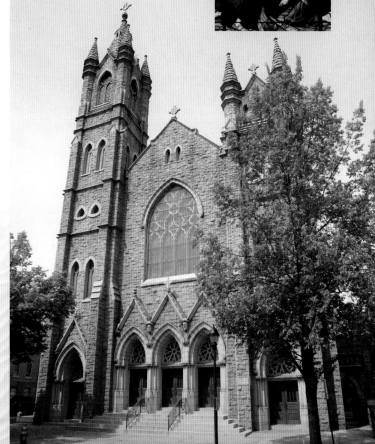

Saints Cyril and Methodius Parish

READING, PENNSYLVANIA

Established 1895

Sv. Curil & Method.

A handful of Slavic immigrants first came to Reading around 1880. A group of men banded together in 1893 to form the Slovak Society of Reading in 1893. A Greek Catholic rite building was purchased in Oakbrook located outside the city boundary and named the Church of the Assumption of the Blessed Mother in 1895. Anxious to move to the central city, the Slovak families resolved to begin a church fund and property located at Sixth and Laurel Streets was later purchased.

In September 1906, the cornerstone of the church was laid and the parish was renamed as Saints Cyril and Methodius. The structure initially had only a lower level prayer area. The present church was finally dedicated on July 5, 1914. In September 1916, religion classes were begun by the Missionary Sisters of the Sacred Heart in a converted building on the opposite corner of Sixth and Laurel Streets. Property for a new parish school was in 1939 but construction on the building did not begin until 1950. Groundbreaking for the new school took place on April 2, 1950. The cornerstone was laid and the dedication took place on April 1, 1951. The school was closed in the mid-1970s.

From these humble beginnings grew a vibrant community which celebrated the parish Centennial on October 1, 1995. During the intervening years, a new Convent and new Rectory were built and blessed. In the late 1990s, the stained glass windows were restored and a new roof was put on the church. The church

basement was later renovated for use as a parish activities center. The last Sister of the Third Order of Saint Francis left the parish in late 2007. The former convent building was transformed into parish CCD instructional classrooms in 2009. Father Charles S. Sperlak is the current pastor of Saints Cyril and Methodius Parish.

COMMEMORATION OF THE
CENTENNIAL ANNIVERSARY
SS. CYRIL & METHODIUS
SLOVAK CATHOLIC CHURCH
1895 - 1995

Saint Mary Parish

RINGTOWN, PENNSYLVANIA

Established June 3, 1923

Saint Mary Parish in Ringtown was established on June 3, 1923 by Archbishop Dougherty of Philadelphia. On June 9, 1923, Father Patrick Dougherty was named the first pastor. The first Mass was celebrated in Scheider's residence on June 17, 1923, and continued to be held there until the fall of 1924. In January 1924, the parish decided to erect a combination church and rectory at 82 North Center Street, on a site donated by the Franey Estate and John O'Hearn of Shenandoah. The church building was completed in the fall of 1924.

In 1923, Mass was also celebrated in Brandonville at the Brandon School and continued there until 1927. Thereafter, the services were held in Smith's Inn, the Schypin home, and the elementary school in Brandonville. In 1950, services ceased and were transferred to the mother church in Ringtown.

Father Wierzalis became pastor on July 20, 1950. He undertook the task of building a larger church on ground adjoining the rectory. On April 16, 1951, permission to build was received from the Cardinal. The blessing and groundbreaking of the new church took place on April 29, 1951. The opening of the new Saint Mary's took place on November 30, 1952. The church was dedicated by

Archbishop John O'Hara on June 14, 1953. Father Wierzalis also saw the need for a parish cemetery and purchased three acres at the present site. The Good Shepherd Shrine was soon constructed at the cemetery. On May 30, 1960, the cemetery was blessed by Monsignor Joseph O'Donnell. Extensive renovations to church and rectory were made in 1973. Saint Mary Parish currently serves 316 families.

Saint Frances de Sales Parish

ROBESONIA, PENNSYLVANIA

Established September 1, 1982

As Catholic families continued to settle in western Berks County, the pastor of Saint Ignatius Loyola Parish in Sinking Spring petitioned the Diocese of Allentown to create a new parish in the western part of the county in July 1980. In October 1980, ten acres of land in Robesonia were purchased for a new parish and church. In May 1982, the Oblates of Saint Francis de Sales were entrusted with the care of the parish. On August 11, 1982, the soon to be parish was named for Saint Francis de Sales.

Saint Francis de Sales was established as a parish by Bishop Thomas Welsh on September 1, 1982. Father William Nessel, O.S.F.S. was named as the first pastor. Due to the lack of a church facility, the first Mass was celebrated at the Blue Velvet Restaurant (now Ozgoods) in Robesonia on September 5, 1982. Until a Parish Center was constructed, Sunday Masses were celebrated first at

Blue Velvet Restaurant and later at Conrad Weiser High School. Trinity Lutheran Church in Robesonia was the site of Masses on Saturday and the Brenner Building at Wernersville State Hospital was used for Masses on Holy Days. Daily Masses were held in the living room of the parish house.

Construction of the parish building took place during 1984 and was completed by January 1985. On January 24, 1985, Father Nessel celebrated the first Mass in the present church. Saint Francis de Sales Parish celebrated its 25th anniversary in 2007. The parish currently serves over 600 families. Father Mark Wrightson, O.S.F.S. has served as pastor since June 2010.

Our Lady of Mount Carmel Parish

ROSETO, PENNSYLVANIA

Established 1897

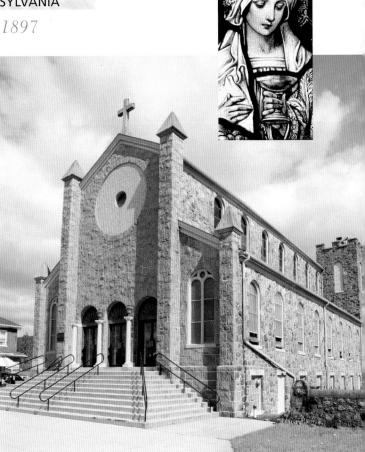

In 1892, a group of hopeful men arrived from Roseto Valfortore in Italy. This small cohesive group formed a village in the Slate Belt that would become known as Roseto. In early 1893, they were able to acquire a small tract of stony woodland in Washington Township and quickly broke ground for the first Roman Catholic Church in the Slate Belt. This first church was a small wooden structure but was without a priest until Father Pasquale DeNisco was appointed as the first pastor in 1897.

As the parish grew, the church became too small and the building was enlarged twice. Father DeNisco died on July 16, 1911. He was succeeded by Father Luigi Fiorillo and then Father James Lavezzari, who built the first rectory and was the first Vincentian priest. Under the direction of Father Peter Montiani, work began on a new church in 1920. The first Mass was celebrated in the beautiful new church in 1923.

In 1932, Father Joseph Ducci, C. M. became pastor and successful in securing a group of Salesian Sisters to come to the parish and staff the school in 1938. The Sisters conducted classes in different homes until their convent was built in 1940. They immediately began a kindergarten class in the basement of the convent. Shortly thereafter, Father Ducci saw a need for an elementary school. In 1946, ground was broken for the school on a piece of land across from the church. In 1953, a new elementary school was built on a large tract of land near the convent. Our Lady of Mount Carmel High School was opened in the original school building in 1951. The school was renamed Pius X High School in 1953 and staffed by the Sisters of Saint Joseph. A new brick rectory adjacent to the church and high school was completed in 1968. Additions to the elementary school building were added in 1960, 1990 and 2002. Our Lady of Mount Carmel serves over 2800 parishioners. Father James Prior, C.M. is the current pastor.

School

Saint Clare of Assisi Parish

ST CLAIR, PENNSYLVANIA

Established July 15, 2008

Saint Clare of Assisi Parish in Saint Clair was established on July 15, 2008. Monsignor William Glosser was appointed as the first pastor. Saint Clare Parish was formed by the consolidation of five older neighboring parishes that included: Saint Boniface Parish in Saint Clair, Saint Mary Parish in Saint Clair, Immaculate Conception Parish in Saint Clair, Saint Casimir Parish in Saint Clair and Saints Peter and Paul Parish in Saint Clair.

Saint Boniface Parish in Saint Clair was established in February 1853. Father Wincellaus Joames Repis was appointed as the first pastor. In 1852, Bishop John Neumann had given permission for a church to be built in Saint Clair. The dedication of the church by Bishop Neumann took place on October 30, 1853. A new church and school were built in the 1890s. Father Albert M. Korves became pastor in 1902. He constructed a new rectory. Father Joseph Schaeffer served as pastor from 1911 to 1945. He remodeled the church and school buildings. The interior of the church was renovated in 1976. Father Kevin Gallagher, M.A. was the last pastor of Saint Boniface Parish.

Saint Mary Parish in Saint Clair was established on September 2, 1863. As more English speaking Catholics settled in Saint Clair, they decided to petition Bishop Wood of Philadelphia to create a parish for them. He agreed and named the new parish as the Church of Saint Mary, the Immaculate Mother of God. Father N.J. Walsh was appointed the first pastor. Construction of a church was begun in September 1863. Mass was held in the rented Walker's Hall at the corner of Third and Carroll Streets. The first Mass celebrated in the new church was held on December 25, 1864. On March 17, 1914, ground was broken for a new school. The cornerstone was blessed on July 26, 1914. The school was opened

by the Sisters of Saint Joseph in September 1915. The Sisters of St. Joseph remained at the parish until 1984. Father Kevin Gallagher, M.A. was the last pastor of Saint Mary Parish.

Immaculate Conception Parish in Saint Clair was established in 1905. In the early 1900's, a priest by the name of Father Peter Schaaf was acquainted with the problem of the local Slovaks. Father Schaaf began plans for a Slovak parish. The Slovaks soon acquired the property known as Dormer's Place. The parish was founded by Archbishop Patrick Ryan in the autumn of 1905. Father John Stanek was appointed as the first resident pastor. In October 1905, a dance pavilion on the property was converted into a temporary church. A new church was dedicated on November 27, 1913. In 1921, the church was condemned because of structural defects in the roof. The parish was forced to move to the original church. The parish would worship in the old church building until a steel structure was built under the roof of the new church in 1929. The church was rededicated on July 27, 1930. Father John Matlos became pastor in 1937. Under his pastorate, the church acquired a convent and engaged the services of the Missionary Sisters of the Sacred Heart for religious instruction. Many renovations to the church were made from 1952 to 1954. The Lourdes grotto was dedicated on May 24, 1953. Renovation of the church interior was completed in 1980. On August 15, 1991, the Chapel of the Most Blessed Sacrament in the basement of the church was dedicated by Bishop Welsh. Father Ronald Jankaitis, Th. M. was the last pastor of Immaculate Conception Parish.

Saint Casimir Parish in Saint Clair was established in 1912. The spiritual needs of the area Lithuanians were served by Father Vincent Dargis around 1900. Later, Father J. Dumicus came to Saint Clair at least once a month to celebrate Mass for the Lithuanians at Immaculate Conception Slovak Church. Saint Casimir Parish was founded in 1912 by Father A. Kutas, who celebrated Mass weekly in the Missions Hall, Saint Mary's Church and the Columbia Hose House. In 1915, the Lithuanian and Polish speaking peoples were combined into one parish under Father M. Durickas. However, the Poles soon split to form their own church. After the Poles began their own church, the Lithuanians bought a plot of ground on South Nichols Street. The church cornerstone was laid on May 30, 1917. The building was completed on October 22, 1917. In 1937, the church's interior and auditorium were renovated. Father Ronald Jankaitis, Th. M. was the last pastor of Saint Casimir Parish.

Saints Peter and Paul Parish in Saint Clair was established in 1918. Beginnings of the Polish congregation can be traced back to 1906 when a priest from Minersville said the first Mass in Columbia

Hall. Archbishop Prendergast appointed Father John Dudzik to care for Saints Peter and Paul Mission in 1912. He celebrated his first Mass in Columbia Hall and later arranged to use the basement of Saint Mary's Church in Saint Clair. In 1913, Father Stanislaus Olesinski took over and directed the purchase of property on North Mill Street. The church was built in 1918 and Father Albert Sulek became the first resident pastor. In 1980, Father Frederick Skotek was named pastor. Under his tenure, a new rectory was built and the church interior was remodeled. Bishop Welsh rededicated the church in 1987. Father Kevin Gallagher, M.A. was the last pastor of Saints Peter and Paul Parish.

Saint Boniface Parish, Saint Mary Parish, Immaculate Conception Parish, Saint Casimir Parish and Saints Peter and Paul Parish were all closed on July 15, 2008. The new Saint Clare of Assisi Church now occupies the former Saint Mary Church building in Saint Clair. The former Saints Peter and Paul Church building was converted into the Saints Peter & Paul Education Center.

Saint Ambrose Parish

SCHUYLKILL HAVEN, PENNSYLVANIA

Established 1851

Saint Ambrose Mission in Schuylkill Haven was established in 1847. Priests from Saint Patrick's Church in Pottsville came to celebrate Mass each Sunday in the home of Patrick White, located near Broadway in a section of town called the "Irish Flats." Saint Ambrose Parish was established in 1851. A church building located at Dock and Broadway was purchased from a Lutheran Congregation in 1863. In 1865, two missions were established in Port Clinton and Auburn. A priest from Saint Patrick's in Pottsville continued to say Mass weekly in Schuylkill Haven and three times per year in Auburn and Port Clinton. Father Philip McEnroe was appointed as the first resident pastor in 1868.

The cornerstone for Sacred Heart Mission Church in Port Clinton was laid in 1887. A rectory adjoining the church on Dock Street was built in 1898. Improvements were made to the interior of the church in 1901. Saint Ambrose School was opened in the basement of the church by the Sisters of Saint Joseph on August 31, 1914. The Convent was built adjacent to the rectory in 1914. A school building and auditorium were built on Dock Street in 1928. In April 1955, Saint Kunegunde's Chapel was opened in Deer Lake under the direction of Father William Powers. Sacred Heart Mission Church in Port Clinton was closed and the last Mass was celebrated on April 14, 1955. Saint Ambrose Church was renovated in June 1964.

By 1971, plans were underway to relocate the church. In 1973, 14 acres of property were purchased by Father Alfred Ott. On February 22, 1976, he announced the decision to proceed with the relocation and building of a new church. Groundbreaking ceremonies were held on Thanksgiving Day 1976. The first daily Mass in the church was held on February 17, 1978. The first Sunday Mass was held on March 4, 1978. A new rectory to the left of the church was built in 1981. Ground was broken for a new school on August 18, 1985. On September 14, 1986, the new school and parish center were dedicated. A Pre-School was started by the parish in the basement of the rectory in September 1993. In July 1996, Saint Kunegunde's Chapel in Deer Lake was sold. Bishop Cullen celebrated the 150th Anniversary of the parish with a Mass on October 7, 2001. Father Michael Stone is the current pastor of Saint Ambrose Parish.

Annunciation of The Blessed Virgin Mary Parish

SHENANDOAH, PENNSYLVANIA

Established April 1, 1870

Annunciation of the Blessed Virgin Mary Parish in Shenandoah was established by Bishop James Wood on April 1, 1870. Father Henry O'Reilly was appointed as the first pastor. The church was begun in a building erected during the late 1860's in Mayberry Alley (now Columbus Street). This modest building had originally been built for use as a mission church. Father O'Reilly built a pastoral residence, moved the original church building and built a larger church to accommodate the growing Catholic population. Father O'Reilly died on November 23, 1908 and was succeeded by Father Lemule Norton. A new rectory was built in 1912. The erection of a new church was begun in July 1914. The cornerstone was laid on November 26, 1914 and the church was dedicated on October 10, 1915.

Father John Dever became pastor in 1921. He established a parochial elementary school which opened in September 1923. A high school, Shenandoah Catholic, was added in 1925. The Church of the Annunciation was destroyed by fire on October 29, 1925. Plans were made to rebuild but delays followed. During the early years of the depression, efforts were made to salvage as much as possible from the original church building. The basement of the church was renovated as a temporary solution in 1930. The basement church was used until the new church was completed 40 years later.

Father John Nugent became pastor on November 29, 1967. He began a renovation program, financial drive, and building plans for the new church in 1968. Ground was broken in November 1969 and the first Mass in the new church took place on December 23, 1970. The church was dedicated by Bishop McShea on March 28, 1971. Monsignor Bernard Flanagan was pastor from 2006 to 2010.

Our Lady of Mount Carmel Parish

SHENANDOAH, PENNSYLVANIA

Established August 2, 1914

Our Lady of Mount Carmel Parish in Shenandoah was established on August 2, 1914. Our Lady of Mount Carmel began as an Italian mission of Sacred Heart Parish in Mahanoy City. Father Thomas Antenni, pastor of Sacred Heart Parish in Mahanoy City, conducted services for the Italian Catholics of Shenandoah in Holy Family Church prior to 1914. The Italian population of Shenandoah increased so rapidly, that it became necessary to erect a church of their own.

After months of planning and raising funds, the church was dedicated on August 2, 1914. During the latter years of Father Antenni's pastorate, the church was relocated from Washington Street to its present site on Diamond Avenue due to a number of cave-ins. In 1925, ground was purchased for a parish cemetery. In early 1926, the church was damaged by a fire. Remodeling began and was completed during the pastorate of the next pastor, Father Joseph Megna.

In 1989, the church was completely renovated and a beautiful grotto was erected in the church yard in honor of the Blessed Mother. Monsignor Bernard Flanagan was pastor from 2006 to 2010.

Saint Casimir Parish

SHENANDOAH, PENNSYLVANIA

Established 1872

In 1872, Saint Casimir Parish was established in Shenandoah originally to serve the Lithuanian community. With the aid of the Saint Casimir Beneficial Society, funds were soon raised and two lots were purchased on North Jardin Street. The first Casimir's Church was erected in 1873, on the site of the present church. Father Andrew Strupinskas was appointed the first pastor and served the parish until 1879.

Father J. Alexis Lenarkiewicz, a Polish priest, was appointed pastor in 1879. Sometime later, an error was discovered by the parishioners that Saint Casimir Parish was originally registered as a Polish church and not a Lithuanian church. Much dissention followed and plans were made to form a strictly Lithuanian parish at a meeting on March 31, 1891. More than 1500 Lithuanian parishioners left Saint Casimir's to form their own church in April 1891. With the blessing of Archbishop Ryan of Philadelphia, Saint George Parish was established in Shenandoah as a Lithuanian parish and Saint Casimir's would remain a Polish parish.

Father Lenarkiewicz remained as pastor until 1904. Under his pastorate, the church structure was enlarged and the building transformed into a red brick church. The rectory, school and convent were also constructed. The parish school was entrusted to the Bernardine Sisters from Reading. In 1915, a new church was built with additions to the rectory and convent. In 1944, Father Julian Zagorski was assigned as pastor. He made many repairs, renovations and improvements throughout the parish. These included much needed work on the church, school, rectory, convent and cemeteries. Monsignor Edward Sarzynski was appointed pastor in 1994. During his tenure, major renovations to the church were completed. Monsignor Ronald Bocian has served as pastor of Saint Casimir Parish since 2001.

Saint George Parish

SHENANDOAH, PENNSYLVANIA

Established April 1891

With the blessing of Archbishop Ryan, Saint George Parish was established in April 1891 and ground was purchased on South Jardin Street to build the church. On October 26, 1891, the cornerstone was laid by Father F. H. O'Reilly. The frame church was completed in early 1892 and Father P. Abromaitis was appointed pastor. The church was enlarged in 1901-1902. In 1907, alterations and renovations were made including the addition of two towers. On January 1, 1908, the renovated church was dedicated. In 1915, a renovation and enlarging of the church took place. In October 1934, property was acquired for a school and convent on North Chestnut and Highland Streets. The school was staffed by the Sisters of Saint Casimir. On March 1, 1938, a horrible fire damaged the entire church. Temporary repairs were made immediately. Permanent renovations continued for a period of two years.

The church underwent an extensive renovation that was completed in 1989. The sanctuary and sacristies were renovated, many stained glass windows were replaced and the parish hall was renovated. On October 6, 1991, the church was rededicated by Bishop Welsh in honor of its centennial anniversary. In 2006, profound structural problems were found in Saint George Church and social hall. The church building was closed in May 2006 due to safety issues. On September 24, 2009, Bishop John Barres was on hand at a parish meeting at which it was announced that the church building would be demolished. Saint George's parishioners continue to worship at Annunciation BVM in Shenandoah.

Saint Stanislaus Parish

SHENANDOAH, PENNSYLVANIA

Established May 1898

Toward the end of the eighteenth century, the rich deposits of coal attracted a great number of Polish immigrants to Shenandoah. The small Polish Church was not sufficient to meet their spiritual needs and a committee was formed to organize another Polish parish in Shenandoah. In March 1898, the committee acquired the property of the Evangelical Congregation located on the corner of Cherry and West Streets. Saint Stanislaus Parish in Shenandoah was established by Archbishop Patrick Ryan of Philadelphia in May 1898 with parishioners. Father Miecislas Kopytkiewicz was appointed as the first pastor.

Due to a shortage of Polish priests, Father V. Matulaitis and other priests from neighboring parishes cared for Saint Stanislaus from January 1899 to June 1900. Father Stanislaus Olesinski was appointed pastor in July 1900. His first concern was to establish a parochial school, which he conducted himself for one year. In 1901, he entrusted the school to the care of the Bernardine Sisters from Reading. Father Olesinski undertook the work of building a new brick church in place of the old wooden structure in June 1903. The present church was completed in 1905 and dedicated by Archbishop Symon from Poland. In November 1907, Father Thomas Grenbowski, became pastor. Through his efforts, the church was artistically decorated with altars and hand carved statues. In May 1913, a rectory and convent were completed.

Father Stephen Zmich was appointed pastor in September 1924. Ground was broken for a new school across from the church and was completed in 1926. The new school was opened in September 1926. In 1941, the church interior was renovated and improvements included new floors and kneelers. Father Leonard Merook became pastor in 1973. During his pastorate, improvements were made to the school and church following the Second Vatican Council. Monsignor Ronald Bocian has served as pastor of Saint Stanislaus Parish since 2001.

Saint Stephen Parish

SHENANDOAH, PENNSYLVANIA

Established 1899

Many Slovaks from Shenandoah and the immediate area attended church at St. Mary's Parish in Mahanoy City. After six years, the pastor began to come to Shenandoah on Sundays to say Mass in rented halls. In 1899, Father Kasparek purchased a building at 14-16 East Oak Street that had formerly been used as All Saints Episcopal Church. Repairs and alterations soon allowed for Sunday services to begin there. Three priests served the parish intermittently until, in 1907, Father Francis Kabctka was appointed as the first pastor. Saint Stephen's in Shenandoah was established as an independent parish in 1907. In 1914, the parish purchased land for a cemetery. A rectory was purchased in 1917.

Father Stephen Basovsky was appointed pastor in 1935. Under his guidance, the former church building was razed and a new structure erected. On October 31, 1937, the cornerstone of the

new church was laid and blessed. Dedication of the new brick church took place by Father Basovsky on November 25, 1937. In 1942, the School Sisters of the Third Order of Saint Francis arrived in Shenandoah to offer catechetical instruction and operate summer school. In 1947, Saint Stephen's School opened by the Sisters of Saint Francis with 75 students.

In the fall of 1962, extensive remodeling was done to the church. Beautiful marble altars replaced the old wooden ones. Also installed were new floors, side altars, tabernacles and bronze sanctuary gates. Father Charles Sperlak became pastor in 1974. Under his pastorate, the face of the church was renovated and the old rectory and convent were razed to make way for a new rectory. Saint Stephen's Hall was also renovated and reduced from a three-story structure to a one-story building. Monsignor Ronald Bocian is the current pastor of Saint Stephen Parish.

Saint Joseph Parish

SHEPPTON, PENNSYLVANIA

Established 1894

Saint Joseph Parish in Sheppton was established in the fall of 1894. A group of men from the area organized the building of a church on the corner of East Oak and Shepp Streets. Mass was first offered in Recla's Hall until continued until 1896. Father John Pribyl came from Saint Joseph Parish in Hazleton to administer to the spiritual needs of the early parishioners in Sheppton. Soon, Father John Kasparek, pastor of Saint Mary of the Assumption in McAdoo, realized that Saint Joseph Church was in Schuylkill County and should be served by the Archdiocese of Philadelphia. After a meeting with Archbishop Ryan, Saint Joseph's became a part of the Archdiocese of Philadelphia in 1895 and was served by Father Kasparek.

The cornerstone of the church was laid in the fall of 1895. The church also purchased adjoining property and land for a cemetery. The first Mass in the new church was celebrated by Father Kasparek in April 1896. He was officially appointed Saint Joseph's first pastor on May 30, 1896 and remained pastor until August 1897, when Saint Joseph once again became a mission to Saint Mary in McAdoo. In March 1905, Father John Jaskovics was appointed pastor.

An hour after Mass was held on March 19, 1940, a devastating fire destroyed Saint Joseph's Church. Within days, Father Joseph Baran and the parishioners began to build a new stone structure. The cornerstone for the new church was laid on November 28, 1940. Mass was celebrated for the first time in the not yet completed church on December 25, 1940. On March 19, 1941, the church was completed. The new church was dedicated on November 27, 1941. On August 25, 1955, Father Sverchek became pastor and served the parish for 37 years before retiring in 1992. Saint Joseph's Parish currently serves over 145 families.

Saint John Baptist de la Salle Parish

SHILLINGTON, PENNSYLVANIA

Established October 4, 1948

Saint John Baptist de la Salle Parish in Shillington was established on October 4, 1948 and Father Hasson was appointed as the first pastor. On October 24, 1948, Father Hasson offered the first Catholic Mass in Shillington at the Shillington Community Center for about 200 people. The same congregation remained faithful through the inconvenience and make-shift arrangements at Sunday Mass for the six months at the Community Center. A private residence was soon purchased and converted for use as a church by April 1949. In February 1952, extensive renovations converted a local factory into a combination church-school with the chapel in the center surrounded by 8 classrooms. Four Sisters of Mercy came to Shillington to teach in the parochial school. The Sisters utilized the old church as their convent. Saint John Baptist de la Salle School was opened on September 11, 1952. The new church and school were dedicated by Archbishop John F. O'Hara of Philadelphia on November 2, 1952.

Groundbreaking for new church took place in May 1969. The final interior work on the church was completed in early July 1970. The first Mass celebrated in the new church was on July 18, 1970.

Bishop McShea dedicated the church on March 21, 1971. Father Thomas Birch became pastor in 1987. The most pressing need at the time was to build a new school. In May 1988, a capital campaign was initiated by now the three parishes that feed LaSalle Academy (Saint John's, Saint Anthony's, and Saint Benedict's). The result was a beautiful $2.3 million dollar school. In the late 1980s and early 1990s, other building projects included the construction of the Father Lyons Meeting Room, renovations to the sanctuary, and new stained glass windows and doors in the church.

Father David Gillis became pastor in 1996 and recognized the need to enlarge the school building. The addition of a new school wing with four classrooms was completed in 2002. In recent years, some modifications to the interior of the church included a new lighting system and chandeliers. A larger entrance to the church was completed. Father Richard Clement, M. Div. has been pastor of Saint John Baptist de la Salle Parish since June 2005.

Saint Ignatius Loyola Parish

SINKING SPRING, PENNSYLVANIA

Established June 1, 1965

was celebrated in the new church. The church was dedicated by Bishop McShea in 1968.

Monsignor James A. Treston has served as pastor since August 1983. Under his pastorate, the parish experienced astounding growth. In the course of two major capital campaigns, the parish education center was added to the school and the church also underwent an extensive renovation in 1996-97. Saint Ignatius Loyola Parish currently serves more than 3000 families.

Saint Ignatius Loyola Parish in Sinking Spring was established on June 1, 1965 by Bishop Joseph McShea for 475 families that had previously attended Sacred Heart in West Reading. Father Joseph P. Radocha was appointed as the first pastor. During the first two years of the parish, Sunday Masses were celebrated in the social quarters of the West Lawn Fire Company and daily Masses took place in the converted garage of the first rectory.

By August 1967, the auditorium of the recently constructed school accommodated parishioners for Sunday Masses. Saint Ignatius Loyola School was opened with 230 students in September 1967. The Easter Vigil of 1968 marked the first occasion that Mass

Assumption of The Blessed Virgin Mary Parish

SLATINGTON, PENNSYLVANIA

Established 1883

Assumption of the Blessed Virgin Mary Parish was established by Archbishop James Wood of Philadelphia in 1883, with a membership of 200 parishioners. After acquiring land on Washington Street, between Sixth & Seventh Streets, parishioners erected the first church building and celebrated the first Mass on September 16, 1883. Father John Vitt was appointed as the first resident pastor on March 29, 1906.

In 1908, a rectory was built as an addition to the church. In August 1908, the Missionary Sisters of the Most Sacred Heart began a school in their convent. In 1912, the students began attending school in Palmerton until the renovation of the church basement for use as the school was completed. The present school building was erected in 1955.

Assumption of the Blessed Virgin Mary School was merged with Saint Nicholas in Berlinsville and Sacred Heart in Palmerton to form Saint John Neumann Regional School in 1978. In 1986, a new church was built and dedicated under the direction of Father James Stilwell. Father Joseph Grembocki, M. Div. is the current pastor. Assumption of the Blessed Virgin Mary Parish in Slatington serves over 1200 parishioners.

Saint Joseph Parish

SUMMIT HILL, PENNSYLVANIA

Established 1850

By 1826, infrequent visits were made to the area by Father Courtney, Father Cummings and Father John Fritzpatrick from Pottsville. A decade later, Father Wainwright was made pastor at Pottsville and he began making regular visits Summit Hill. In 1840, Father James Maloney was transferred to Tamaqua and began tending to the spiritual needs of the Catholics in Summit Hill. By the early 1840s, Thomas Connahan had provided a stable to hold Masses. A church was built in 1844. Father Maloney prepared a schoolroom in the basement of the church and then began the enlargement of the church building. Saint Joseph's was established as a parish in 1850. Father Ambrose Manahan became the first resident pastor in February 1852 and completed the church enlargement.

In October 1854, Father Basil Shorb became resident pastor and built the first rectory. In August 1858, Father Hugh Magorien became pastor. He built the office of the residence and improved the church. In August 1860, Father James Kelley became pastor. In the fall of 1860, he removed the rooms from the church, built a sanctuary, added 21 pews and connected the pastoral residence to the church. Father James Wayne came to Saint Joseph's in April 1877. He purchased land on White Street for a cemetery and also built a portion of the rectory. On June 21, 1882, the cornerstone was laid for a new church by the Very Reverend Maurice A. Walsh. Father James McConnon became pastor on September 29, 1903. He enlarged the rectory. Father William Barrington arrived in March 1911. He went to work on repairs on the church and enclosed the entrance from the sacristy to the basement.

In December 1926, the parish purchased property for a convent and the erection of a school. The new school was to be erected on Ludlow Street, opposite the rectory. On June 19, 1927, the cornerstone was laid by Father William Sullivan and the Sisters of Mercy from Merion agreed to staff the school. The school building was not ready for the opening day on September 6, 1927, so the Sisters began teaching in the basement of the church. On October 16, 1927, the new school located near the center of town behind the convent was dedicated by Monsignor Hugh Lamb. Father William Begely became pastor in September 1944. He made repairs to the church that had been neglected during the depression years. Father Joseph McPeak came to Saint Joseph's on September 15, 1948 and made many repairs to the church. He renewed the pews, painted the interior and added new confessionals. Father James Burdess is the current pastor.

Saint Jerome Parish

TAMAQUA, PENNSYLVANIA

Established 1833

Early Jesuit missionaries were the first to come to Tamaqua on their way through the Schuylkill Valley to Pottsville. As early as 1827, Father John Fitzpatrick came regularly to celebrate Mass in both Pottsville and Tamaqua. Father Edward McCarthy assumed the work of caring for the Catholics of Schuylkill County and promised to visit them at regular intervals from Bally. In November 1833, Father Arthur Wainwright became pastor of the Pottsville parish and built the first Catholic Church in Tamaqua. Saint Jerome Church in Tamaqua was established in 1833 and

erected on the crest of the hill where the old cemetery stands. The church was dedicated by Bishop Kendrick on June 6, 1834. Father Martin Kelly became the first resident pastor in 1850. His successor, Father James Kelly, began planning for the new stone church and rectory. The cornerstone was laid on June 8, 1856 by Father Joseph O'Keefe, pastor of Saint Patrick's in Pottsville. Bishop John Neumann attended the ceremonies but was too ill to officiate. He did return to dedicate the new church on August 21, 1859. Saint Patrick's Chapel in Seek was established as a mission chapel of Saint Jerome in 1886.

Father Henry Baker became pastor in 1912. He purchased a house for use as a convent for the Sister Servants of the Immaculate Heart of Mary. Groundbreaking for the school took place on September 23, 1919. The school was dedicated by Archbishop Dougherty on May 30, 1921. Saint Jerome's School was opened in September 1921. A major church renovation was completed in 1923. Archbishop Dougherty blessed the church on September 30, 1923. Saint Jerome's High School was opened in 1927. On December 16, 1934, the Our Lady of Lourdes shrine was dedicated. A second major renovation of the church took place in 1948. The deteriorating stucco on the church exterior was replaced with yellow brick plaster to match the school and the church interior was redecorated. Saint Jerome's High School was closed in 1954 when Marian High School was formed. A third major renovation of the church took place in 1958. The marble altar was installed along with marble around the interior walls.

In 1983, the church was renovated for the 150th anniversary of the parish. In 1997, the parish purchased the Salvation Army building for use as an annex to the parish center. The Parish Center (Annex) was dedicated in 2001. Saint Patrick's Chapel in Seek was closed in 2003. In 2005, the Sister Servants of the Immaculate Heart of Mary completed their tenure at Saint Jerome Regional School. On July 15, 2008, Saint Bartholomew Parish in Brockton and Saint Bertha Parish in Tuscarora were closed and consolidated into Saint Jerome Parish. Saint Bartholomew Parish in Brockton was originally established in 1846. Saint Bertha Parish in Tuscarora, formerly known as Saint Raphael Parish, was originally established in 1922. Father James Bechtel, M. Div. is the current pastor of Saint Jerome Parish.

Saints Peter & Paul Parish

TAMAQUA, PENNSYLVANIA

Established 1911

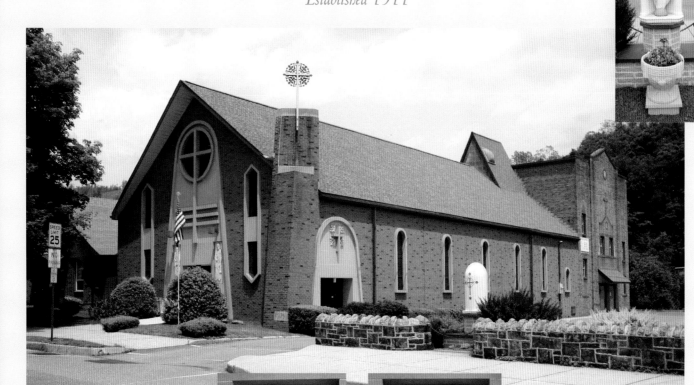

Lithuanians began immigrating into Tamaqua as early as 1898. By 1911, there were 106 Lithuanian families. On January 21, 1911 an organization called the Saints Peter and Paul Society declared their intention to form a Lithuanian Parish in Tamaqua and overtures were made to the ecclesiastical authorities requesting a Lithuanian priest. Services were first held by Father M. Durickas, who arrived on January 3, 1911.

Saints Peter and Paul Parish in Tamaqua was established in 1911. Father Peter Gudaitis arrived on October 20, 1911 to assume the pastorate. Services were originally conducted in Seitzinger's Hall on Center Street and Father Gudaitis would commute from Coaldale by trolley for services. To secure a functioning parish in Tamaqua, attempts were made to purchase some property for services and a pastor's residence. After a long and diligent search, it was decided to purchase the Weldy Home at 307 Pine Street on December 7, 1912. The first floor of the building was set aside for services and the second floor was the residence of the

pastor. Father Gudaitis assumed residence on January 1, 1913 and commuted to Coaldale from Tamaqua. In 1913, it was decided to build a temporary wooden church building. The blessing and dedication of the church by Father J. Kaulakis took place on April 13, 1914.

Father Joseph Shucavage was appointed pastor in September 1936. He brought the Sisters of Jesus Crucified to the parish. These Sisters conducted religious instruction, directed the choirs, and were active in the Apostolic works of the parish. Father Clarence Batutis was appointed pastor on May 10, 1946. During his pastorate, a convent was purchased and extensive renovations were made to the church and convent. A parochial school was also established and staffed by the Sisters of Jesus Crucified. In 1975, the old church hall and rectory were razed. In May 1976, the construction on a new church and rectory was completed. Father William J. Linkchorst, M. Div. has served as pastor of Saints Peter and Paul Parish since December 1, 1983.

Most Blessed Trinity Parish

TREMONT, PENNSYLVANIA

Established July 15, 2008

Most Blessed Trinity Parish in Tremont was established on July 15, 2008. Father Dominik Kalata, M. Ed. was appointed as the first pastor. Most Blessed Trinity was formed by the consolidation of three older neighboring parishes that included: Immaculate Conception Parish in Tremont, Saints Peter and Paul Parish in Tower City, and Sacred Heart of Jesus Parish in Newtown.

Immaculate Conception Parish in Tremont began in 1853 when Father Barr was sent by Bishop John Neumann of Philadelphia to conduct a spiritual census of West of Pottsville to the Dauphin County Line. Father Barr was assigned the responsibility of setting up a mission for the Catholics of this area. The erection of a church in Donaldson was begun. Mass was celebrated in Tremont at the residence of Peter Laux on the Main Street. As the mission grew, it began necessary to hold Mass temporarily in the German Lutheran Church. Father Barr was then given a gift of land in Tremont and construction of the church in Donaldson was discontinued in favor of a church in Tremont. Saint Mary's Mission in Tremont was established in 1853. The transition of mission to Parish changed the name from Saint Mary to Immaculate Conception Parish in 1854. Father Sylvester Eagle became the first pastor of Immaculate Conception Parish. In 1855, the laying of cornerstone took place and the new church was blessed by Bishop John Neumann on June 25, 1856. In 1925, Immaculate Conception School was opened and staffed by the Sisters, Servants of the Immaculate Heart of Mary. In 1946, a fire destroyed the interior of the church but a rebuilding and renovation of the church soon followed. In 1964, Immaculate Conception School was merged with Saint Mary's in Branchdale.

Father Michael Ahrensfield, M. Div. served as the last pastor of Immaculate Conception Parish.

Sacred Heart of Jesus Parish in Newtown was founded in 1896 and was originally part of the Diocese of Philadelphia. The earliest existing records for the parish date to 1908 and record the first baptism in the parish was performed on December 27, 1908. Father Charles Abt was listed as the first pastor of the Newtown parish. Father David Loeper, M. Div. served as the last pastor of Sacred Heart of Jesus Parish.

Saints Peter and Paul in Tower City began as a mission as early as 1865, when Tower City Catholics would meet in various Catholic homes and a priest from Tremont would come to celebrate Mass. This practice continued until 1880. One of the earliest locations where Masses were held was Bettinger's Hotel, Muir. In the fall of 1880, a petition was approved by the Tower City Board of Education that allowed Catholics to use the old brick school building for Sunday worship. Masses were held there for the next 8 years. In 1888, the Catholics acquired a lot for their own building. The construction of the church followed and the first Mass in the new mission church was celebrated in the fall of 1889. In 1896, the mission church in Tower City was elevated to that of a parish church and became Saints Peter and Paul Parish. Father Francis M. Ward was appointed as the first pastor. Father Michael Ahrensfield was appointed in 2003 as the last pastor of both Saints Peter and Paul and Immaculate Conception Parishes.

Immaculate Conception, Sacred Heart and Saint Peter and Paul were all closed on July 15, 2008. The new Most Blessed Trinity Church now occupies the former Immaculate Conception Church building in Tremont. On April 12, 2009, Saints Peter and Paul Church reopened as the Chapel of Most Blessed Trinity Parish. Most Blessed Trinity Parish currently serves over 361 registered families.

Saint Nicholas Parish

WALNUTPORT, PENNSYLVANIA

Established 1974

Saint Nicholas Parish in Walnutport was established in 1974. The history of the parish can be traced back to Nicholas Glasser, a German immigrant who settled in Lehigh Township by 1840. He allowed a small building to be built on his land for the purpose of Catholic worship. This first log church was named for Saint Nicholas and built in Berlinsville by Father Tanzer of Easton about 1840. A small cemetery was located beside the church.

The Saint Nicholas Congregation in Berlinsville was formally established as a mission and the cemetery blessed by Bishop John Neumann of Philadelphia on August 23, 1855. Nicholas and Catharine Glasser deeded the land and church to Bishop Neumann on March 7, 1856. Bishop Neumann blessed the church on December 7, 1856. The second Saint Nicholas Church was built in 1872. Nicholas and Catharine Glasser sold the property with the newly constructed church to Bishop James Wood of Philadelphia on August 19, 1873.

Saint Nicholas became a mission church of Assumption Parish in Slatington in 1906 and was attended to by the priests from Slatington. On October 8, 1967, the new Saint Nicholas Church in Walnutport was dedicated by Bishop McShea. The congregation of

Saint Nicholas remained a mission church for 119 years until it was established as a parish by Bishop McShea in 1974. Father Robert Reed was appointed as the first resident pastor. Father Ed McElduff was the second pastor and served for 20 years. Father Francis Schoenauer, M. Div. has served as pastor of Saint Nicholas Parish since June 2003. In 2008 additional land was purchased for future developement.

Our Lady of Lourdes Parish

WEATHERLY, PENNSYLVANIA

Established July 15, 2008

Our Lady of Lourdes Parish in Weatherly was established on July 15, 2008. Father Floyd Caesar Jr. was appointed as the first pastor. Our Lady of Lourdes Parish was formed by the consolidation of two older neighboring parishes that included: Saint Mary Parish in Beaver Meadows and Saint Nicholas Parish in Weatherly.

Saint Mary Parish in Beaver Meadows was established in 1841. The first Catholics who arrived in Beaver Meadows were Irish immigrants who were ministered to by Jesuit missionaries. The first Mass was celebrated in the log house of James Mooney. Saint Mary's was founded in 1841 as a mission of Saint Jerome Parish in Tamaqua. Bishop Francis Kenrick of Philadelphia purchased land on January 17, 1842 in Beaver Meadows for a church. The church was completed by 1847.

Saint Mary's Mission became a parish in 1849. Father Hugh McMahon was appointed as the first resident pastor on July 23, 1849. Father Francis Brady became pastor in 1898. He had the church moved in 1900 from the cemetery lot to a site near the present church. A rectory was built in 1902 and construction on a new church began on October 2, 1904. A major renovation of the interior of the church took place in 1980 under the direction of Rev. John J. Duminiak. Father Floyd Casear Jr. was the last pastor of Saint Mary Parish.

Saint Nicholas Parish in Weatherly was established in May 1902. Saint Nicholas was founded as a mission of Saint Joseph Parish in Laurytown in late October 1874. Father Eugene McElhone was appointed the first pastor in 1874. A chapel was erected in 1875. In May 1902, the mission was elevated to a parish and Father Francis Wastl was appointed pastor. He was responsible for the construction of a rectory and Columbus Hall. Our Lady of Lourdes in Buck Mountain was established as a mission church of Saint Nicholas on May 30, 1915. A parochial school was opened in Columbus Hall by the Sisters, Servants of the Immaculate Heart of Mary in 1921. The school flourished and a new school building was erected in 1926. In 1950, a fire destroyed the rectory and a new rectory was built in 1951. Our Lady of Lourdes Mission was closed in 1957. Saint Nicholas School closed in June 1981, when it was merged into McAdoo Catholic Elementary. The church interior and exterior was renovated in the late 1990s by the Rev. William J. Onushco. Father Floyd Casear Jr. was the last pastor of Saint Nicholas Parish.

Saint Mary Parish and Saint Nicholas Parish were both closed on July 15, 2008. The new Our Lady of Lourdes Church now occupies the former Saint Nicholas Church building in Weatherly. The mission church thus becomes the parish church.

Sacred Heart Parish

WEST READING, PENNSYLVANIA

Established 1917

O n the recommendation of Monsignor George Bornemann of Saint Paul Parish in Reading, Archbishop Prendergast erected Sacred Heart Parish to provide for the spiritual needs of Catholics living west of the Schuylkill River in 1917. Monsignor Bornemann purchased a plot of land at the southwest corner of Eighth and Hill Avenues in Wyomissing. Father Charles Bornemann was appointed the first pastor of the new parish of 180 people. He celebrated the first Mass on July 8, 1917 in the Wyomissing town hall. The site was the parish's place for worship until the two-story brick combination church-school was completed at the end of 1917. The church occupied the first floor and a two-room school was on the second floor. To the rear of the classrooms were the living quarters for two Sisters, Servants of the Immaculate Heart of Mary. A rectory was also purchased at 917 Franklin Street.

Father John Wachter became pastor in 1928. In exchange for the Hill Avenue property, Father Wachter received $50,000 and a parcel of land in West Reading. The new building, on the corner of Franklin St. and Seventh Ave, would be a combination church-school. The cornerstone was laid in 1929 and the new church was blessed by Archbishop Dougherty in 1930. Father Theodore Wagner was appointed pastor in September 1943. He undertook the expansion of the school and planning for a new church in 1956. The first Mass in the new church was celebrated on April 8, 1962.

A new parish center, offices and rectory were completed in October 1982. The interior of the church was renovated in 1987. Father James Reichert became pastor in 1989. The parish soon undertook a school renovation and addition that included a library on the first floor and the Immaculate Heart of Mary Room on the second floor. The Immaculate Heart of Mary Sisters left the parish in 1993. In 2000, it was determined that the bell tower was no longer structurally sound. Monsignor Joseph DeSantis has served as pastor since June 2003. A major restoration of the church was undertaken beginning in June 2006. The project was completed and the altar consecrated by Bishop Cullen in December 2006.

Holy Trinity Parish

WHITEHALL, PENNSYLVANIA

Established June 1928

In June 1928, Holy Trinity Parish was founded in Egypt, Pennsylvania. Early families of Slovak descent living near Egypt were traveling to Saint Andrew Church in North Catasauqua and later Assumption of the Blessed Virgin Mary Church in Northampton. In 1928, 56 Slovak families petitioned Archbishop Dougherty of Philadelphia to establish a parish of their own. Father Michael Holly was appointed the first pastor. Initially, he lived at Saint Andrew's and traveled to Egypt every Sunday to celebrate Mass. A building was soon offered for services by the Giant-Portland Cement Company in Lower Egypt.

In February 1929, Father Holly obtained the property at the corner of Main and Church Streets from Eugene M. Long. With about sixty families, the parish began renovating a barn on the property to be used as the first church in June 1929. Until this project was completed, the present rectory and church office were used for services as well as the pastor's residence.

Father John Matlos was appointed pastor in 1930. He continued to upgrade the property and purchased a new church organ and church bell. Father Michael Ditsky was appointed pastor in 1939 and held the position for the next 36 years. In 1961, a Building Committee was formed to begin raising funds for a more adequate church building. The excavation for the new church began in September 1964 and was completed in May 1966. The church was formally dedicated by Bishop McShea on September 18, 1966. Monsignor Daniel Yenushosky was appointed as pastor on June 16, 2009.

Saint Elizabeth Parish

WHITEHALL, PENNSYLVANIA

Established November 19, 1941

Monsignor Leo Fink, pastor of Sacred Heart Parish in Allentown, petitioned Archbishop Dennis Cardinal Dougherty to establish a mission for 70 Catholic families in Fullerton in December 1927. On January 1, 1928, permission was granted to established Saint Elizabeth Mission and Monsignor Fink purchased a lot from George Boyle on January 3, 1928. The mission chapel was under construction by April 14, 1928. The first Mass was offered in the mission on June 24, 1928. The priests from Sacred Heart served the needs of the mission. By Christmas 1928, the interior of the church was completed and furnished.

A third petition by Monsignor Fink to establish Saint Elizabeth as a parish was granted on November 19, 1941. Father John G. Engler was appointed as the first pastor. In July, 1942, the parish purchased the Keppel estate adjoining the church grounds. There were two buildings on the property and the acquisition provided the parish with a rectory and parish hall. Ground was broken for a parish school by Monsignor Leo Fink on January 11, 1953. The

school was opened by the Sisters of Mercy of Merion in September 1953. A new parish hall was dedicated on November 10, 1957.

By July 1968, preliminary plans for a new church were completed. The facilities included not only the church but a wing of parish offices behind the main sacristy and joined to the rectory.

Groundbreaking for the new church complex took place on October 27, 1968. The church complex was dedicated by Bishop McShea was on May 9, 1971. In November 1985, a second Cry Room was added in the rear of the Church. The Cry Room adjacent to the Altar was then transformed into a Weekday Mass Chapel.

Monsignor Anthony D. Muntone has served as pastor since June 21, 1987. He established the 50th Anniversary Building Campaign with the main emphasis placed on the completion of the church sanctuary. The main altar was moved forward and a special area provided for the baptismal font. The walls of the church were repainted, the ceiling and choir loft refinished, and the Weekday Mass Chapel was renovated. All the church renovations were completed by 1992.

School

Saint John The Baptist Parish

WHITEHALL, PENNSYLVANIA

Established June 16, 1927

the Sodality and the Altar and Rosary Society. Father Koenig also purchased four acres of land for a parish cemetery.

Father Charles Ruffenach was appointed the second pastor of Saint John the Baptist in 1934. He purchased 11 plots of land adjoining the rectory for a new church, school and social hall. In 1942, the new school building was completed. Shortly thereafter, it was determined that the original church was too small to hold the increasing number of parishioners. The basement of the school was then excavated and used as a temporary church for many years. Due to the continued growth of the parish, groundbreaking for a new church took place in 1959. The new church was dedicated on December 18, 1960.

Beginning with the original eighteen Catholic families in the 1920s, Saint John the Baptist Parish has grown to include almost 600 families in 2009. Father Joseph Campion, M. Div. is the current pastor of Saint John the Baptist Parish.

Saint John the Baptist Parish in Whitehall was established on June 16, 1927 to serve the 18 Catholic families of Whitehall. The first church and school were located in a building that had previously had both a butcher shop in one hall and the West Coplay Maennerchor in the other hall. Father Joseph Koenig was appointed as the first pastor. He established the Holy Name Society,

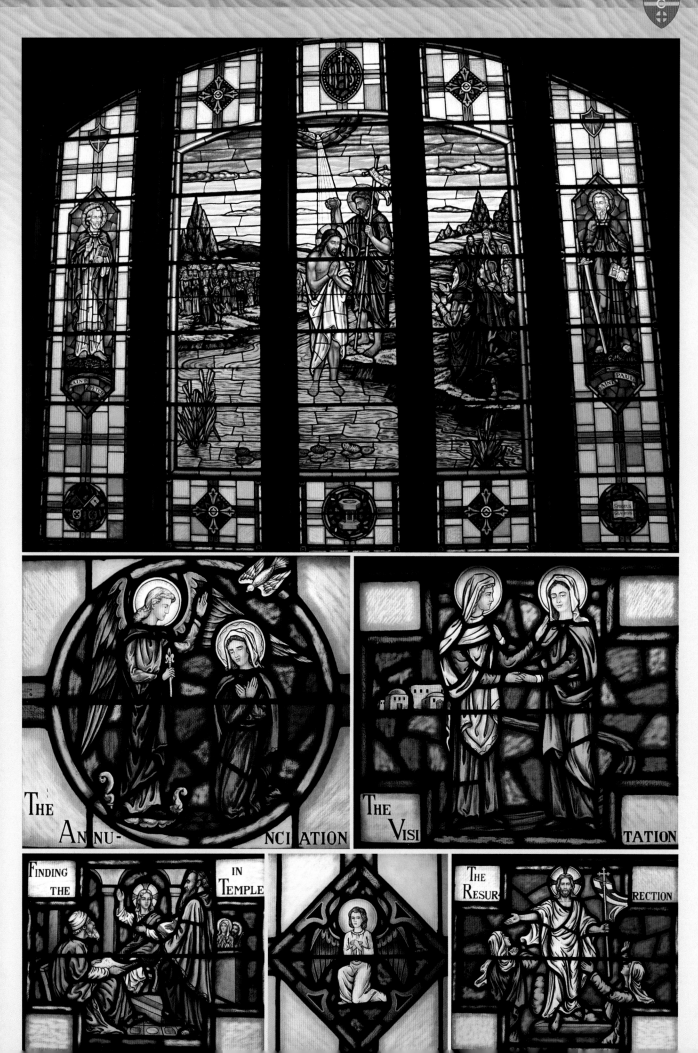

ECCE
AGNUS DEI

FAMILY OF SAINT JOHN

BEHEADING OF ST JOHN

ST. JOHN PREACHING

ST. JOHN IN THE WILDERNESS

Closed Churches

IN THE DIOCESE OF ALLENTOWN

On July 15, 2008 a restructuring and consolidation of parishes, in keeping with the statutes of the Second Synod of Allentown went into effect. The churches pictured on these pages were closed after special closing Masses the previous Sunday. They are pictured here to honor the many generations who, by their fidelity, sacrifice, and worship, have handed on to us the Catholic Faith.

Assumption BVM Mahanoy City

Immaculate Conception Kelayres

Immaculate Conception Saint Clair

Mary Queen of Peace Pottsville

Our Lady of Mont Carmel
Allentown

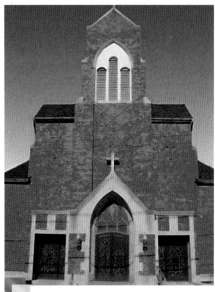

Our Lady of Mount Carmel
Minersville

Our Lady of Pompeii Bethlehem

Our Lady of Mount Carmel
Nesquehoning

Our Lady of Siluva Maizeville

Sacred Heart Mahanoy City

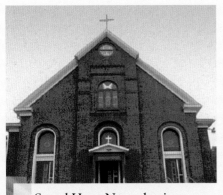

Sacred Heart Nesquehoning

Sacred Heart New Philadelphia

Sacred Heart Newtown

SS. Cyril and Methodius Coaldale

SS. Peter and Paul Lansford

SS. Peter and Paul Saint Clair

SS. Peter and Paul Tower City

St. Ann Lansford

St. Anthony of Padua Cumbola

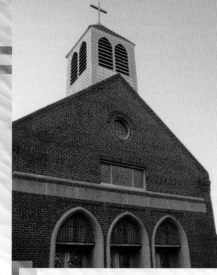
St. Barbara Minersville

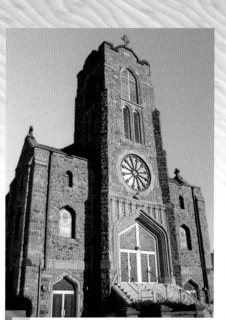
St. Bartholomew Brockton

St. Bartholomew Tresckow

St. Bernard Easton

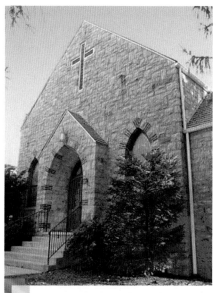
St. Bertha Tuscarora

St. Boniface Saint Clair

St. Canicus Mahanoy City

St. Casimir Mahanoy City

St. Casimir Saint Clair

St. Fidelis Mahanoy City

St. Francis de Sales Mount Carbon

St. Francis of Assisi Minersville

St. John Capistrano Bethlehem

St. John the Baptist Coaldale

St. Joseph Bethlehem

St. Joseph Pottsville

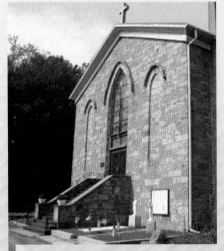

St. Kieran Heckscherville

St. Kunegunda McAdoo

St. Mary Beaver Meadows

St. Mary Coaldale

St. Mary of the Assumption
McAdoo

St. Mary Star of the Sea
Branchdale

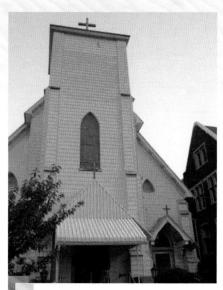

St. Michael Easton

St. Michael Northampton

St. Michael Tresckow

St. Roch West Bangor

St. Stanislaus Bethlehem

St. Stanislaus Summit Hill

Catholic Schools

IN THE DIOCESE OF ALLENTOWN

Catholic education began in what is now the Diocese of Allentown with the first school established by Father Theodore Schneider, S.J. at Goshenhoppen (Bally) back in 1743. That tradition continues over 250 years later with the fifty-three Catholic schools of the Diocese of Allentown including two colleges, eight diocesan high schools, twenty-one regional schools, nineteen parish schools and three special learning centers. The colleges and high schools in the Allentown Diocese include: Alvernia University (1958), DeSales University (1965), Allentown Central Catholic High School (1927),

Bethlehem Catholic High School (1926), Holy Name High School (1964), Marian Catholic High School (1954), Nativity of the Blessed Virgin Mary High School (1955), Notre Dame High School (1957), Pius X High School (1951), and Reading Central Catholic High School (1940).

Alvernia University in Reading was founded as Alvernia College in 1958. In 1926, the Bernardine Sisters of the Third Order of Saint Francis established a Teacher's Seminarium for the education of the Sisters. Alvernia

Father Bally and children outside St Aloysius Academy 1866

Alvernia University- Francis Hall

College began in 1958, when the institution was expanded into a four-year liberal arts college. Alvernia College received its charter from the Commonwealth of Pennsylvania in 1960. The first male students were enrolled in 1971. On September 25, 2008, officials announced that it had attained university status and was renamed as Alvernia University.

DeSales University in Allentown was founded as Allentown College of Saint Francis de Sales in 1965. The groundbreaking was held on May 17, 1964. On August 17, 1964, Bishop McShea presented the Oblates of Saint Francis de Sales with a deed to 301 acres of land in Center Valley for the college. Allentown College was opened on September 15, 1965. The college was dedicated by Bishop McShea on October 6, 1965. Although initially an all male institution, Allentown College made the transition to a coeducational college in 1970. The name was changed to DeSales University on January 1, 2001.

Allentown Central Catholic High School in Allentown was founded as the Monsignor Masson Memorial High School in 1927. The name was changed to Central Catholic High School in 1928. Central Catholic and

DeSales University

Allentown Central Catholic High School

Holy Name High School

Bethlehem Catholic High School

Allentown Catholic High Schools were merged in 1943. Ground was broken for a new high school annex on June 2, 1962. Bishop McShea dedicated the new Barry Hall Annex on February 24, 1964.

Bethlehem Catholic High School in Bethlehem was founded by five Sisters of Saint Joseph on September 5, 1926. On January 4, 1963, Bishop McShea purchased 26 acres of land in Bethlehem for a new building and ground was broken on May 21, 1963. The new Bethlehem Catholic High School was dedicated on December 6, 1964. On December 7, 1964, over 720 students moved from the old school on the South Side of Bethlehem to the new campus.

Marian Catholic High School

Holy Name High School in Reading was founded in 1964. On September 23, 1962, Bishop McShea blessed the site for the new high school in Reading and ground was broken on May 10, 1963. On August 30, 1964, Holy Name High School was dedicated by Archbishop Egidio Vagnozzi, Apostolic Delegate to the United States.

Marian Catholic High School in Tamaqua was founded in 1954. Bishop McShea announced the purchase of 40 acres of land north of Tamaqua for a new building in June 1962 and ground was broken on September 24, 1962. Construction began on the new high school building on March 28, 1963. The new Marian Catholic High School was dedicated on August 23, 1964.

Nativity of the Blessed Virgin Mary High School in Pottsville was originally founded as Pottsville Catholic High School in September 1955. Monsignor John Boyle was commissioned by Archbishop John O'Hara of Philadelphia to purchase ground for the new diocesan high school. The school was dedicated to the Blessed Virgin Mary on April 14, 1956. The school was expanded to include another 300 students in 1963-64.

Notre Dame High School in Easton originally began as Easton Catholic High School in 1957. On April 24, 1963, Bishop McShea announced plans to enlarge Notre Dame High School. The new 12-room addition was dedicated by Bishop McShea on January 21, 1964.

Nativity of the BVM High School

Notre Dame High School

Pius X High School

Reading Central Catholic High School

Religious communities of women that have served in Catholic schools in the Diocese over the years

Community

Angelic Sisters of Saint Paul
Missionary Sisters of the Precious Blood
Sisters of Holy Family of Nazareth
Daughters of Divine Zeal
Sisters, Servants of the Immaculate Heart of Mary, Immaculata
Sisters, Servants of the Immaculate Heart of Mary, Scranton
Missionaries of Charity
Missionary Sisters of the Most Sacred Heart of Jesus
Carmelite Nuns of the Ancient Observance
Dominican Daughters of the Immaculate Mother
Sisters of Saint Benedict
Bernardine Sisters of the Third Order of Saint Francis
School Sisters of the Third Order of Saint Francis
Sisters of Saint Francis of Philadelphia
Sisters of Saint Francis of Philadelphia (Glen Riddle)
Poor Sisters of Saint Joseph
Sisters of Mercy (Merion)
Sisters of Christian Charity
Sisters of Saints Cyril and Methodius

Sisters of Saint Joseph of Chestnut Hill, Philadelphia
Sisters of the Village of Peace Pentecost

Historical

Daughters of Mary, Help of Christians
Poor Sisters of Jesus Crucified and the Sorrowful Mother
Felician Sisters
Sisters of Saint Casimir
Sisters of the Holy Family of Nazareth
Grey Nuns of the Sacred Heart
Sisters of Saint Francis of Christ the King
Religious Sisters of Mercy
Daughters of Divine Charity
Sisters of Saint Francis of the Providence of God
Daughters of Charity of Saint Vincent de Paul
Daughters of the Most Holy Redeemer
Missionary Sisters of the Most Blessed Trinity
Sisters of Jesus Crucified
Daughters of Charity of Saint Vincent de Paul

Pius X High School in Bangor was established as Our Lady of Mount Carmel High School in 1951 by the Salesian Sisters. It was renamed as Pope Pius X High School and staffed by the Sisters of Saint Joseph in 1953. The school was expanded to include another 200 students in 1963-64.

Reading Central Catholic High School in Reading was opened in the old William Luden mansion in 1940. The school was staffed by three Sisters of Charity with an initial enrollment of 75 students. An addition was made to the building in 1941.

Our Lady of Hungary Regional School in Northampton

The Allentown Diocese is also home to twenty-one regional schools, nineteen parish schools and three special learning centers. The regional schools in the diocese include: Sacred Heart Regional School in Allentown (1995), Saint John Vianney Regional School in Allentown (2010), Saint Francis Academy in Bally (1993), Seton Academy in Bethlehem (2006), Christ the King School in Coplay (1983), Saint Joseph Regional Academy in Jim Thorpe (1980), Our Lady of the Angels Academy in Lansford (1999), Saint Michael the Archangel School in Limeport (1977), McAdoo Catholic Elementary School in McAdoo (1985), Our Lady of Hungary Regional School in Northampton (1982), Saint John Neumann Regional School in Palmerton/ Slatington (1978), Immaculate Conception School in Pen Argyl (1955), Saint Stephen Regional Elementary School in Port Carbon (1991), All Saints Regional Elementary School in Pottsville (1983), Holy Guardian Angels Regional School in Reading (2001), Our Lady of Mount Carmel School in Roseto (1938), Trinity Academy at the Father Walter J. Ciszak Education Center in Shenandoah (2006), La Salle Academy and Early Childhood Center in Shillington (1989), Saint Jerome Regional School in Tamaqua (1992), Saint Ignatius Loyola School in Sinking Spring (1966), and Saint Elizabeth Regional School in Whitehall (1984).

The nineteen parish schools of the Allentown Diocese include: Our Lady Help of Christians in Allentown (1927), Saint Thomas More School in Allentown (1969), Sacred Heart of Jesus Parish School in Bath (1925),

Saints Peter and Paul school children in Lehighton- early 1900s

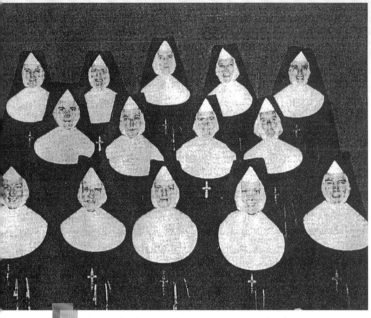
Sisters of Saint Joseph at Notre Dame School in 1961

Holy Infancy School in Bethlehem

Holy Infancy School in Bethlehem (1894), Notre Dame School in Bethlehem (1955), Our Lady of Perpetual Help School in Bethlehem (1964), Saint Anne School in Bethlehem (1949), Immaculate Conception Academy in Douglassville (2003), Saint Jane Frances de Chantal School in Easton (1926), Saint Ann School in Emmaus (1949), Saint Theresa School in Hellertown (1939), Saints Peter and Paul School in Lehighton (1886), Holy Family School in Nazareth (1910), Saint Joseph the Worker School in Orefield (1997), Saint Catharine of Siena School in Reading (1938), Saint Margaret School in Reading (1922), Saint Peter School in Reading (1859), Saint Ambrose School in Schuylkill Haven (1914), and Sacred Heart School in West Reading (1919). The three special learning centers of the diocese include: Mercy Special Learning Center in Allentown (1954), Saint Joseph Center for Special Learning in Pottsville (1955), and John Paul II Center for Special Learning in Shillington (1982).

Saint Margaret School in Reading